/// GOD AT WORK ///

DAVID W. MILLER

/// GOD AT WORK ///

The History and Promise of the
Faith at Work Movement

OXFORD
UNIVERSITY PRESS
2007

OXFORD
UNIVERSITY PRESS

Oxford University Press, Inc., publishes works that further
Oxford University's objective of excellence
in research, scholarship, and education.

Oxford   New York
Auckland   Cape Town   Dar es Salaam   Hong Kong   Karachi
Kuala Lumpur   Madrid   Melbourne   Mexico City   Nairobi
New Delhi   Shanghai   Taipei   Toronto

With offices in
Argentina   Austria   Brazil   Chile   Czech Republic   France   Greece
Guatemala   Hungary   Italy   Japan   Poland   Portugal   Singapore
South Korea   Switzerland   Thailand   Turkey   Ukraine   Vietnam

Published by Oxford University Press, Inc.
198 Madison Avenue, New York, New York 10016

www.oup.com

Oxford is a registered trademark of Oxford University Press

Library of Congress Cataloging-in-Publication Data
Miller, David W. (David Ward), 1957–
God at work : the history and promise of the Faith at Work movement / David W. Miller.
   p. cm.
Includes bibliographical references and index.

ISBN-13 978-0-19-531480-9

1. Faith at Work (Organization)   2. Work—Religious aspects—Christianity.
3. Work—Religious aspects.   4. Employees—Religious life.   I. Title.
BT738.5.M575 2006
267'.13—dc22   2006014123

9 8 7 6 5 4 3 2

Printed in the United States of America
on acid-free paper

To *Avodah*

ACKNOWLEDGMENTS

Certain clichés exist because there is an inescapable truth that lies behind the utterance. That is indeed the case here, as there are many people without whom I could not have written this book. All credit goes to them and all errors belong to me.

I am indebted to many in the academy, with special thanks to my Doktorvater Max L. Stackhouse, Peter Paris, and Robert Wuthnow who took special interest in helping me transition from a senior business executive to a junior scholar. Further, deep appreciation to Miroslav Volf, my friend and colleague at the Yale Center for Faith & Culture (YCFC) for partnering and sharing a vision of faith as a way of life. I also thank other colleagues at Yale for their friendship and support, including Yale Divinity School Dean Harold Attridge, the staff of the YCFC, the YCFC Advisory Board (Denise Adams, George Bauer, Michael Donovan, Lord Griffiths, John Hare, Dale Jones, Jim Lane, Gene Lockhart, Bill Pollard, Steve Reinemund, Scott Smith, Yolanda Smith, John Tyson, and Debra Waller), and my Yale School of Management colleagues, including Dean Joel Podolny, Jeff Sonnenfeld, and Jeffrey Garten.

I have been fortunate to have many special conversation partners, advisors, and journeyers in the Faith at Work movement. Together, you are too numerous to mention, but I would be remiss if I did not give special thanks to André Delbecq, George Bauer, Dick Broholm, Howard E. Butt, Jr., Buddy Childress, Bill Diehl, Jack Fortin, Mark Greene, Pete Hammond, Larry Herr, Buck Jacobs, Pat Kidd, John Lewis, Judi Neal, "Mac" McQuiston, Mike McLoughlin, Paul Minus, Bill Pollard, David Prescott, Shirley Roels, Martin Rutte, Sally Simmel, John Tyson, and José Zeilstra.

Many others have encouraged and helped me during the different chapters of my work. While only a partial list, I thank Kerry Alberti, Clarence Ammons, the board members and constituents of the Avodah Institute,

John Beckett, Bob Buford, Ken Blanchard, Tillie Chase, Tom Charles, Chris Clark, Jim Charlesworth, Ellen Charry, Howard Dahl, Jane Douglass, David Dunkel, Whit Ferguson, Ann Fudge, Steve and Marian Gaultney, Lou Giuliano, the members of the Greenwich Leadership Forum, Stephen Green, Walter Hansen, Hank and Erika Higdon, Doug Holladay, Bill Johnson, Kathryn Johnson, Laurie Beth Jones, Charles Kerr, Paul Klaassen, Dwight Lacy, attendees of Leaders Offline events, Linda and Phil Lader, Ed McVaney, Ted Malloch, Pete McDonald, Bob and Jane McLennan, Ken Melrose, Pat Miller, Morgan Mitchell, Dick Murphy, Bob Naegele, Laura Nash, Kathy Nelson, Pat O'Neill, Ray Owens, Greg Page, Dale and Jill Pemberton, Eric Pillmore, Tad Piper, Sid Reber, Russ and Debbie Reynolds, Jim Reese, Dudley Rochelle, Edwin Robertson, Dave Robinson, Nancy Rockwell, Kathy Sakenfeld, Richard Scurry, Bob Slocum, Pat Spainhour, Jack Stewart, John Stott, Tom Tewell, Brian Walker, Glynn and Mandy Walker, Jon Ward, Craig Weatherup, David Wessner, Don Williams, Ollie Williams, Dave Williamson, Rick Woolworth, Peter Wodtke, and Mike Volkema.

I am also in debt to Susan Richardson and Rose-Anne Moore for their meticulous help, and to Cynthia Read and her team at Oxford University Press for their vision to undertake this subject and their exceptional assistance. And I thank my immediate and extended family, who have accompanied me during the writing of this book and throughout my life.

Yes, there is one person missing in this acknowledgment. Indeed, without the sacrifice, support, love, encouragement, red pen, and prayers of Karen Lyn Kahn Miller, my wife, best friend, and conversation partner, I would still be on page one. Thank you, Karen, and thank you all.

David Ward Miller
Soli Deo Gloria

CONTENTS

	Introduction	3
ONE	"Faith at Work"?	9
TWO	The Social Gospel Era (c. 1890s–1945)	23
THREE	The Ministry of the Laity Era (c. 1946–1985)	39
FOUR	The Faith at Work Era (c. 1985–Present)	63
FIVE	Response of the Church and the Theological Academy to FAW	79
SIX	Faith at Work as a Social Movement	105
SEVEN	Analyzing and Understanding the Faith at Work Movement	125
EIGHT	The Future of the Faith at Work Movement	143
	Notes	155
	Selected Bibliography	197
	Index	219

/// GOD AT WORK ///

INTRODUCTION

"Whatever else you learn here, just don't forget, religion and business simply don't mix. Customers want solutions to their business problems, not their spiritual problems." Thus spoke my IBM instructor in a new employee training class in 1979. That may have been true then, but fast-forward twenty years, and we find a new conversation taking place in the boardrooms and cafeterias of workplaces across the United States, as well as in the media that cover them.

"God and Business," "Religion in the Workplace," and "How the Church Has Failed Business" are titles of just three among dozens of recent cover stories in respected journals and periodicals.[1] With headlines talking about God, religion, and the church, we might expect to find these articles in peer-reviewed theological journals, such as the *Journal of Religious Ethics* and the *Journal of the American Academy of Religion*, or in respected religious magazines like *Christian Century* and *Christianity Today*. Instead, these particular stories on God, religion, and the church boldly graced the covers of three venerable business journals: respectively, *Fortune*, *BusinessWeek*, and *Across the Board*.[2] The simple fact that these stories exist—let alone where they were published— points to the crucial nature of the theological and ethical questions they raise, and the increasingly blurred boundaries between faith and work. Today, contrary to the advice I was given in the late 1970s, growing numbers of businesspeople of all levels are attending conferences and management seminars on spirituality and work, participating in small prayer and study groups on faith and leadership, and reading books, magazines, and newsletters for self-help as regards integrating biblical teachings with marketplace demands. This change was already well under way before the terrorist attacks of September 11, 2001, and has only gained momentum since.

So what is going on today at this intersection of faith and work, how did we get here, and how do we theologically interpret and engage this phenomenon? This book is an attempt to answer these three questions, drawing on theological, historical, and sociological resources. While startling to some, these headlines point to a story that has deep theological and sociological roots. Yet as influential and widespread as the FAW movement has been, scholarly research into its contemporary incarnation is limited and insufficient.[3] There is no definitive text that describes the movement as a whole, its forms, and its genesis or trajectory, nor one that offers critical reflection and a theoretical framework to help guide the movement. Given the movement's scope, scale, and potential social and economic impact, as well as its continuing evolution, the church and the theological academy will be left behind and become mere spectators, unless they seek to understand and engage the issues driving the movement and the participants themselves. Toward that end, methodologically, this study draws on the ethical and theological traditions of the church, the sociological and historical analytical tools of the academy, and the practical wisdom and experience of people in the workplace. Using those tools, my goal is to understand the historical roots and formation of the modern-day Faith at Work movement, to describe and analyze its scale and diversity, to analyze the factors driving the movement today and the church's response to the movement, and finally to place it all into a critical yet coherent framework that helps to make sense of the movement, including the needs it reveals and the solutions it proposes. In addition, I also propose new language and a model to help people integrate faith claims and workplace demands and to assist the academy and the church in the training of future clergy.

This book takes as its point of departure and focus the Faith at Work movement in the United States. However, the movement has global dimensions, as parallel efforts can be found to varying degrees in Europe, Asia, and Latin America. Moreover, this international dimension has exerted an influence on the FAW movement in the United States, particularly in the earlier waves of activity, as discussed in chapters 2 and 3 on the history of the FAW movement.

Before proceeding, the name of the movement and focus of this volume require some explanation. The "faith" part of the Faith at Work movement is highly diverse, comprising nearly all of the major religions, including Judaism, Christianity, Islam, Hinduism, Buddhism, and noninstitutional forms of spirituality. This study, reflecting the religious demographics of the United States, where Christianity is the majority religion, focuses primarily on the Christian dimension of the movement, with recognition of and reference to other religions and forms of spirituality in the movement. Further, the primary emphasis is on the Protestant expressions of faith at work, though several significant Catholic-Protestant connections and points of cross-pollination are included. The Catholic-Protestant distinction is more apparent in the first two waves of the movement (chapters 2 and 3) in which specific strands and influences coming from the Catholic tradition are readily identifiable. However, though some Christian FAW groups still maintain clear Catholic-Protestant distinctions, by wave three in the late twentieth century, most of these confessional differences tended to blur and in many cases fully disappear (chapters 4, 5, and 6), such that participants in the movement today pay little heed to Protestant-Catholic distinctions.

A complete historical analysis of Christian thought on faith and work would include most of Judeo-Christian history. While beyond the scope of this book, one could trace the relationship between faith and work starting with the Old Testament teachings, moving to the New Testament writings, and then on through the patristics, the monastic orders of the High Middle Ages (such as the Benedictine practices), the gradual decline of agrarian life, and the parallel development of cities. The Reformation and its interest in Christian vocation in daily life and work, the Enlightenment, the Industrial Revolution, the resulting Marxist critique of religion and capitalism, and the Weberian response further shaped the historical understanding of the relationship between faith and work. The beginning of the modern Catholic social teaching tradition and the early roots of the Social Gospel in the late nineteenth century also had an impact on the modern dialogue about faith and work.[4] This rich theological history has fluctuated in emphasizing the spiritual and the material, at times lauding work as prayer and a virtue, while at other times viewing it as a curse and an earthly burden to be escaped; at times recognizing work as a spiritual calling, and at other times as mere secular labor; at times understanding that faith should be part of and inform all aspects of daily living, including work, and at other times seeing expressions of faith as limited to Sunday worship. Thus, though known by different names over the ages, the concept of "faith at work" is not new.

The "work" part of the Faith at Work movement also merits definition, raising the question, "What is work?" While the nature and content of the work involved may vary greatly, the FAW movement has been generated largely out of and focuses on what we commonly call our "jobs": paid work in our place of employment.[5] In today's complex and ever-changing economy, that work can include a wide range of job types (from manual labor to knowledge work), job functions (sales to service), industry sectors (agriculture to manufacturing), geographic locations (Buffalo to Beijing), and settings (home office to office park). Thus, for the purposes of this inquiry, the term *work* means that activity that is undertaken in a paid job, occupation, position, function, or profession and the place in which one performs that work. Further, the FAW movement, while most vibrant in the business community, is not limited to the marketplace and can be found in other professions and lines of work.

As noted, what draws most people to the FAW movement is the desire to live an integrated life, where faith teachings and workplace practices are aligned. Workers of all types, whether data entry clerks or senior executives, are no longer content to leave their souls in the parking lot. Businesspeople today want to find moral meaning and purpose in their work. Regardless of job level or salary, today's employees want their work to be more than just a way to put bread on the table and pay the rent. This modern quest for integration has ancient theological roots. In particular, the Hebrew word *avodah*, which conjoins these points, is illuminating. Found throughout the Hebrew Scriptures, the root of the word *avodah* means "work and worship," as well as "service," thereby suggesting that our work can be a means of honoring God and serving our neighbor, thus providing greater meaning and purpose to our work while also providing the conditions for our basic living and leisure. The concept of *avodah* is a premise that underlies the FAW movement and this book.

The changing societal, economic, and ecclesiastical environments of the late twentieth and early twenty-first centuries are together driving this fresh interest in faith and work. Some of the changes were brought about by religious traditions, which helped to produce a new context in which work could be undertaken, while others were driven by different social forces. Taken together, these changes have prompted new and varying theological and ecclesiastical attitudes toward work itself, those who work in business, and the capitalist structure in which the global economy increasingly functions.

In the 1980s, a complex set of relatively independent developments emerged that, taken together, can be called the Faith at Work (FAW) movement. At its core, the FAW movement is organized around a quest to integrate one's personal faith teachings with one's professional work responsibilities. Workers and professionals of all kinds no longer want to live bifurcated lives, where work and spiritual identity are compartmentalized into disconnected and unrelated spheres. Those involved in the movement see integration as a healthy antidote to the emotional, spiritual, and professional costs of compartmentalization and bifurcation. Integration recognizes the different spheres of life, such as government, family, religion, arts, and economics, but argues for a holistic lifestyle in which the whole self—body, mind, and soul—is important.[6] While many in the FAW movement are driven by a quest for integration at a personal level, such integration of faith and work also has profound ethical and moral ramifications for corporations as a whole and life in the broader economic sphere and, thus, has the potential to play a powerful and positive role in today's global economy. The opposite is also true. Business leaders need to be attentive to the potential for divisiveness and discrimination if religion and spiritual practices in the workplace are not implemented in inclusive and respectful ways.

For these reasons and more, the Faith at Work movement, with its many forms, member profiles, and modes of expression, is of theological and social importance. Rightly understood and engaged by theologians and the church, the FAW movement has the power to influence and give new ethical shape to those in the workplace—from secretaries to CEOs—and to the marketplace structure itself. Similarly, rightly understood and engaged by people in the workplace, the FAW movement has the potential to help reshape aspects of theological education and reenergize the church itself. Indeed, the movement's historical roots, as well as its current forms and ways of grappling with the relationships among faith, ethics, and the lived experience of the modern workplace under contemporary economic conditions, all point to the fact that, as both a theological and a sociological phenomenon, the Faith at Work movement demands our attention.

Chapter 1 of this study introduces the Faith at Work movement and defines its key terms. Chapters 2 and 3 describe and analyze the late nineteenth-century to mid-twentieth-century waves of the movement, tracing the antecedents of the modern (post-1980) phase. The first wave, called here the Social Gospel era (c. 1890s–1945), has the Protestant Social Gospel period and the Roman Catholic social encyclical, Leo XIII's *Rerum Novarum* (*The Condition of Labor*), in 1891 as its symbolic beginnings. This wave was interrupted by World War I and fully receded with the Great Depression and World War II. The mid-twentieth century saw the movement's second wave, the period of the ministry of the laity (c. 1946–1980). It began in the wake of World War II and continued until the early 1980s, accenting ecumenism and lay ministry.

After tracing the shape and development of the first two waves, the remainder of this volume focuses on the third phase, beginning in the mid-1980s, in which we still find ourselves, referred to here as the Faith at Work era. During this period, members of the baby-boomer generation began to take the reins of power in the corporate and political spheres, seeking meaning and purpose in their work. At the same time, tectonic changes in information technology, telecommunications, transportation, manufacturing, globalization, and political ideologies began to challenge old paradigms and fundamentally to transform how we work and the society in which we live. This current wave of FAW activity has not yet given any indication of receding and, to the contrary, appears to be gaining momentum and spreading around the globe. Moreover, in tandem with my analysis of current FAW activity (and the needs it fulfills) is an analysis linking the movement's formation and existence to the societal and religious conditions out of which it has arisen.

Chapter 4 describes and analyzes the third and current wave of the Faith at Work movement, from the standpoint of the laity, particularly in terms of the societal context and the needs that the movement addresses. Chapter 5 explores what the movement offers its participants by focusing on the inadequate response by the church and the academy to the questions and issues surrounding the integration of faith and work. Chapter 6 looks at FAW as a movement, analyzing its member profiles and modes of expression, using theological and sociological categories. Chapter 7 constructs and proposes a new framework and language for discussing the FAW movement that allows for critical analysis of the movement and the different ways in which it manifests. Finally, chapter 8 offers prescriptive ideas and constructive critiques to help guide the movement's participants, the church, and the theological academy, while also looking ahead to outline the issues and research that could be explored to better learn from and contribute to the Faith at Work movement.

With this book, I hope to help begin to address the paucity of scholarly study of the Faith at Work movement and its history and to serve as a guide to further research. At the same time, I seek to increase understanding within the church and the academy of a powerful, contemporary movement that has the potential to affect—positively or negatively—countless individuals, the corporations and organizations in which they work, and the broader marketplace itself. In an era when membership in mainline denominations has plummeted and churches are radically rethinking how to reach out to people, it is my hope that study of the Faith at Work movement will highlight and encourage further exploration of both the need and the opportunity that is knocking at the church's door.

ONE

"Faith at Work"?

They might as well have just posted a sign outside the church: "Corporate types not welcome to worship here." My friend Steve, the chairman and chief executive officer of a large multinational company, tells the story of being excluded—indeed, derided—within his own congregation, not because of race, ethnicity, gender, sexual preference, or doctrinal disputes, but because of his work. Sitting in an adult education class one Sunday morning, he listened to the pastor berate "the greed of all multinationals" and the "self-serving nature of their executives." The apex of the pastor's scolding message left this question hanging in the air: "How could a Christian work at this company?" My friend, a committed and thoughtful Christian, was the head of that company.

Steve is not alone. Hundreds of thousands of women and men around the country have come to feel an urgent need to integrate their faith and their work and, at the same time, have found the church to be of little help. Their stories, which make up the Faith at Work movement, have emerged both within and in response to the dramatically changing social, economic, technological, geopolitical, and ecclesiastical conditions that began in the 1980s and that continue today. During that time, the conditions surrounding work, the employee, and the workplace have changed significantly as a result of several factors. These include large-scale corporate mergers and acquisitions, restructurings, layoffs, plant closures and the resulting relocation of factories to low-cost overseas manufacturing sites, advances in technology and telecommunications, mobile capital, lower global transportation costs, and reduced trade barriers.

In the midst of these changes, many people report feeling that they live increasingly bifurcated lives, where faith and work seldom connect. Many who are Christians complain of a "Sunday-Monday gap," where their Sunday worship hour bears little to no relevance to the issues they face in their Monday workplace hours. Though notable exceptions exist, sermon topics, liturgical content, prayers, and pastoral care rarely address—much less recognize—the spiritual questions, pastoral needs, ethical challenges, and vocational possibilities faced by those who work in the marketplace and world of business.

When speaking to clergy gatherings of a variety of denominations around the country, I often ask this question: "Who here prays for and commissions your teenagers as they go off on a mission trip?" Invariably, all hands go up. Then I ask: "Who here prays for and commissions your Sunday school teachers each September as the new church year starts?" Most of the hands go up again. Finally, I ask: "Who here prays for all the certified public accountants in your congregation around April 15, and who here prays for all the salespeople and those working on commission at the end of the month and end of the year, when quotas are due?" Silence. Eyes drop to the ground. Usually, not a single hand is raised.

Whether conscious or unintended, the pulpit all too frequently sends the signal that work in the church matters but work in the world does not. It is perhaps no surprise, then, that workers, businesspeople, and other professionals often feel unsupported by the Sunday church in their Monday marketplace vocations. Increasingly, businesspeople—whether correctly or incorrectly—perceive the clergy's lack of interest in, unawareness of, and generally pejorative view of the business world and, by association, of those who work in it. Of course, responsible theological and ethical criticism of immoral business structures, practices, and people is certainly in order. But the often presumptive and pervasive suspicion shown by religious professionals blocks consideration of the theological and practical possibility that there could be redemptive, creative, productive, ministerial, and transformative possibilities in the world of business, and in the lives of those called to live out their Christian vocation in the marketplace and other workplaces.

In light of the Sunday-Monday gap and the church's distancing itself from the world of business, it is not surprising that the FAW movement has arisen largely outside the church and its usual programs. The movement that has emerged is decentralized, with loosely networked clusters of lay-initiated and lay-led activities that focus on integrating spirituality and work. The result has been the spawning of a plethora of voluntary associations throughout America (and increasingly beyond), comprising many different individuals and types and sizes of groups, as well as a range of ways in which these people express themselves. Indeed, not only has this groundswell of decentralized activity formed largely outside the institutional church, but these groups generally shun doctrinal disputes, transcend denominational boundaries, and include a range of demographic profiles. The people involved in the FAW movement focus on a host of issues, including identity, meaning, purpose, calling, discipleship, ethics, responsibility, witness, evangelization, and transformation in and of the business world. All of these issues can perhaps best be understood and observed through the lens of the following four categories, explained further in chapter 7: ethics, evangelism, experience, and enrichment. This typology, represented by these four categories, illuminates the predominant approaches taken by different individuals and groups within the movement. Like all models, each category functions as an analytical device to observe areas of accent and emphasis; in practice, most people and FAW groups manifest rich combinations, reflecting the multifaceted efforts of people attempting to integrate faith and work.

Ethics and the Faith at Work Movement

Hardly a day goes by when an executive is not faced with an ethical decision that has moral dimensions. For instance, should a CEO (chief executive officer) decide to keep a plant open that employs 25 percent of the residents in a small town, even though high labor costs there result in uncompetitive product pricing, or should she move the plant overseas to save money and let other human beings—who are also created in the image of God—have a chance to gain economic prosperity? Or, should an executive promote a minority female who has less experience but good potential over a majority white male who is currently better qualified for the position? Those drawn to the FAW movement find it insufficient to turn just to lawyers and financial experts for answers to these dilemmas; they increasingly turn to biblical teachings to search for ethical insights and guidance on business matters.

Since any social movement is a response to changing conditions and perceived societal deficiencies, economic or otherwise, a rigorous scholarly analysis can be helpful to reveal and engage those changing circumstances and needs. Specifically, the issues driving and surrounding the FAW movement invite systematic ethical analysis because they are indicative of significant and broader theological, cultural, and economic changes in religion and society. Some scholars distinguish between social ethics—the ethics of setting public policies that impact society as a whole—and personal ethics, the ethics that govern an individual's actions in light of generally accepted conceptions of right and wrong, good and bad, and fitting and unfitting. The question of ethics, both personal and social, is a central part of the FAW movement, and therefore offering an ethical analysis is an essential part of understanding the movement.

Many theologians and sociologists have long recognized that religion and economics, together with government and family, are among society's essential spheres of life.[1] These spheres interact constantly to form society as a whole. The FAW movement finds its primary locus in the economic arena, but it intersects with and has implications for all of these spheres. In an increasingly globalized and interrelated world, such intersection is particularly significant for the field of social ethics, as decisions in the economic sphere wield greater and greater influence on political policy as well as on cultural and family life.[2] If the FAW movement can go beyond personal expressions of piety, virtue, and religious practices, it has the potential to affect and positively alter the larger cultural value system and norms of the economic sphere, both domestically and globally. Conversely, unhealthy manifestations of FAW integration can be the source of conflict and disruption. Indeed, whether someone supports or opposes the growing power of the economic sphere in relation to all others, that influence cannot be ignored—and neither can factors, such as the FAW movement, that affect the choices people make within that sphere.[3]

For these reasons, understanding how the religious sphere fits into this new world order is an urgent ethical need. Many religious institutions and professionals have often sought to remain distinct from and even distance themselves from the economic sphere. However, the dramatic social and economic changes of our times and the issues surrounding globalization challenge ethicists and theologians to renew, rather than deny, their participation in constructively shaping developments in the economic sphere. In particular, Christian ethicists, theologians, and clergy need to understand and engage those involved in the marketplace, so as to assist employees, executives, and professionals as they seek to bring their religious beliefs into the sphere of economics and the workplace. Conversely, it is possible that the church and the academy might also learn from the FAW movement and, in turn, develop fresh ethical resources to guide and support those who seek to integrate faith and work. For these and many other reasons, the FAW movement, which seeks to draw connections between the religious and economic spheres, constitutes a significant phenomenon worthy of ethical reflection—a phenomenon that the church has, so far, largely neglected.

Theology and the Faith at Work Movement

The Faith at Work movement can be linked to a long, rich theological tradition that stresses the doctrine of vocation[4] and the coming kingdom of God,[5] that recognizes work as central to Christian anthropology, and that claims that someone's faith should be a central and informing part of all spheres of life, including work.[6] Indeed, the FAW movement as we know it today has many antecedents and is part of a tradition from which movements, motivated and guided by theological insights, have emerged that shape economic life.

The FAW groups of wave three that emerged in the mid-1980s and continue today are distinct from and have a different theological focus, logic, and genesis, and they have new modes of expression than those seen in earlier twentieth and late nineteenth-century antecedents. Broadly speaking, the current wave of FAW activity can be seen as an heir of the nineteenth-century Social Gospel movement, the mid-twentieth-century ecumenical movement, and the more recent lay-ministry movement. Yet in contrast to some earlier periods of Christian theology, such as the Reformation, much of twentieth-century Protestant scholarship—as seen in the leading divinity schools and seminaries—has moved away from constructive theological engagement and ecclesiastical support of those called to vocations in the business sphere. Instead, broadly speaking, there has been a turn toward a negative critique of work in general and the business world in particular, accenting its problematic aspects and ignoring its constructive and creative dimensions. Indeed, earlier twentieth-century forms of Christian socialism and more recent forms of liberation theology have stood in strong opposition to the for-profit sector, the business community, and its participants. In spite of this—or perhaps in part because of it—the FAW movement has flourished independently from these theological developments and has grown even though it has been little recognized by or nurtured in the church or the academy.

There are, however, many constructive theologies, Catholic and Protestant, which can be brought to bear on the questions that the FAW movement raises. Over the past century, encyclicals and other statements of Catholic social teachings and the theological perspectives grounded in the Reformed tradition have offered great insights and resources. Indeed, heirs of the Reformation tradition arguably had a significant influence on the development of the modern economic structure and business world. The century-long debate about Weber's *The Protestant Ethic and the Spirit of Capitalism*, on the whole, strongly suggests an unintended connection between faith and work. More specifically, the Reformed tradition accents the doctrines of creation (of both the material world and humanity), sin, providence, and vocation, all of which are, from a Christian standpoint, influenced by the doctrine of salvation in ways that bear directly on the issues and concerns that FAW groups address. The Reformed tradition is supplemented in more recent times by several Christian ethicists, including Reinhold Niebuhr and H. Richard Niebuhr. Reinhold Niebuhr's ethical insights included his emphasis on theologically informed engagement in societal discourse (i.e., public theology), his accent on "Christian realism," and a conception of human anthropology having a threefold relationship with God, neighbor, and the self.[7] While his work focused largely on political life, there are many analogues to theologically informed engagement in business life. H. Richard Niebuhr's ethical insights were many, including his lifelong quest to understand the relationship between Christ and culture.[8] His interest in understanding the spiritual forces and social sources that shape individual and organizational life informs many different approaches to faith and work, inasmuch as attitudes toward and participation in the marketplace can be considered a subset of culture. These theologians and their work, on which this study builds, have been decisive influences on the theologically informed social ethics tradition that sees theology, ethics, and the social sciences as mutually illuminating and correcting. Whereas these ethicists have often focused on the political sphere, here I look at the intersection between the economic and religious spheres, as expressed in the Faith at Work movement.

Faith at Work as a Movement

It is important to recognize at the outset, as Laura Nash and Scott McLennan observe in their study of the church and the Sunday-Monday gap, that "the terrain we cover is notably short of common definitions."[9] Until a certain degree of maturity enters or a signature book captures the imagination of scholars or the media, movements are often known only to their participants and often under many different names or catch phrases.[10] In general, the various names of the FAW movement seek to convey the growing interest by businesspeople in bringing marketplace issues and religious, spiritual, and ethical teachings into conversation with each other. The movement under study here is known by its participants under several names, each of which is usually about three words in length, where the first word signifies the religious aspect; the second word is a preposition; and the third word references the arena in which the religious aspect is manifest. Examples of some other names include "spirituality and work," "spirituality in the workplace," "spirit and work," "soul at work," "religion in the workplace," and "faith in the workplace." Each name, with seemingly minor or subtle linguistic differences, often represents or points to significant differences in ethical orientation, theology, or practical implications. In the end, selecting an umbrella term for the movement under study is a tradeoff between specificity and vagueness, given the wide theological diversity within the movement. When moving from the general to the particular, each word has different theological implications and emphases, whether employed in academic discourse or in daily use. Indeed, the groups often signify their theological or economic slant by the names they choose for themselves.

Arguably, the identifier "faith at work" offers the most comprehensive term to describe the movement.[11] Indeed, it is a frequently chosen term of self-reference by participants in the movement.[12] The businesspeople I surveyed for this study liked the open-ended nature and dual meaning of the term *faith at work*. The first meaning locates and legitimizes the spatial presence of faith in the work sphere in general and in the workplace in particular. The second meaning suggests a pneumatological dimension of the activity of God, where God is busy at work—that is, God is working.

We gain further insight into the movement by considering separately each part of the name Faith at Work. There are many terms that could be chosen instead of "faith" to describe the religious or spiritual aspect of the movement. The choice of an umbrella name is complicated by the recognition that many terms have had different meanings over time. These words have distinct historical definitions in Western theological traditions; however, in contemporary American English, many of them have taken on modified or even new meanings, each with different implications.[13] Broadly speaking, however, in a religious context, the term *faith* (and its alternatives) recognizes and acknowledges the existence of and a belief in a "higher power," Creator, theistic being, or divine figure (however broadly or loosely defined) that most people in the West call God. Even if particular conceptions and understandings of God are different, they share the presupposition that how we understand God matters to humanity and should be relevant and applied to daily life. Moreover, in a Western context, many of these terms usually imply the three prominent monotheistic religions of the world: Judaism, Christianity, and Islam.[14]

Of the alternatives to *faith*, the words *spirituality* and *religion* are the most commonly used terms by those in the movement. There is a long tradition of Christian spirituality, particularly in Catholicism, that has affected the Faith at Work movement.[15] Indeed, prior to the twentieth century, the terms *spiritual* and *religious* were used "more or less interchangeably," though this is no longer the case.[16] These two terms typify the issues involved in the debate about what term to choose for the movement. Spirituality, for instance, has become a particularly popular word in public discourse, in part because of its vagueness and perceived inclusiveness. It is often used as a synonym for a belief in God (or a Higher Being) and a yearning for wholeness that transcends the structured dogmatics and doctrines of organized religions. Spirituality does not necessarily imply mysticism or New Age thought, although many adherents of spirituality prefer a personalized, nonstructured, inward-oriented approach to experiencing and knowing God. In contrast, the word *religion* has fallen out of favor in many circles. Indeed, many contemporary Americans, particularly baby boomers and seekers, increasingly describe themselves as spiritual, shunning the word *religious* altogether.[17] Scholars explain this linguistic shift by suggesting that Americans understand religion today in more rigid, public, and institutional terms, which many people increasingly reject, whereas spirituality is understood as more informal, private, and personal, which most people in or outside of the churches increasingly desire.[18]

Three recent studies of spirituality and religion in the workplace have particular relevance to the FAW movement. First, in their empirical research among businesspeople, Ian Mitroff and Elizabeth Denton found that "respondents generally differentiated strongly between religion and spirituality. They viewed religion as a highly inappropriate topic and form of expression in the workplace. Conversely spirituality was viewed as highly appropriate."[19] Religion was viewed as formal, organized, dogmatic, intolerant, and divisive. In contrast, spirituality was considered to be informal, personal, universal, nondenominational, and broadly inclusive and tolerant.[20] On the basis of their research, Mitroff and Denton conclude, "Spirituality is the basic desire to find ultimate meaning and purpose in one's life and to live an integrated life."[21]

The second study, mentioned previously, by Nash and McLennan, contains similar findings from their empirical research into companies and businesspeople seeking to straddle the Sunday-Monday gap. "Spirituality is not the same as organized religion," they state.[22] Spirituality is "access to the sacred force that impels life . . . stressing discovery of the inner, sacred self."[23] Further, they argue, "[t]he parameters of religion include spirituality," but go beyond the personal and experiential accents of spirituality.[24] Indeed, they note that the "new spirituality" does not try to "replicate an ethic of total selflessness, suffering, and sacrifice as found in some traditional Christian theologies modeled on the suffering of Jesus."[25] Nash and McLennan recognize religion as containing three essential elements that are generally lacking in definitions of spirituality: (1) source narratives, (2) source disciplines and rituals through which people personally discover these truths and apply them to daily life, and (3) ethical rules and practices that followers believe are demanded by these understandings.[26]

A third study, by management scholar William Judge, is an empirical analysis of values and business leadership.[27] Judge finds similar distinctions between spirituality and religion. However, Judge inverts the conclusion of Nash and McLennan, arguing, "Spirituality is a more encompassing term than religiosity."[28] Basic differences such as this, even among scholars, highlight the problem of terminology and the importance of careful attention when selecting and defining the movement's key words. However, from the practitioners' perspective, "a good number of those who embrace spirituality programs have no trouble with the vagueness of the terms; it allows them to customize the new spiritual messages to their own deeper beliefs."[29] Indeed, this customization process results in a form of cafeteria spirituality in which seekers pick and choose what they find pleasing, utilitarian, and helpful, while discarding or ignoring the aspects of a religious tradition they find difficult, offensive, or not useful. Such cafeteria spirituality has a wide range of formulations and adherents, including Christians, but also New Age enthusiasts who sample from Eastern religious traditions, humanist philosophy, and the human potential and self-improvement movements that captivate American pop-culture interest.

Contrary to most of these findings, it is arguable that the term *religion* could provide a larger theological umbrella than *spirituality* and that the attributes generally ascribed to spirituality can also be found in most forms of religious practice. Many who reject the label of religion and prefer spirituality do so out of deficient knowledge of the breadth of religious practices (even in their own tradition) and in reaction to the claims by some Enlightenment philosophers and some social pundits of today that many political and social travesties have been solely due to religion. Moreover, retreat from the word religion is often reactionary and fails to appreciate that religion's pursuit of truth and its formation of disciplined faith communities reflect a "binding together" (*religio*) of believers to the insights of centuries of theological reflection. Such communities of faith often include theological teachings that accent ethical concerns, social justice, and the self-sacrificial act of serving one's neighbor, as opposed to the often inward and narcissistic accent of some forms of modern spirituality.

However, according to current research, the view that religion is a better overarching term to describe the movement is in the minority in the court of public opinion, so it is not the best term to describe the movement under study, particularly as people in the movement generally do not use it themselves. Thus, in light of this seemingly oppositional relationship between the perceptions of the open and inclusive nature of spirituality and the closed and exclusive nature of religion (notwithstanding the argument that religion includes spirituality), I propose here an alternative term—faith—that has both mediating and overarching possibilities, thus transcending the tired debate of religion versus spirituality.

Like spirituality and religion, faith is another commonly used term in the movement under study and is often a synonym for and used interchangeably with spirituality and religion. Faith can have a highly subjective meaning, as in "my faith" or "her faith." Faith can also have a highly objective and specifically defined meaning, as in "keeping the faith." Faith's simultaneous subjective and objective meanings allow for the inclusion of the various interpretations of both spirituality and religion. For some, the word faith is merely a generic expression of belief in some form of transcendent being and resists location in a specific religious tradition. For others, faith is a synonym for a specific religion, such as Christianity, and a belief in Jesus Christ.[30] Indeed, from a Christian perspective, faith is often defined as "being sure of that which we hope for and certain of that which we do not see" (Heb. 11:1). Thus, the term *faith* recognizes the generalities and openness of spirituality and at the same time includes the particularities of the more codified and institutionalized nature of religion. While faith usually implies belief in a monotheistic God, it seems also a broad enough term to be employed by polytheistic religious systems and more loosely defined New Age adherents.

Just as the theistic part of the faith at work label merits definition, so too does the final term, *work*. Those in the movement employ several meanings for *work* somewhat interchangeably, including a specific job or productive activity and the broader workplace, also known as the marketplace, the economy, business, the business world, the corporate world, and the commercial arena. Broadly speaking, these terms are different ways of referring to human activity that generates income—in other words, the economic sphere of life. While the economic sphere itself can be broken down into various classifications and subsectors and is composed of privately held and publicly traded corporations (small and large), the Faith at Work movement is located across all of these areas.[31] FAW incorporates occupations traditionally thought of as the professions, such as law and medicine, and white- and blue-collar occupations. Yet it also includes those who work in government and nonprofit organizations. It seems, however, that the majority of the movement's activity—and, therefore, the focus of this volume—is composed of people engaged in some form of marketplace activity for which they are paid.[32] Moreover, the word *work* often refers to the location or venue in which one does one's particular job, which is usually but not exclusively outside the home,[33] such as a factory, a retail store, an office building, or some other facility in which one works, regardless of the industry sector or type of company.

Thus, the work aspect of faith at work is both an activity and an institutional location. And as Keith Thomas, editor of *The Oxford Book of Work*, observes, "Work is harder to define than one might think."[34] Indeed, "the large *Oxford English Dictionary* gives the noun 'work' no less than thirty-four different meanings and the verb thirty-nine."[35] Over the centuries, many prominent economists, philosophers, social critics, ethicists, and theologians have ventured different views of the nature of human work.[36] From an ethical perspective, work has been seen in deontological, teleological, and ethological terms.[37] Deontologically speaking—that is, in Kantian terms of obligation and duty—ethical work is seen as having boundaries where right and wrong kinds of work and ways of doing work can be defined. Teleologically speaking—that is, in Millian terms of purpose and utility—ethical work must aim toward a *telos*, a good end, and avoid bad or societally destructive goals or results. And ethologically speaking—that is, in Stackhousian terms of the mores or ethos of a culture—ethical work must discern what is fitting or not fitting in particular circumstances and in accordance with social customs and norms. These and other approaches, such as a Marxist understanding of work, often contain particular philosophical presuppositions or prescribe methodologies of analysis that frequently predetermine the outcome of a given study. At the end of the day, all of these perspectives on work—analytical categories of dialectical materialism, class, liberation, race, gender, and monetary supply—agree that work matters.

Taking these factors and perspectives into account, work can be defined as human activity that has both intrinsic and extrinsic value; that involves physical and emotional energy; that can be both tedious and exhilarating; and that often is done out of necessity and in exchange for financial remuneration but also is done out of joy and in return for self-fulfillment and accomplishment. Work can be drudgery or creative delight, paid or unpaid, voluntary or compulsory, necessary or optional, rewarding or tedious, and intrinsically satisfying and purposeful or destructive and meaningless. What often distinguishes whether it is one or the other is whether one's work is imbued with theological meaning and purpose. Even the most humble of tasks and positions, when seen in a broader perspective of *avodah*—honoring God and serving neighbor—can become holy work. Indeed, as Martin Luther King, Jr., noted, "If it falls to your lot to be a street sweeper, sweep the streets like Michelangelo painted pictures, like Shakespeare wrote poetry, like Beethoven composed music; sweep streets so well that all the host of Heaven and earth will have to pause and say, 'Here lived a great street sweeper, who swept his job well.' "[38]

Consistent with the observation about the historical and cultural conditioning of the word work, from a theological perspective Christians have interpreted work over the centuries in a wide variety of ways.[39] Over time, meaning sets and theological accents for work vary and overlap, including understanding work as a curse (Genesis), a duty of faith (the letter of James), a necessity (the Apostle Paul), a vocation (Martin Luther), a manifestation of being elect (Jean Calvin), as having intrinsic and extrinsic value (Pope John Paul II), a moral calling (Michael Novak), a gift of the spirit in an eschatological framework (Miroslav Volf), and a divine calling that requires a profession as a response (Max Stackhouse).[40] More recently, theologian Paul Stevens seeks to go beyond the blessing-curse dialectic and defines work simply as "purposeful activity involving mental, emotional, or physical energy, or all three, whether remunerated or not."[41] Notably, Volf recognizes that "work cries out for a conceptual demarcation of work from other human activities."[42] In the end, Volf interprets "work as cooperation with God in the eschatological transformation of the world," which he calls "work in the spirit."[43] Thus, while the theological accents and interpretations of work may vary, the act of work—its praxis and its *telos*—is central to theological reflection and to life as a Christian.[44]

The final definitional matter to be addressed is my assertion that this FAW activity actually rises to the level of being a bona fide movement. The media and other social commentators use the term *movement* fairly freely and loosely, often failing to distinguish it from fads, temporary popularity, and other forms of collective activity, such as interest groups, political parties, ad hoc protest events, coalitions, mass hysteria, and small-scale religious sects.[45] Sociologists who specialize in analyzing and understanding collective activity often disagree on definitions and the criteria of what constitutes a movement. A full analysis of the historical and contemporary developments of collective behavior and social movement theory within the field of sociology is beyond the scope of this book.[46] Yet an overview of the scholarly literature reveals, as sociologist Mario Diani argues, enough commonality among different theorists to develop a working definition of a social movement.[47] Specifically, Diani suggests that the concept of a movement is sharp enough to differentiate social movements from related concepts, such as interest groups, political parties, protest events, and coalitions, and has a specific identity that can be investigated and theorized upon.[48] Agreeing with Diani, I conclude that bona fide social movements can be defined as "networks of informal interactions between a plurality of individuals, groups and/or organizations, engaged in political or cultural conflicts, on the basis of shared collective identities."[49] Further, Diani argues that "the characteristics of networks may range from the very loose and dispersed links . . . to the tightly clustered networks which facilitate adhesion,"[50] the former described by Gerlach and Hine and the latter by Della Porta and Diani.[51] Thus, a social movement has three main components: (1) a loosely networked collection of individuals or groups that are (2) reacting against something they find unsatisfactory and unlikely to be resolved by normal cultural institutions or resources, and are (3) grounded in some common identity, world view, or organizing principle.[52] As we shall see throughout the rest of this book, the FAW movement meets all three of these characteristics, thus deserving recognition as being a bona fide social movement. The FAW movement is a loosely networked group of individual and collective activity, reacting against the church's lack of support for those called to a life in the marketplace, and whose common drive is a deep desire to live a holistic life with particular attention to the integration of faith and work.

In addition to or even independent of how the FAW movement meets these criteria, there is also a plethora of anecdotal evidence that suggests "something is happening." This evidence is found in the frequency of press coverage, informal stories and narratives, books, articles, Web sites, conferences, and other activities that many social observers have begun to notice and record (see chapters 4–7 and the bibliography).

Finally, Diani claims that "movements may also develop" over the course of different stages and that the phase of "collective effervescence" is not necessarily or immediately followed by institutionalization.[53] Indeed, "movements often oscillate between brief phases of intense public activity and long 'latent' periods . . . in which activities involving inner reflection and intellectual development prevail."[54] This observation is consistent with the FAW movement's prior and current waves of activity, each with a certain ebb and flow, containing various levels of intensity, informality, and institutionalization. In addition, as a result of many factors, including inner reflection and intellectual development, the FAW movement has experienced various changes and developments, as the research in the subsequent chapters illustrates. In short, for all of its diversity, the FAW movement's internal coherence and commonalities underline its presence as a social movement and raise the question of its eventual place in history.

TWO

The Social Gospel Era (c. 1890s–1945)

One of the vanities of all generations is that we often think we are the first ones to raise an issue or to identify a concern. Yet about a hundred years ago, a businessman and a pastor each blew the clarion call for integrating Sunday and Monday. The businessman was interested in what lessons he could find in his faith to help his work. The pastor was interested in what lessons he could find in his faith to help society.

Bruce Barton, a successful New York advertising executive and later a U.S. congressman, read the Bible for the first time and discovered that Jesus was not a mild, meek, domesticated God whose relevance is relegated to quiet once-a-week visits. Rather, Jesus was a strong, vibrant being who lived in the rough and tumble of daily life, who assembled a management team made of both winners and losers, and who built an organization from scratch that has outlasted most other known businesses, governments, and societies. Walter Rauschenbusch, a pastor in New York's "Hell's Kitchen" for years and later a theologian, also looked at Jesus differently than did many of his day. He, too, saw Jesus as a vibrant figure, someone who made some rather specific demands of his followers in the here and now. Rauschenbusch seems to have had a multifaceted attitude toward business. He was always quick to criticize its abuses, yet he also thought that Christians should engage in manufacturing and commerce so as to make the structures and organizations more humane, more Christ-like.

Foundational to an analysis of the current Faith at Work movement is the understanding that it is not completely new.[1] Just as the modern Civil Rights movement did not start with Rosa Parks, neither did the current Faith at Work movement start with Rauschenbusch, Mark Gibbs, or William Diehl.[2] Indeed, study of the movement's antecedents and their respective trajectories helps to identify the major theological, ethical, and sociological contours, shapes, and forms of the activity evident today. An understanding of the movement's history, why it arose and receded in different periods and why some forms of expression left a deeper impact than others, yields insight into the formation and ongoing evolution of the movement's current phase.

Two different but compatible theoretical frameworks help us to understand, organize, and analyze the variety of activities within the FAW movement. The first is sociological in nature and emphasizes ways of looking at the relationship between the spiritual and the material, that is, between faith and work. It draws on the work of sociologist Robert Wuthnow and his conception of "orientations."[3] Wuthnow argues that people tend to have one of three orientations toward the spiritual and the material, which I extend, by way of analogy in the current study, to the correlates of faith and work. These orientations are "broad categories or styles, each of which encompasses much internal variety."[4] Wuthnow identifies these three orientations as compartmented, harmonious, and conflictual. The first orientation avoids conflict between faith and work by compartmentalizing them and keeping them conceptually isolated from each other. The second believes that faith and work can be harmonized, that there is no inherent conflict. The third concludes that they are in fundamental conflict with each other and cannot be reconciled.[5] While different religious traditions have predispositions to each of these three orientations, Wuthnow notes that today a significant amount of convergence exists.

The second framework, based on David Bosch's recent study of Christian understandings of mission,[6] is theological in nature and focuses on the historical paradigm shifts in mission and the resulting impact and trajectories of premillennialism and postmillennialism.[7] Bosch observes that the concept of mission has undergone six major paradigm shifts since New Testament times, concluding that mission is "an indispensable dimension of the Christian faith and that, at its most profound level, its purpose is to transform reality around it."[8] Indeed, Bosch argues that Christian mission is, in essence, all about transforming—"it refuses to accept reality as it is and aims at changing it."[9] This understanding of mission and transformation is manifested in millennialist theology in the late nineteenth and early twentieth centuries, particularly in premillennialists, who emphasize saving the individual soul, and postmillennialists, who emphasize saving society. These different conceptions of transformation form a helpful framework to understand the theological and ethical emphases of various Faith at Work groups. Indeed, most people involved in the FAW movement refuse to accept the marketplace reality as it is; they wish to change or transform it in some fashion, driven by the teachings of their faith. Premillennialist FAW participants tend to focus on the personal (transforming the individual) while the postmillennialist FAW participants focus on the social (transforming society). Some in the premillennialist tradition limit their understanding of personal transformation to the development of a personal and salvific relationship with Jesus Christ, while others build on that to include transformation of personal habits, character, and behaviors.

Bosch also traces how the individual and organizational heirs of these two theological millennialist paradigms evolved during the twentieth century and the notable convergence and intermingling of their accents in contemporary times.[10] As the current form of the FAW movement shows, changing societal and ecclesiastical conditions render this framework less helpful, as the two millennialist strands have begun to commingle and converge. In light of this, many scholars in the Reformed tradition and in the contemporary mainstream academy find the language and theology of millennialism to be anachronistic and outdated.[11] However, a more extensive look at the premillennialist roots of evangelical Protestantism and the postmillennialist roots of mainstream Protestantism is a helpful method to illuminate and understand their respective orientations toward faith at work, particularly during waves one and two of the FAW movement.

For instance, premillennialism spawned fundamentalism, Adventism, the holiness movement, Pentecostalism, and conservative evangelicalism.[12] These premillennialist strands focused on preparing for the eschaton by emphasizing personal salvation through Jesus Christ, ecstatic experience, and overcoming personal sin. Less attention was paid to saving society or overcoming structural sin, though evangelism was indirectly understood to have social consequences in the form of a moral uplift that invariably followed conversion. As such, most premillennialists "saw little hope for society before Christ returned to set up his kingdom."[13] Indeed, this group saw the Social Gospel as the opposite of true faith and developed "an ever more absolute antithesis between evangelism and social concern."[14]

In contrast to premillennialists, Bosch argues that postmillennialists felt that much had to be done structurally to prepare for Christ's return. Over time, postmillennialist "belief in Christ's return on clouds was superseded by the idea of God's kingdom in this world, which would be introduced step by step through successful labors in missionary endeavors abroad and through creating an egalitarian society at home."[15] This expectation of bringing in the kingdom of God on earth was exemplified by the early twentieth-century clergyman Walter Rauschenbusch's conception of the Social Gospel and found expression in the phrase "the fatherhood of

God and the brotherhood of all men." The heirs of postmillennialism are found in mainstream and liberal Protestant denominations and ecumenical groups, such as the National Council of Churches and the World Council of Churches.

There is a body of Protestant literature that reveals this postmillennialist strain, reflecting on matters of economic justice and Christian thought that began somewhat cautiously as far back as the 1850s to 1870s during the antislavery movement and the Civil War period. Later, from the 1890s to World War II, the issue of economic justice became a greater focus of mainstream Protestantism, and accordingly the writings were more theologically developed and scholarly.[16] Protestant thinking on issues of economic justice became articulated in new ways at about the same time that Pope Leo XIII issued his landmark social encyclical *Rerum Novarum* (*The Condition of Labor*) in 1891, the symbolic beginning date for wave one of the FAW movement.[17] The early Social Gospel essays and *Rerum Novarum* were written during a time of great social and economic change and concern. Along with the extraordinary social advances, this era experienced significant changes in science, industry, agriculture, philosophy, political thought, and city life. It also brought large-scale social and economic problems, which Social Gospel writings and Catholic encyclicals sought to highlight and redress.

Pope Leo XIII's concerns in *Rerum Novarum* paralleled many theological assertions shared by a growing number of Protestants of the period. He spoke of the special consideration that must be given to the weak and the poor (foreshadowing later liberation theology motifs), the dignity and respect owed to all types of work and workers (foreshadowing much of the modern human rights tradition), and the payment of decent wages, while at the same time rejecting socialism and endorsing the virtues of private ownership. He set an optimistic tone in *Rerum Novarum* and staked out several themes that become the blueprint for Catholic social teaching for the next one hundred years. For instance, Leo XIII offered a moral vision of the common good in the economic sphere, while also insisting on individual human rights in the economic order. He rejected the extremes of laissez-faire capitalism and of radical collectivism, seeking instead a path of reform of the market-driven economy. Further, he established that labor has certain inviolable rights, and he discussed labor conditions, employer-employee relations, money, the dignity of labor, workers' rights, child labor, just wages, and the right to organize. Here lies the nascent support of workers' organization into unions and what we today refer to as a "living wage."[18]

It was in this context that many Protestant pastors in the United States, such as Walter Rauschenbusch, began to speak and act against the economic injustices they saw, particularly with regard to the inner city and working-class populations. Indeed, Rauschenbusch started his ministry in 1886 and was writing his first book on Christianity and society when *Rerum Novarum* appeared.[19] This period of economic development saw two powerful but often devastating trends develop. First, manufacturing efficiency and specialization techniques were combined with mass-production methods. The assembly lines created a voracious appetite for low-cost labor, often drawing women and children into dangerous, monotonous jobs with long hours. Second, this demand for labor in the cities where the factories were situated caused huge social unrest both in these cities and in the rural towns the workers left behind. The cities did not have the infrastructure or social services to absorb the influx of workers, and the family unit was often torn apart as the historic models of family farms and small family businesses were forever changed. City pastors were overwhelmed with new levels of affluence in their congregation, as well as with increasing levels of poverty, crime, alcoholism, hunger, and spiritual thirst.

Wuthnow argues that, during most of the nineteenth century, moralism and its variants kept economic behavior in check. He notes how pastors and theologians drew on biblical teachings for a form of "ascetic moralism." In parallel, thinkers influenced less by Christianity and more by Enlightenment and Romantic thought utilized a form of "expressive moralism" to contain the excesses of material life. While grounded in a different logic, both types of moralism "attempted to situate economic commitments in a moral framework and thereby imposed moral restraints on these commitments."[20] Nevertheless, by the end of the nineteenth century, the "economic realm was regarded as a separate domain impelled by its own incentives, conducive to human betterment for all who lived by its principles, and needing legal restrictions only to curb its worst excesses."[21] The compartmentalization of faith and work into separate domains or spheres of life became the norm.

Along with these developments, and in response to increasing concern about escalating social problems, Marxist ideology, and waning biblical influence, several new streams of social Christian thought emerged. The optimism and confidence of wave one's various forms of theologically motivated social activity were disrupted by World War I, threatened by the Depression, and shattered by World War II. While sympathetic to many of wave one's Social Gospel aims, later theologians such as Reinhold Niebuhr criticized them under the rubric of Christian realism, charging that Social Gospelers had a weak understanding of the doctrine of sin and an overestimation of human agency. In this sociohistorical context of wave one, three broad streams of FAW activity developed whose vestiges we still see today: (a) the Social Gospel, (b) special-purpose groups, and (c) the popularization of Jesus.

The Social Gospel

The Protestant response to the growing individualism-communitarian debate going on in political, economic, philosophical, and religious circles took the form of the Social Gospel. The Social Gospel sought theological legitimacy in and gave hermeneutical primacy to the doctrine of the kingdom of God. The Social Gospel comprised many shapes and forms, often with overlapping interests.[22] However, it can be organized into three main substreams: conservative social Christianity, radical social Christianity, and progressive social Christianity.[23]

First, *conservative social Christianity* was characterized by compartmentalization and an inward orientation, where stress was laid upon individual conversion and transformation. It was essentially premillennialist with a focus on individual salvation, with only little or tangential interest in addressing the structural or material causes contributing to society's woes. This substream of the Social Gospel sought to "rescue" the individual from his or her plight and took the form of urban evangelical rallies, rescue mission projects, and settlement houses. Second, *radical social Christianity*, in many ways the antithesis of conservative social Christianity, focused on society, not the individual. In the postmillennialist tradition, many in this substream concluded that society's economic and social structures were in need of total repair and radical renewal. Its orientation toward spiritual and material forces was often one of conflict. The radical and progressive substreams of the Social Gospel movement were sympathetic to Marxist critiques of society and often employed Marxist social analysis tools. Third, *progressive social Christianity* was characterized by an interest in the transformation both of the individual soul and of society's unjust structures. Although the theological accent was more social and in the postmillennial tradition, in many ways it was a hybrid of the first two substreams that sought reformation of both the individual and society, with an orientation toward the harmonization of the spiritual and the material.[24]

Of the leading Social Gospel figures, perhaps Rauschenbusch came closest to arguing for both individual and social transformation. While millennial thinking appears not to have driven his kingdom of God theology per se, his form of Social Gospel is highly consistent with postmillennialism. As such, Rauschenbusch can be located in the progressive social Christianity substream, although at times he was also radical. For instance, critical of the unbridled capitalism of the "robber baron" era, he wrote, "Capitalism has generated a spirit of its own which is antagonistic to the spirit of Christianity; a spirit of hardness and cruelty that neutralizes the Christian spirit of love; a spirit that sets material goods above spiritual possessions."[25]

However, Rauschenbusch could also write eloquently of his desire to transform business and the hope he held for the constructive role of business in society.[26] It is this hope that resonates with the Faith at Work movement. For instance, in his essay "Wanted: A New Kind of Layman," he essentially argued for what in wave two is ministry of the laity and in wave three is faith at work. He lamented that the church singles out young people "with evidence of gifts and consecration" solely for ordained ministry, neglecting the fact that "we need laymen sent of God even more."[27] In addition, he rejected the typical concept of a good layman who attends church, tithes, and is a member of church committees doing good works.[28] Instead, he argued, "what we want is young men who will carry the determination to live consecrated lives into the workshop and office and clear a track for their determination by revolutionizing the conduct of business in which they are engaged."[29] Further, Rauschenbusch talked of the "heavy dough of business life" as "unleavened still" and in need of "real captains of industry." His vision of faith in the workplace was to give "business men and laborers that glorious consciousness of serving God in the totality of their lives."[30]

In the context of Wuthnow's sociological framework, and my extension of it to faith and work, Rauschenbusch's substream of progressive social Christianity is most akin to the category of harmonizers. In contrast, the conservative social Christianity substream of the Social Gospel was more akin to compartmentalizers, who saw the image of a "Christian businessman" mostly in a philanthropic sense, that is, exterior to how he conducted his business,[31] whereas Rauschenbusch criticized those who were "good Christians in one part of their lives and scoundrels in another."[32] Rauschenbusch rejected the tendency to compartmentalize faith and work. He spoke of "a life consecrated to God in all its departments," that would "break the present business methods in pieces and reconstruct our commercial life, as our political life had already been partly reconstructed by the spirit of Christian Democracy."[33] He developed a strong following among his fellow clergy, through both his Brotherhood of the Kingdom group and the students he taught in seminary. As a pastor, he was critical but affirming of businesspeople and their calling.

Despite Rauschenbusch's powerful insights into the "new kind of layman," arguably his message never seemed to catch on nationally among the laity in the pews. One scholar observed, "there is evidence to indicate that [the Social Gospel] movement was probably too clerically dominated, and that the clergy failed to take the laity along in their thinking."[34] With its perceived labor orientation, the Social Gospel never gained a nationwide or grassroots following in the broader church and found its popularity limited largely to congregations in the more liberal northeastern states.[35] Others argue that some mainstream denominations, such as Presbyterians, were reluctant to participate in the Social Gospel not only for doctrinal reasons, but also for social reasons, as many of its members were from upper socio-economic groups.[36] Moreover, Rauschenbusch's theological accent on the kingdom of God was later criticized for having too high a doctrine of humanity and too low a doctrine of sin (see Niebuhr's *Christian Realism*). Further, conservative congregations in the premillennialist tradition felt threatened by the accent on the communal and the deemphasis of personal conversion. However, that is not to say that ideas do not matter nor that Rauschenbusch's teachings on the Social Gospel did not eventually contribute to changes in public policy.[37] Indeed, Rauschenbusch sowed the theological and ecclesiastical seeds of a new ethos that affected missional thinking and public policy by highlighting the shameful nature of urban squalor, poor labor conditions, and low wages.[38] Thus, these three substreams of the Social Gospel—conservative, radical, and progressive—represented a stage of Christian development that struggled with understanding the right orientation toward faith and work. In addition, these groups exemplified the tension between the paradigms of mission focused on salvation of the soul versus transformation of society.

Special-Purpose Groups

Wave one of the FAW movement also produced what Wuthnow calls religiously motivated "special-purpose groups." These special-purpose groups addressed "issues both specific to the churches and of more general concern to the broader society."[39] These religiously motivated groups are part of the American tradition of voluntary associations. New religiously motivated groups tend to emerge out of "interior and exterior church movements," noting both their place of origination and their arena of activity, relative to the church.[40] Many special-purpose groups started in the second half of the nineteenth century and were active well into wave two and beyond. Examples of earlier nonworkplace-related groups include the Sunday school movement, various youth movements (e.g., Young Men's Christian Association and student Christian groups at Harvard and Yale), women's movements (particularly missionary societies and the Young Women's Christian Association), the antislavery movement, and the temperance movement.[41]

Starting in the early twentieth century, several new special-purpose groups were formed that focused specifically on the workplace. Many of these new special-purpose groups related to the workplace were spawned and led by lay Christian businessmen (in contrast to the Social Gospel stream, which was largely clergy-led and often labor-oriented). Three separate substreams of special-purpose groups illustrate this pattern: ecumenically oriented lay and clergy groups (e.g., the Life and Work group); clergy-led small-group networks (e.g., the Oxford Group and its offshoots); and lay-founded, lay-led groups (e.g., the Gideons and the Christian Business Men's Committee).[42]

The substream of ecumenically oriented lay and clergy groups was largely spawned by theologically educated lay Christians in concert with clergy. These special-purpose groups, ecumenically oriented, lay- and clergy-led, had their origin in the Student Volunteer movement (founded by D. L. Moody, a former shoe salesman) and the Student Christian movement (which also included international entities, such as the Dutch and British SCM groups). In many ways, these groups and their heirs led to the Life and Work group, climaxing in 1937 in the Second Life and Work World Conference, held in Oxford. These special-purpose groups gathered for conferences, assemblies, and discussions attended by both laity and church professionals, although in time, these groups and their successor entities (e.g., the Faith and Order group) came largely to be led by, composed of, and oriented toward the interests of theological professionals and clergy.[43]

Joseph H. Oldham (1874–1969), a theologically trained Anglican layperson and one of the movement's key leaders spanning waves one and two, had a broader vision for the Life and Work group that would go beyond the guild of theologically trained church professionals. Oldham was a pioneer in the ecumenical missionary movement, led efforts to help restore colonial Africa to its native governance, and was a leader in gathering lay and secular groups to discuss and engage the deep issues of society. He was an early advocate of Christian social responsibility in modern society. He wrote, "If the Christian faith was to bring about changes in the present and in the future," it could only do so through the "working faith" of laypeople in the "ordinary affairs of life."[44] Even as early as 1937, Oldham realized that the church stood "before a great historic task—the task of restoring the lost unity between worship and work."[45] The promise of his theological insight into the close connection between faith and work was interrupted by World War II. However, his vision and drive to unify work and worship reemerged after the war in the form of the Ecumenical Institute at Bossey and the World Council of Churches (see wave two). This substream continued in wave two and increasingly was identified with the mainline Protestant church, heirs of the postmillennialist tradition, whose orientation toward the world was one of reform and harmonization.

The second type of special-purpose group in wave one, clergy-led small-group networks, had its roots in an organization called A First Century

Christian Fellowship, later renamed the Oxford Group. This group gave birth to many interesting special-purpose groups both inside and alongside the church, including Alcoholics Anonymous. The Oxford Group's founder, Frank Buchman, formerly secretary of the YMCA, was a charismatic and strong leader who felt called to "minister to the disillusioned and the sophisticated post–World War I generation."[46] He employed and organized a small-group format dedicated to the so-called evangelical four absolutes of honesty, purity, unselfishness, and love. The Oxford Group soon took on international proportions, such that Buchman ultimately sought to "reach the world's masses with his moral conviction," and in 1938 he changed the name to Moral Re-Armament.[47] In addition, he shifted the accent from making Christian disciples (typical of most lay-sponsored special-purpose groups of wave one) to interfaith dialogue, allowing people to find the four absolutes within whatever religious system they embraced. Buchman's new organization, Moral Re-Armament (MRA), captured the imagination of high-profile post–World War II international government and business leaders. MRA bought a château in Caux, Switzerland, to serve as a meeting and conference facility. This discreet but powerful group of leaders included prime ministers and corporate chairmen and aimed at reconciling opponents. Buchman and Caux played vital roles in reconciliation efforts between Germany and France after the war and then, in Japan, helped it to reconcile with its Asian neighbors. In 2001, MRA changed its name to Initiatives of Change.

Buchman's shift from a Christian to an interfaith focus[48] led one of his disciples, clergyman Samuel Shoemaker, to branch off and start a new small-group ministry in New York called Faith at Work, which retained an expressly Christian identity. This group held intimate house gatherings, where laypersons witnessed to the upwardly mobile, and began publishing a widely read newsletter. In many ways (e.g., the name, small-group methods, and target audience), Shoemaker's early Faith at Work ministry became the prototype for much of what we shall see in wave three of the FAW movement, with the notable exception that most wave three groups are not clergy-founded or -led. While modified in many ways, two special-purpose Faith at Work groups—the Pittsburgh Experiment and Faith at Work, Inc., both of which retain a Christian identity—still exist today, and they can trace their roots to Samuel Shoemaker's Faith at Work group in wave one. And the two other groups that no longer emphasize Christian or other religious world views or underpinnings—Initiatives of Change (formerly MRA) and the Caux Roundtable—trace their roots to Frank Buchman; they focus, respectively, on international peace and reconciliation and business ethics standards.[49]

The third kind of special-purpose group in wave one, lay-founded and lay-led groups, differed in many ways from the increasingly clergy-driven and -oriented groups such as the Life and Work and Faith and Order ecumenical bodies. While not hostile to the church, these new lay-founded, lay-led groups existed structurally outside the formal church. They formed across denominational boundaries and barriers, often with the primary aim to evangelize or "christianize" the business community. Typically, they were conceived, organized, led by, and aimed at businesspeople. For instance, the Gideons were founded in 1899 by two businessmen—traveling salesmen—who, in trying to cut expenses, accidentally ended up sharing a hotel room. They discovered that they were both Christians, prayed together, and discussed the need for an organization to support the spiritual needs of traveling businesspeople. The original name of the Gideons was the Christian Commercial Travelers' Association of America. Their initial goal was to help bring "Christian commercial travelers together for mutual recognition, personal evangelism, and united service for the Lord."[50] This led, over time, to the decision to place Bibles at the reception desk and ultimately in every hotel room, "as a silent witness remaining in these hotels when they were elsewhere."[51] The primary function today of the Gideons is still "placing and distributing Bibles and New Testaments in the human traffic lanes and streams of national life. Gideons as laymen, stand shoulder to shoulder as 'missionaries' of local churches and their pastors in going to the four corners of the world to win others for the Lord Jesus Christ."[52] Today, the Gideon group serves "as an extended arm of the church and is the oldest Christian business and professional men's association in the United States," according to its literature.[53]

Another example of a lay-founded, lay-led special-purpose group in wave one is the Christian Business Men's Committee (CBMC). Founded in Chicago in 1930 by a handful of businessmen in the wake of the Great Depression and a local revival, an informal committee was convened to pray for a spiritual revival of the city and the business community. This group of men continued to meet after the revival ended and eventually decided to establish a formal organization. Their weekly prayer and testimony meetings attracted more than eight hundred businessmen. They soon discovered that "similar groups were being started in San Francisco, Seattle, and several other large cities throughout the country. These separate groups linked together and established CBMC in 1937."[54] One of the key businessmen behind this was R. G. LeTourneau, a successful entrepreneur and founder of the LeTourneau heavy moving equipment business. CBMC relocated to Chattanooga, Tennessee, and now markets itself under the name Connecting Business and the Marketplace to Christ. The new name did not change CBMC's male orientation or its mission, which is "to present Jesus Christ as Savior and Lord to businessmen and professionals and to develop them to carry out the Great

Commission."[55] Today, CBMC reports that it has "grown from a small group of men in Chicago to over 18,000 members in 700 teams across the United States. Worldwide, CBMC is active in over 70 countries with over 50,000 members total."[56] Both the Gideons and the CBMC are still active organizations with a global reach. Even now in wave three, they maintain their theologically motivated male focus and premillennialist accent on individual salvation in preparation for Jesus' second coming.[57]

The Popularization of Jesus

In addition to the Social Gospel and special-purpose groups of wave one, the late nineteenth and early twentieth centuries were characterized by a third major stream of faith in the workplace activity. Largely seen in popular literature, a style of writing and speaking emerged that sought to contemporize and popularize a practical Jesus for modern times. In particular, two influential books and one popular speaker represent the stream's mixture of pre- and postmillennialist Protestant influences.

The first example is the book *In His Steps: What Would Jesus Do?* written in 1896 by a young pastor, Charles Sheldon, for his congregation.[58] His goal was to shock them out of their indifference to the suffering of the unemployed in their community. *In His Steps* became a runaway bestseller throughout the decades of wave one and is still in print today. The basic thesis of the book is for people to ask, "What would Jesus do?" in response to any and all modern issues that Christians might encounter. Indeed, *In His Steps* is the literary forerunner of the modern popularity of WWJD (What Would Jesus Do?) bracelets and t-shirts. Sheldon's book was a clarion call to Christian social action to transform one's community, with particular emphasis on the workplace, always seeking to discern what Jesus would do and then to do it. Sheldon is somewhat of a bridge figure between the premillennialist strand (and its evangelical trajectory) and the postmillennialist strand (and its mainstream/liberal Protestant trajectory). While criticized for its utopian nature, this "Social Gospel novel" and others in this genre helped to bring "social religion to the attention of millions of laymen who might never had heard of it otherwise."[59] What began as a simple sermon series in Topeka, Kansas, asking what would happen if people really modeled their lives on Jesus, turned into a mass-marketed book phenomenon paralleling the popularity of today's *Purpose Driven Life* by Rick Warren. Today, *In His Steps* enjoys great popularity with evangelicals and other heirs of the premillennialist stream, while most in the postmillennial strand of mainstream Protestantism are unfamiliar with the book.[60]

A second book in this stream of popularized literary accounts is Bruce Barton's 1925 *The Man Nobody Knows*. This also became a runaway bestseller (foreshadowing wave three authors such as Laurie Beth Jones and her bestseller *Jesus: CEO*).[61] Barton, a layperson and successful advertising executive, discovered in Jesus all of the leadership attributes of a successful business executive. Barton bemoaned that the church had distorted the image of Jesus, portraying him as sissified, sorrowful, meek, and lowly, whereas his reading of the Gospels revealed a vibrant, strong, life-enjoying, and popular leader. He noted that Jesus "picked up twelve men from the bottom ranks of business and forged them into an organization that conquered the world."[62] Barton wrote *The Man Nobody Knows* to "tell the story of the founder of the modern business," in hopes that "every business man will read it and send it to his partners and salesmen" as a means to spread Christian culture throughout the world.[63] While some scholars may scoff at Barton's hermeneutic, his book struck (and still strikes) a chord with those whose church experience echoed Barton's and with those who had never considered Jesus as having any relevance to the business world. For instance, the chief operating officer of a major retail food business wrote in 2001, "This book had a major impact on my life! I read it at a crucial time, a time of extreme intellectual and spiritual struggle. Since that day, I have read *The Man Nobody Knows* every year. I have given copies to hundreds of people and recommended it to thousands."[64]

The final example of a popularized and practical Jesus was portrayed through the teaching and lectures of Russell Conwell, a successful lawyer and world traveler turned Baptist preacher and lecturer. In the late 1800s, he taught hugely popular Bible classes in Boston, stressing "the application of the truths taught to the everyday problems of life," which attracted "thousands of business men."[65] Later, he built a thriving church in Philadelphia but was active most days of the year as a traveling lecturer. His signature speech, "Acres of Diamonds," was given more than six thousand times and reached tens of thousands of listeners. Its central theme was that wealth could be found where we are planted and not in faraway exotic places. Moreover, he stressed that people should become wealthy: "I say you ought to be rich; you have no right to be poor."[66] This early version of the Faith at Work movement easily harmonized faith and work, noting that "we ought to get rich by honorable and Christian methods, and these are the only methods that sweep us quickly toward the goal of riches."[67] A cynic might brand him pejoratively as merely an early form of the prosperity gospel preacher, yet that would be reductionist and inaccurate. Conwell argued that people ought to be rich because money has power—power to pay scholarships for poor people, to build hospitals and schools, and to take care of one's family. Faithful to his teachings, Conwell died with little money to his name, having used his fame and money to fund worthy causes; his particular interest in education for the poor led to his vision of what later became Temple University.

In the wake of two world wars and the Great Depression, the Social Gospel receded, as did this first wave of faith at work activity. Much of the Social Gospel's adherents' optimism and hope for the transformation of people and society was disappointed in the face of the inconceivable magnitude of pain, suffering, and death caused by the two world wars and the displacement of workers and farmers during the Depression. Indeed, Reinhold Niebuhr's theology of Christian realism charged that the Social Gospel and other analogous missional thinking were naive in their optimism and failed to account for the depth of sin and the structural reality of evil. Thus discredited, these three streams—the Social Gospel, special-purpose groups, and the popularization of Jesus—of wave one of the FAW movement receded. However, they did not retreat entirely. The spirit of this movement reemerged in wave two, accommodating itself to new societal and economic circumstances. Indeed, many dimensions of Social Gospel teaching and theology became routinized in the departments of mission and social action in the ecumenically oriented churches. Moreover, the legacy of wave one, particularly the Social Gospel goals of improving the conditions of industrial workers, can be found in many later public policy and government initiatives limiting monopolistic abuses and protecting basic workers' rights.

The shift from the first to the second wave of twentieth-century FAW activity was observed by Elton Trueblood (1900–1994), another influential figure in the history of the movement. A lifelong Quaker, Trueblood was a noted philosopher, theologian, writer, and speaker, who taught at Stanford University and later at Earlham College. An astute social commentator, he observed the significance of the emerging lay-spawned and lay-led organizations that occurred during wave one. In 1949, looking back over that period, Trueblood noticed a broad level of grassroots activity and commented on the "beginnings of the enlargement of the sense of Christian vocation in some associations of our time."[68] Trueblood approvingly took note of this pattern of lay-initiated activity, including that commercial travelers had formed the Gideon Society, that many cities had associations of Christian businessmen, that even a society of Christian professors had been formed, and that in Washington, D.C., a small group of legislators met regularly to pray. What all of these groups had in common, he concluded, was that they came to look upon their work as a holy calling. Of this first wave of grassroots (or special-purpose) associations, he wrote, "this movement is small, and seems to have little chance in a city where the normal basis of a meeting is not prayer but a cocktail party, yet it is a step in the right direction in which we must turn if our common life is to escape ultimate decay."[69]

Trueblood was correct to identify the wave of the future as "associations of Christian businesspeople," but he erred in assuming that it would have little chance in the cities.[70] Indeed, the evidence suggests that the special-purpose groups and the popularizers of Jesus did at least as much to reach, teach, and transform the average person's view of faith in the workplace as did the clergy and theologians who led the Social Gospel and early ecumenical movements. Special-purpose groups and the popularizers, for all of their theological simplicity and occasional imbalance, knew how to organize, communicate, and sustain the energy of their organizations. This is not wholly surprising, as many of these groups were founded and led by commercially successful businesspeople who by training and instinct had strong organizational, communication, and leadership skills. In many ways, including their relevance, sustainability, and effectiveness, the lay-spawned and lay-led special-purpose groups of the early twentieth century became the paradigm for much of the faith at work activity seen today.

THREE

The Ministry of the Laity Era
(c. 1946–1985)

In 1962, Episcopal priest and lay ministry advocate Francis Ayres wrote:

> Fifteen years after the war, the ministry of the laity is widely acclaimed.
> Convention addresses, pamphlets, articles on the present state of the
> church, sermons calling for advance, special conferences—all have urged
> a development of the ministry of the laity. . . . But with what a radi-
> cally different meaning! The layman remains a second-class citizen, an
> assistant to the clergy, primarily a maintenance man in the institu-
> tional church.[1]

Was Ayres overly pessimistic? Apparently not. In 1976, William Diehl,
Bethlehem Steel sales executive and active Lutheran layperson commented:

> When my church preaches about the ministry of the laity, it speaks in
> broad and idealistic terms; but when it comes down to reality, my church
> sees my ministry purely in terms of service to the institutional church.
> My church proclaims the ministry of laypersons in the world; it prac-
> tices the encouragement of lay ministries solely within the church—in
> teaching, leading worship, visiting members . . . and giving time and
> money to the organization.[2]

As the Social Gospel era of the FAW movement receded, ending with
World War II, it was soon refueled through the midcentury developments
that comprise the Ministry of the Laity era. Though this second era built on
aspects of earlier twentieth-century activity from wave one, this phase of
FAW was different. In large part, it was characterized by a shift away from
the institutional church and toward an ecclesiastical emphasis on ministry of

the laity, including its popularization, and the proliferation of special-purpose groups.

The mid-twentieth-century FAW movement emerged in a context of the international political, military, and religious coalition building and conversations that evolved during World War II. After the war, many of these coalitions, even those with differing interests and ideologies, remained intact and took new shape and form. In virtually all spheres of life, new groups formed, including the military (the Allied Forces and later the North Atlantic Treaty Organization), politics (the United Nations), jurisprudence (international law courts), finance (the Bretton Woods system of the International Monetary Fund and the World Bank), trade (the General Agreement on Tariffs and Trade and, later, the World Trade Organization), and religion (the World Council of Churches and the World Council of Reformed Churches). Participants believed that these international coalitions might rein in the threats posed by totalitarianism and excessive nationalism, thereby helping to prevent another world war. Paralleling these developments, the commercial promise and the military threat of nuclear power served as a new geopolitical reality, serving in some cases to heighten differences, alliances, and suspicion among various countries. Indeed, wave two also saw the Cold War, the Korean War, and the Vietnam War—evidence that the new coalitions did not necessarily prevent conflicts and may have even contributed to them.

In parallel, rapid developments had an impact on virtually all aspects of economic life, including agriculture (centralized and large scale farming), manufacturing (mass production), transportation (cargo and container ships and jet airplanes), technology (cathode ray tubes, transistors, and early computers), and communications (telephones, airmail, facsimiles, and photocopiers). These fueled changes in the nature and structure of modern business, leading to vastly expanded global corporations, whose size, power, and societal impact in some cases exceeded that of nation-states. Living patterns were altered with the middle-class exodus from the city to the suburbs, and family life changed as women became increasingly active and accepted in the workplace.

The church, too, saw many changes midcentury. After enjoying steady levels of attendance early in the century and in the immediate postwar era, mainstream churches began losing membership. By the 1960s, a mood of anti-institutionalism and anti-establishmentarianism became the ethos for baby boomers, with the result that many young people sought alternative forms of community and spiritual expression. There were also powerful centripetal forces at work in the church. Despite embracing decentralized forms of ministry, such as ministry of the laity, and the exploration of other new modes of addressing a rapidly changing culture, the church, by the end of this era, inevitably seemed to turn back in on itself and retained its institutional way of thinking and acting. But before this occurred, both the Protestant church (as represented in the World Council of Churches) and the Roman Catholic church recognized the need to respond to the new social realities of the day and embarked on historic changes. For instance, the Vatican II Council, held between 1962 and 1965, wrought significant changes in the Roman Catholic church, certain of which I explore later in this chapter. For purposes of this volume, however, the elevated appreciation for and role of the laity was the most profound. Indeed, the Vatican II Council became one of the powerful forces internal to the midcentury church that affected the character and possibilities of the FAW movement.

In light of all these changes, both societal and ecclesiastical, the theoretical frameworks put forward by Wuthnow and Bosch, albeit helpful in wave one, require revision to be effective in analyzing the Ministry of the Laity era. Wuthnow's sociological understanding of religion's three orientations toward the spiritual and the material—harmonious, compartmentalized, and conflictual—still has its analogues in a businessperson's attitude toward faith and work. However, these three orientations alone prove insufficient for certain midcentury developments. Businesspeople and other churchgoers ultimately felt that the goal of harmonization, at least this side of heaven, was naïve and unrealistic. Instead, many found the paradigm of conflict—an unbridgeable chasm between faith and work—to be the only way to make sense of the tension between faith and work.[3] To survive, many midcentury businesspeople opted to compartmentalize their work and their faith,[4] although this strategy, too, eventually proved to be not only unsuccessful but theologically problematic. By the end of wave two, a fourth option began to evolve as a possible new paradigm—*integrating* faith and work—which contributed to the revitalization of the FAW movement and the unfolding of wave three in the late 1980s.

Bosch's millennialist paradigm continues to shed light on midcentury developments in FAW, yet his framework also requires modification to accommodate effectively the significant societal changes of this era. Increasingly, premillennialists moved toward a hybrid position, gradually accepting the importance of saving society, as well as souls. Postmillennialists also made a shift, but not in the direction of soul saving. Rather, postmillennialists moved toward a mode of amillennialism in which millennialist thought was no longer a central theological question or defining problem. Generally speaking, their focus remained on ministering to the world by improving the material condition of humanity. Perhaps the growing spirit of ecumenism and internationalism, and the gradually receding impact of the divisive

Scopes "monkey trial" (1925), which pitted science and reason against biblical authority and fundamentalism, led both traditions to be somewhat less doctrinally rigid and socially homogeneous than their forebears and comparable groups in wave one.

Many midcentury FAW groups began to shift away from their theological and social traditions, becoming less predictable than before. By the 1980s, many premillennialist FAW groups were moving toward the new orientation, a hybrid combining the orientations of harmony and conflict, to stress integration and even social transformation. Indeed, Bosch notes that twentieth-century evangelicals struggled to recognize the two biblical mandates of evangelization (i.e., the Great Commission, Matt. 28:19–20) and social concern (i.e., the Great Commandment, Matt. 22:37–39). By the late 1970s, they began to move past the either-or dichotomy and cautiously began to link the two. For years, evangelizing had exclusive priority over social concerns (see the Wheaton Declaration,[5] 1966). However, after the 1974 Lausanne conference, the declaration's primary author, John Stott, wrote, "Not only the consequences of the commission but the actual commission itself must be understood to include social responsibility, unless we are to be guilty of distorting the words of Jesus. Thus evangelism and social responsibility are inseparable."[6] At the 1983 World Evangelical Fellowship consultation in Wheaton, the dichotomy between the two mandates of evangelism and social justice was finally overcome. The resulting Wheaton '83 Statement (paragraph 26) stated, "The mission of the church includes both the proclamation of the gospel and its demonstration. We must therefore evangelize, respond to immediate human needs, and press for social transformation."[7]

In like fashion but in a different direction, by the end of wave two, the postmillennialist streams began to change, making an inward turn to focus on the soul and the therapeutic transformation of the self. Indeed, by around 1980, most mainstream Protestant heirs of postmillennialism were essentially amillennial. Millennial thinking, while perhaps subconsciously still operative in their theology, ceased to be central to mainstream and liberal Protestant denominations. These trends in millennial thinking continue in wave three.

As noted, during wave two, ecclesiastical and theological representatives referred to FAW issues under the general rubric of *Ministry of the Laity*, which might be defined as a people called to be Christ's representatives in the world, engaging, serving, and seeking to transform the world. Broadly speaking, the Ministry of the Laity era had three streams of activity: the Bossey Institute and the ecumenical movement, special-purpose lay ministry groups, and the popularization of lay ministry.

Ministry of the Laity

In many ways, the midcentury emphasis on lay ministry and ecumenism grew out of J. H. Oldham's work earlier in the twentieth century. Similarly, the ecumenical orientation of and lay participation in many international ecclesiastical gatherings and groups helped to fuel interdenominational dialogue and lay participation, raising many of the questions that would later interest wave three participants. For instance, the Student Volunteer Movement (SVM) moved away from an early twentieth-century focus on foreign missions and evangelism to accent ecumenism instead. This caused dissent and fissure from many of the evangelical or premillennialist members, who gravitated toward the newer InterVarsity Christian Fellowship organization (founded in 1941). SVM's eventual successor entity, the Student Christian movement, moved in the direction of ecumenical, humanitarian, and social concerns. Finally, the later Life and Work group, formed out of two ecumenical conferences (Stockholm in 1925 and Oxford in 1937), paved the way for the founding of the World Council of Churches (WCC).

While several factors combined to affect the midcentury FAW movement, four were predominant: the emergence of strong leadership figures; the development of a theology of the laity; the rise and decline of a focus on lay ministry by the Ecumenical Institute at Bossey and the WCC; and the parallel influence of and dialogue with Roman Catholicism. As regards leadership, three individuals consistently championed the ministry of the laity: J. H. Oldham, a theologically trained Anglican lay leader; Hendrik Kraemer, a Dutch missionary and scholar; and Hans-Ruedi Weber, a Swiss Reformed theologian and self-described "disciple of both Kraemer and Suzanne de Diétrich."[8] All were professionally trained theologians and scholars who spent most of their lives serving the church, yet only Weber was ordained. They collaborated over the decades spanning waves one and two (the late 1930s to the early 1960s), seeking to construct a theological and practical foundation for ministry of the laity. Their hope was that lay ministry would be fully incorporated into the core of the ecumenical movement and mainstream churches via the WCC and the Ecumenical Institute at Bossey. However, despite their collective passion for lay ministry, Oldham, Kraemer, and Weber faced a Sisyphean task, trying to elevate the level of theological, ecclesiastical, and practical attention paid to the ministry of the laity. As such, this Ministry of the Laity era mirrors the way in which the wave one Social Gospel had its luminaries but never became part of the core of church life or a true mass movement. However, to say that these three men and their colleagues failed is also inaccurate. Indeed, in light of a two-thousand-year debate in the church over the relationship between ordained clergy and laity, in which laity often ended up in a role secondary to that of clergy,[9] the significance of their contribution to legitimize, heighten the role of, and raise new conceptions of lay ministry becomes clear in many ways.

These three leaders' organizational skills, passion, and writings gave rise to excellent theological contributions that underpinned and validated the relationship between laity and work in daily life. While never fully absorbed into the mainstream of the church, this branch of the Ministry of the Laity wave served at least as a theological corrective and an attempt to return to the insights of the Reformers. Second, this stream of wave two serves as a reminder of how the church, like all institutions, can be resistant to changes in the roles, functions, and expectations of its leaders and members. Behind such changes lies the subtler question of the transfer of power and authority.

Oldham was the driving force behind the question of the role of the laity and a pioneer in the development and shaping of the ministry of the laity stream.[10] Oldham was active in both of the Life and Work world conferences prior to the formation of the WCC and was the movement's continuity and bridge between the prewar and postwar eras of FAW. He was one of the first to point to "the great gap between the concerns normally discussed in the assembled church and the reality experienced by laypeople in their world of daily work."[11] Kraemer credits Oldham with initiating the lay ministry dialogue in preparation for the 1937 Oxford conference, titled Church, Community, and State, of the Life and Work movement and developing a thesis "on the strategic importance of the laity of the church for a new and fruitful relation of the church and the world."[12] Further, Oldham viewed "the laity as an expression of the Church and its calling and function in the world."[13] In 1950, he wrote *Work in Modern Society*,[14] in which he articulated his lifelong dedication to the intertwined themes of the relationship between secular society and the church, and an underlying theology of the laity to support the Christian's role in both.[15] With unfortunately accurate prescience, Oldham expressed his concern in the book that the WCC would steer Bossey away from work issues and toward the natural sciences.

In 1958, Kraemer published *A Theology of the Laity*, which for years was and in many ways remains a landmark modern theological text on ministry of the laity. Kraemer's "deep concern," he wrote, was "to show as well as discover in quite new ways the relevance of the Christian Faith to all fields of life and to all modern needs and perplexities."[16] He sought the practical integration of a world that seemed to function according to its own rules and principles and a Christian whose teachings and vision are of a world beholden to higher principles of human action and an eschatological vision of the kingdom of God. He understood the problems of laity, asking questions that are still relevant in wave three, such as, "Do not most of the Church-members live a schizophrenic life having two different sets of ethics, one for the private Sunday life and the other one for their behavior in the workday world?"[17] Further, Kraemer asserted that "the laity, generally speaking, feels itself spiritually powerless and illiterate as to its witness" in the secular world, "which is the very place where most of its life is spent."[18] Finally, he concluded, "the church does not primarily exist on behalf of itself, but on behalf of the world."[19] Thus, painting an outward-oriented ecclesiology, he resolved that the church is mission, the church is ministry, the church is diakonia, and all are stamped with theological certainty; that is the true meaning of ministry of the laity.

Hans-Ruedi Weber was another pivotal figure, whose work spanned waves two and three, just as Oldham and Kraemer spanned waves one and two. In his book on ministry of the laity, *Salty Christians* (1963), Weber laid out the thesis that our lives should not be compartmentalized into a religious department and a rest-of-the-world department.[20] Instead, they should be integrated, each informing and relevant to the other. In his historical account of the ecumenical movement, Weber lauds Kraemer's "rediscovery" of lay ministry and rejects two common misunderstandings about lay movements: they are "not anti-clerical movements, fighting for a better status of the laity in the church," nor are laypeople "mere auxiliary troops helping the ordained ministry."[21] Instead, Weber asserts, "The basic intention is to recover the necessary rhythm of the Church which is being assembled and sent out."[22] Moreover, this rediscovery places an "emphasis on the charismata promised to each baptized person and giving each one his own irreplaceable function within Christ's ministry."[23] This foreshadows the innovative theology of work developed by Miroslav Volf late in the twentieth century and his elevation of gifts and eschatology as a fresh way of understanding our relationship to work.[24]

After World War II, Europe was fertile soil for lay ministry. Evangelical academies (meeting places for dialogue between the church and the world) and the *Kirchentag* (aimed at laypeople and their responsibility in the world) emerged in Germany; the worker-priests experiment began in France, ending with Vatican II; industrial missions flourished in England; and the Ecumenical Institute at Bossey was launched in Switzerland. The focal point for much of the international ecumenical work, the Ecumenical Institute at Bossey was made possible by a large gift from J. D. Rockefeller, Jr., in 1945. The formation of the institute preceded that of the WCC, although soon Bossey fell under its control. Bossey's mission and original intent were to focus on the intersection of Christianity and secular society. Bossey was designed to focus on three subjects:

the Bible, the world, and the church universal. It was sometimes referred to as a laboratory by its early sponsors, such as Oldham, Kraemer, and de Diétrich, and as a place where ecumenism was being lived. From the outset, however, this mission was under threat. Indeed, Oldham became "incensed at the initial omission of the subject of 'work' from the study" designed to underpin Bossey's mission, and he strongly urged Dutch clergyman Willem Visser 't Hooft, co-founder and first general secretary of the WCC, to reinstate it.[25]

Kraemer, known for his interest in lay ministry, was the logical choice to be Bossey's first director (1946–1955). In the reconstruction after World War II, Kraemer felt that "laypeople would have to play an important role, and the training of pastors would have to be directed towards helping church members to be present as Christians in their professional life, in public affairs and families."[26] Notably, in an era dominated by men, the lay ministry movement had a prominent female leader, Suzanne de Diétrich. She was Bossey's assistant director and is generally acknowledged as being a central part of Bossey and the broader ministry of the laity stream of activity.[27] She worked alongside Kraemer for years, and Weber heavily credits her influence on Bossey and the development of lay ministry. As one of France's first university-trained engineers, de Diétrich became one of the leading lay theologians of her time, and she authored several books. In many ways, her life paralleled her vision of lay ministry and the early goal of Bossey to be a place where lay leaders from all spheres of life studied Scripture alongside theologians, enriching each other through dialogue and the resulting transformative possibilities.[28]

In its early years, Bossey held interdisciplinary conferences and even vacation courses for laypeople. However, as early as 1952, the original vision "that would have maintained the strong emphasis on the vocation of laypeople in their secular professions, was in fact never fully considered and [was] soon forgotten," Weber reported.[29] In effect, a "takeover by professional theologians" occurred, thereby permanently shifting the emphasis away from lay empowerment and from equipping Christians for service in the world.[30] The new focus was graduate-level academic training and degree certification for theologians and clergy, and "the majority of participants were now theologically trained church workers."[31] In 1954, Kraemer warned against the shift, but his voice was not heeded. From 1955 to 1970, a few "frontier conferences" on issues pertaining to the business and economic spheres were held, but such topics were the exception, and attendees were largely church workers, clergy, and theologians.[32] Finally, paralleling the emerging tone in the WCC, Bossey became increasingly critical of those who participated in free-market modes of economic organization, and Marxist-influenced

Christian socialist critique became the de facto standard of theological analysis and dialogue. By the 1960s, the "clerical takeover" of the Bossey lay institute was complete.

Although Bossey's mission was in flux during the 1950s, the WCC appeared to embrace lay ministry during that period. Oldham hosted a conference at Bossey on the meaning of work, leading to the discussion of "The Laity: The Christian in His Vocation" at the Second World Council of Churches Assembly at Evanston, Illinois, in 1954.[33] The Evanston assembly issued the following famous statement:

> [T]he real battles of the faith today are being fought in factories, shops, offices and farms, in political parties and government agencies, in countless homes, in the press, radio and television, in the relationship of nations. Very often it is said that the Church should go into these spheres; but the fact is, that the Church is already in these spheres in the persons of the laity. . . . It is the laity who draw together work and worship.[34]

While Evanston's statement served as a rallying cry for lay ministry, the church was unsure how to proceed from theological proclamation to practical reality.

Some denominations responded during the 1950s to the Evanston charge by creating a staff position at the judicatory level responsible for lay ministry and by conducting research, organizing programs, and developing congregational literature. Mainstream denominations, such as Lutheran, Episcopalian, Presbyterian, and Methodist, were the most visibly and financially committed to this type of judicatory-level staff support. Many mainstream denominations also wrote position papers, made formal statements, or offered proclamations on the importance of lay ministry. However, hindsight suggests that the institutional church and its leaders never fully embraced or understood lay ministry. Some clergy and religious professionals resisted empowerment of lay ministry, as it signaled a possible loss of institutional authority, a diminution of their power, and a transfer of ecclesiastical focus from Sunday liturgy to Monday life outside the church walls. Much as some religious figures in medieval times resisted translating the Bible into the vernacular, and thereby reducing ecclesiastical authority, so too the problems of clericalism and control have continued in modern times. Indeed, by 1960, Kraemer felt compelled to challenge the Faith and Order Commission to take seriously "the theological and ecclesiological implications of the laity in the life and mission of the church."[35] Facing resistance, Kraemer concluded by predicting that "the laity would be lost to the Church within twenty-five years."[36]

Some twenty-five years later, writing at the end of wave two, Weber concluded that Kraemer was right, noting, "The upsurge of lay activity during the Fifties was nothing more than 'temporary effervescence.'"[37] Weber realized that the future of lay ministry was in finding a way to reach laypeople directly. Some writings, such as his own *Salty Christians* (1963), foreshadowed the wave three demands for practical texts and support for laypeople in their daily work. While Kraemer and Weber were correct in their pessimistic assessment of the WCC's approach toward lay ministry, they seemed unaware or unappreciative of other forms of the lay ministry movement, such as the parallel stream of special-purpose groups, particularly those coming from the premillennialist tradition. A theological Eurocentricity may also have contributed to the nonrecognition or dismissal of the emerging lay-spawned, lay-led special-purpose groups and popularizing movements in America.

Paralleling this ecumenical stream in Europe, Elton Trueblood's writings in the United States also contributed to the development of a theology of the laity and has continued to be a touchpoint for many in the movement.[38] For instance, Trueblood argued powerfully that it was a misnomer to talk of "full-time Christian work" in reference to ordained ministry, missionary, or charitable work, because the logical implication is that all others are only "part-time Christians."[39] Instead, he said, "We would do well to speak of 'full-life Christian service.'"[40] Moreover, Trueblood observed, "The world is one, secular and sacred, and . . . the chief way to serve the Lord is in our daily work."[41] Later, he contended that lay ministry is the only response to the despair, societal problems, and appeal of Marxism to enable a new reformation of the church.[42] Indeed, he argued that lay ministry, rightly understood, allows a congregation to spring from one pastor to five hundred overnight.[43] With echoes of Rauschenbusch's essay "Wanted: A New Kind of Layman," Trueblood wrote some fifty years later that only "a minority ought to leave their secular employment in order to engage in full-time work for the promotion of the gospel, but this is not true of most. Most men ought to stay where they are and to make their Christian witness in ordinary work rather than beyond it."[44] Trueblood, an admirer of Reinhold Niebuhr, did not romanticize the work world; rather, he honored it. He asserted that even the most boring jobs, while perhaps not enviable, could be redeemed and brought into a Christian experience providing that the human relationships are fully developed; that the worker contributes to a good end; and that the worker's free time, outside the factory, is creatively employed.[45]

A review of the conditions that helped to form a Protestant theology of the laity and its ministry would be incomplete without considering the influence of developments from the Vatican II Council and the more prominent Catholic theologians and experiments. Indeed, as William Diehl, a leading FAW lay figure in wave three, expresses it, "Had it not been for the pronouncements of Vatican II and the resultant actions of Catholic Laity, I would have given up on my work a long time ago. What came out of the Catholic Church convinced me that I was part of a broad Christian movement in this country. There is no such thing as a purely Protestant lay movement."[46] Indeed, in the early 1960s, Diehl says, Vatican II offered ground-breaking pronouncements that "electrified" the laity by "the strong affirmation of what they themselves had concluded: they have a special Christian ministry in and to the world."[47] In particular, the laity were profoundly inspired by sections from three particular writings that emerged from the conciliar and postconciliar documents emerging from Vatican II Council: first, *Gaudium et Spes*, which offered a new framework for understanding the self in the modern world, including life in the economic sphere; second, the Dogmatic Constitution on the Church, which included a chapter entitled "The Laity," which offered a nascent theology of the laity; and finally, the Decree on the Apostolate of the Laypeople, which continued the new accent on lay responsibility within and outside the church walls.[48]

These new teachings elevating the role of the layperson evoked positive Catholic responses from both clergy and laity around the world. In Europe, Catholic theologians, such as Yves Congar, had anticipated and already argued for new and expanded Catholic conceptions of lay ministry.[49] Some European countries, such as France and Britain, explored radically new clergy roles through the worker-priest movement and the industrial mission.[50] The worker-priest movement was a novel experiment, primarily in France, in which priests took full-time jobs working in factories, joining labor unions, and experiencing firsthand the difficult working conditions of the laboring poor. Industrial mission was an approach undertaken in mostly Great Britain but also in some parts of the United States, where "industrial chaplains" sought to work specifically at the intersection of church, industry, and society. Unlike the worker-priest movement in France, the tradition of industrial mission and chaplains still continues in many parts of Great Britain and in some regions of the United States.

In the United States, one of the more notable Catholic responses to Vatican II was "A Chicago Declaration of Christian Concern"[51] (not to be confused with the similarly titled "Chicago Declaration of Evangelical Social Concern,"[52] a statement by socially concerned evangelicals in 1973). The Catholic Chicago Declaration resulted from a 1977 conference of Catholic laypeople and clergy who were frustrated that the challenging and inspiring rhetoric from Vatican II had yet to be realized in local parish settings.[53] In particular, the Chicago Declaration charged that the elevated role of the laity endorsed by Vatican II had been reinterpreted and redirected to mean simply greater participation and responsibility in ecclesiastical and parish duties, not in one's secular place of work. The Chicago Declaration evoked such a sympathetic response from American Roman Catholics that, Diehl wrote, "the National Center for the Laity was formed to keep alive the discussion of the church/world issue."[54] Notably, the center is a premier Catholic example of a lay-founded, lay-led special-purpose group for faith in the workplace. The National Center for the Laity receives no church funding and has no official standing in the Roman Catholic church. Yet for more than twenty-five years, it has remained a source of high-quality special publications, newsletters, and conferences on the topic of lay ministry in general and faith in the workplace in particular.

Special-Purpose Groups

Along with the midcentury burst of ecumenical activity surrounding the topic of lay ministry came a burgeoning of special-purpose groups. Indeed, Wuthnow observes they grew in such scale and scope that "they now appear to cast their imprint heavily on the character of American religion more generally" and upon society itself.[55] Yet enumerating the organizations is "nearly an impossibility,"[56] even if restricted to the more narrowly focused Faith at Work groups. The diversity of such groups includes the Fellowship of Christian Athletes, the Christian Legal Society, the Association of Christian Economists, the Fellowship of Christian Peace Officers, Executive Ministries International, and even a group called the Race Track Chaplaincy of America.[57] From this wide range of groups, exemplars from the premillennialist and the postmillennialist trajectories reveal wave two's characteristics, although as noted, by midcentury, the crisp millennialist demarcations of wave one had begun to blur.

Special-purpose groups with premillennialist roots comprised two substreams: church-spawned, lay-led groups and lay-spawned, lay-led groups. The ministry of Sam Shoemaker (1893–1963) was representative of the former. He was the master of start-ups and the incubator of several highly effective special-purpose groups, many of which are still active today. Spanning waves one and two, Shoemaker gained international fame (after breaking with Frank Buchman and Moral Re-Armament) during his years as rector of Calvary Episcopal Church in New York City. Many consider him the spiritual founder of Alcoholics Anonymous. He was also influential in founding the popular *Faith at Work* magazine in 1956. The magazine gained worldwide readership through a simple but effective formula: it contained engaging stories of how businesspeople in all walks of life relied on their faith for inspiration and motivation. After being called to Calvary Episcopal Church in Pittsburgh in 1952, he helped businessman Abraham Vereide initiate the International Christian Leadership (ICL) group, which hosted prayer breakfasts with senior executives around the world. Vereide's vision, supported by other businesspeople such as Conrad Hilton, led to the first annual Presidential Prayer Breakfast in 1952 under President Dwight D. Eisenhower, an event that is now part of the core of the Washington political establishment. The Presidential Prayer Breakfast serves as the model for countless state and local prayer breakfasts led by government and civic leaders to this day.[58] Shoemaker was also influential in helping to establish Young Life, a nondenominational Christian ministry founded in 1941 for high school youth, which now is active in all fifty states and more than forty-five countries. It has as its aims evangelism and preparing young people for the future.

Of particular note is Shoemaker's launch in 1955 of what is still known as the Pittsburgh Experiment, whose aim was "to bring dynamic Christianity into day-to-day job situations."[59] Instead of basing the Pittsburgh Experiment staff and events in the church building, Shoemaker chose space in a financial office building in the heart of the business district. From there, he hosted, coordinated, and initiated a steady flow of lunches, discussion groups, and workshops. Each of these adhered to a basic guiding principle: "apply your Christianity to your job."[60] Shoemaker was convinced that God enters the business world in two ways: through converted men and women whose hearts God has changed and who carry God's spirit with them wherever they go and through human relations that are different because God has become a third party to them.[61] So effective was the Pittsburgh Experiment that it was featured in a 1953 article in *Fortune* magazine under the title "Business Men on Their Knees," which, Shoemaker believed, "caused quite a stir throughout the country."[62]

Of the second substream with premillennialist roots—lay-spawned, lay-led special-purpose groups—two exemplars are especially revealing: the Full Gospel Business Men's Fellowship International (FGBMFI) and the Fellowship of Companies for Christ International (FCCI). Both of these groups emphasize the evangelization of businessmen. While in more recent times each has sought to become gender-inclusive, their practical and theological orientation remains male-oriented. The first of these two groups, the non-denominational FGBMFI, was founded in 1951 by successful California businessman Demos Shakarian, who received a vision in which God told him to found this ministry. Operating out of the premillennialist trajectory, FGBMFI is in the Pentecostal tradition of the Four Square Gospel movement that stresses prophecy, speaking in tongues, and visions. Its mission is to reach businessmen in all nations for Jesus Christ, calling all men back to God, helping believers be baptized in the Holy Spirit, and fulfilling the Great Commission (Matt. 28:19–20). FGBMFI envisions "a vast global movement of laymen being used mightily by God to bring in this last great harvest through the outpouring of God's Holy Spirit before the return of our Lord Jesus Christ."[63] Still in operation in 132 countries, FGBMFI is now headed by Demos Shakarian's son, Richard, and is headquartered in California. The group organizes international speakers, conferences, and programs offering a blend of Pentecostal emphasis on prophesy, prosperity gospel teachings that faithful businessmen will be financially blessed, and expectations of miracles and healings. Broadly speaking, FGBMFI fits neatly into the orientation that sees faith and work in harmony, where ethical and theological struggles are not the focus. And theologically speaking, the group also remains strongly based in the premillennialist stream, accenting personal conversion to Jesus Christ as its driving goal. The somewhat hagiographic and "long-awaited personal story of Demos Shakarian" is chronicled in his biography *The Happiest People on Earth*.[64]

The second example of a lay-spawned, lay-led special-purpose group with premillennialist roots, the Fellowship of Companies for Christ International, was conceived in 1978 toward the end of wave two. Notably, the initial inspiration came from a businessman after he read Sheldon's *In His Steps: What Would Jesus Do?* written during wave one of the FAW movement. Formally incorporated in 1981 by a group of businessmen, FCCI's vision is "Transforming our world through Christ . . . one company at a time."[65] FCCI has made its most significant inroads with small businesses and independently owned companies, whereas publicly traded companies tend to eschew participation in its vision and events. Notably, FCCI has been a gathering place for many male executives who later were involved in other significant special-purpose groups, like Christian Financial Concepts and Promise Keepers. FCCI firmly believes that "your company is itself a ministry," and it highlights stewardship, the value of relationships, and high personal standards.[66] However, FCCI's focus on evangelism causes it to gloss over much of the rough side of the business world, the need for structural reform, and issues of economic and social justice. Similar to FGBMFI, the FCCI organization broadly falls into the orientation of harmonizers and into the theological framework of premillennialists. In addition, like FGBMFI, FCCI remains male-oriented, and it struggles in wave three to make its message attractive to businesspeople who reject patriarchally oriented theology and what they feel to be the overly simplistic message of harmonizing or identifying one's company too closely with Christ. Recognizing these challenges, around 2004 FCCI changed its external branding and started using the name "Christ@Work." While still male-dominated and oriented, their marketing now includes women as targets. Evangelization in the workplace still remains paramount, however, FCCI's new branding reveals greater interest in the ethical aspects of conducting one's business and personal affairs in accordance with biblical principles.

Wave two also included special-purpose groups with postmillennialist roots, from which two figures serve well to illustrate efforts to translate a theology of the laity into practical action: Mark Gibbs and William Diehl. Although theologically literate, neither were ordained clergy. Both shared a passion for crossing clergy-laity boundaries and for integrating faith and work. Evangelizing coworkers was not the primary goal or organizing principle of this stream, however, as it was in the special-purpose groups with premillennial roots.

Gibbs was an Anglican layman and former schoolteacher from Manchester, England, who was particularly active in the ministry of the laity wave from the 1960s to the early 1990s. He dedicated his professional life to the propagation of lay ministry and thus has been referred to as the "dean of the lay ministry movement."[67] His focus and strength were connecting people with each other and helping them to integrate their faith and work. A tireless traveler and networker before both were made easier in the Internet era, Gibbs served as the hub of an ever-widening network of international and interdenominational lay businesspeople seeking practical guidance on how to express the Gospel through their jobs and organizations. In 1965, he coauthored *God's Frozen People: A Book for and about Christian Laymen*,[68] followed in 1971 by *God's Lively People: Christians in Tomorrow's World*.[69] Both were thoughtfully written texts aimed at the layperson, with a practical focus on how to live out lay ministry in the scattered church. His more mature work, *Christians with Secular Power* (1981),[70] continued the themes and ideas of his earlier writings but exhibited a more hopeful vein for the lay ministry movement. As a result of the response to his books, writings, and talks, he founded and led the Audenshaw Foundation, based in England, which was affiliated with the Vesper Society of San Leandro, California. Audenshaw gave Gibbs an institutional platform from which to carry out his lay ministry of faith and work. From 1977 to 1992, this link was highly fruitful, generating a regular newsletter called *Laity Exchange*, which was packed with practical examples and theological reflections on life as a Christian in the workplace.[71] Ironically, perhaps, what made Gibbs successful in his work—his engaging personality, abundant energy, networking, and single-minded focus on lay ministry—was what hurt the movement through its absence after he died. The Audenshaw Foundation and the Vesper Society soon lost energy and vision and closed down.[72] However, his work was picked up by many he inspired, directly or indirectly, including William Diehl, Richard Mouw,[73] and others.

The work of Diehl, a Lutheran layperson and retired Bethlehem Steel executive, spans waves two and three. In the 1970s, greatly influenced by Gibbs, Diehl dedicated much of his career and then later in his retired life to speaking, writing, and organizing to help people overcome the Sunday-Monday gap. He spoke for many in his first book, *Christianity and Real Life* (1976), in which he observed that the church was saying the right words about lay ministry but doing very little to support it. When his church did recognize his workplace skills, it usually sought to use them in furtherance of the institutional church, by his serving on the finance committee, the building committee, or the board of trustees. Inspired by Trueblood and Gibbs, he resolved to do something about this.[74] Diehl sought out others experiencing this dichotomy and began both local and national special-purpose groups to address the issue. He became a popular speaker and retreat leader, authoring such texts as *Christianity and Real Life*, a book about the gap between Sunday faith and weekday work and the gap between what the institutional church says about the role of laity and the laity itself; and *In Search of Faithfulness: Lessons from the Christian Community* (1987), a play on the title of Peters and Waterman's bestselling management book, *In Search of Excellence* (1982). In 1991, he wrote *The Monday Connection: On Being an Authentic Christian in a Weekday World*, a further exploration of the themes of and solutions to a life of faith in the workplace. Over time, Diehl shifted away from the term "lay ministry," feeling that it had become hopelessly misunderstood and misused, and began speaking of "ministry in daily life" instead. In 1991, Diehl founded the Coalition for Ministry in Daily Life (CMDL), a loose network of denominationally affiliated lay leaders. In the late 1990s Diehl turned over leadership of CMDL to others (including Sally Simmel, Pete Hammond, Paul Minus, and John Lewis).[75] The group remains active and vibrant today in wave three of the FAW movement, thereby avoiding the fate of the Gibbs' Audenshaw Foundation. Diehl's attempts to move from theory to practice still inspire many FAW participants in wave three.

Others active during the latter decades of wave two included people such as layman Dick Broholm and theologian Gabe Fackre, who launched and led the Center for the Ministry of the Laity (1976–1982) at Andover-Newton Theological Seminary in Massachusetts. The center was an experiment with its roots in the WCC's Department of the Laity under Hans-Ruedi Weber, the U.S. Industrial Mission Project (yet another form of expression of faith in the workplace during wave two), the Metropolitan Associates of Philadelphia (MAP), and interdenominational cooperation. The Center's mission was to train pastors to better equip their laity to approach their daily work and life as ministry. A collection of essays describing the initiative, edited by George Peck and John S. Hoffman, is called *The Laity in Ministry* (1984). The center, while well received by students, never gained full faculty endorsement nor sound financial footing. After the untimely death of George Peck, Andover-Newton's then-president and the main sponsor of the center, it closed its doors in 1982.

Alongside these special-purpose groups with premillennial and post-millennial roots and orientations, there emerged yet a third substream, which in many ways served as a bridge to many of the types of FAW groups found in wave three. Groups in this third substream often have roots in premillennial and evangelical theology but seek to combine questions of personal salvation with social and economic justice in the workplace. Howard E. Butt, Jr., a theologically educated businessman from the evangelical Southern Baptist tradition, exemplifies this combination. "Conservative 'otherworldly' hope and liberal 'this-worldly' hope," he observed, "are dangled like competing pearls of great price before the laity."[76] That is, conservative Christians tend to accent the transcendent God, emphasizing winning souls yet at the same time neglecting Christian responsibility in society, while liberal Christians tend to emphasize the immanent God, concentrating on lay obligation in social causes while neglecting questions of salvation.[77] Butt argues that this either-or conundrum is a false choice for laity and that "transcendence and immanence as they affect Christian discipleship are inseparably linked."[78] In 1978, Butt convened the North American Congress of the Laity in Los Angeles[79] to "encourage lay intellectual prowess as it can contribute to theological reflection and social improvement in this imperfect world where Christians await their Lord."[80] The congress was a voluntary event that assembled a diverse group of Christians, the great majority of whom were laity. Nearly 800 people attended, including keynote speakers Malcolm Muggeridge, Abigail McCarthy, James Reston, Peter Drucker, and Peter Berger.

Butt's promotion of lay ministry and ecumenism during wave two was, in light of his theologically evangelical roots, nothing short of ground breaking. In the 1960s, he worked with Billy Graham to launch the Layman's Leadership Institute for business and professional leaders, which became a model for many of the Christian lay seminars developed subsequently in the United States and Canada; today, it is known as the Leadership Forum.[81] He also established the model of renewal retreats for the laity in an entity called Laity Lodge, located on a large ranch in the Texas hill country, which remains a vibrant and powerful vehicle for equipping the laity.[82] Laity Lodge today is an ecumenical adult Christian organization that in many ways continues to address the themes of the 1978 North American Congress of the Laity: Christian unity, lay intellectual maturity, and the interaction of Christianity and culture. Like Diehl, Butt bridges waves two and three and continues to write books and essays,[83] speak, and underwrite and convene events aimed at equipping the laity for the "high calling of their daily life."[84]

Popularizing the Practice of Lay Ministry

Hendrik Kraemer was fond of saying, "[T]elling a layperson to go into the modern world and live a Christian life is like telling a person to go alone and unprepared to live at the North Pole."[85] In response to this problem, a stream of popular writing emerged in the 1960s and 1970s. This stream, aimed at both clergy and laity, was designed to give laypeople the proper equipment, supplies, and training for their mission.[86] Books were written by and for two distinctly different groups: first, theologians and clergy; and second— increasingly—the laity.

Many books during this era which were intended to popularize the practice of lay ministry were written by theologians and clergy. Some intended the books to be read by both clergy and laity, yet more often than not the writings were not accessible to the average worker or businessperson.[87] These writings tended to focus on broader questions pertaining to economic structures, economic justice, social ethics, and policy questions, seldom delving down to the minutiae of the workaday world. Though high-level theoretical discourse is important and necessary, it often ends up unusable by the average white-collar or blue-collar worker. Moreover, by the late 1970s, with a few notable exceptions, most theologians and clergy seemed to think about lay ministry in one of two ways. One limited and misguided way of thinking about lay ministry is to see it merely as a means to increase lay participation in the interior life of the gathered church, as opposed to equipping laity for the challenges of life in the scattered church. Many critics of this view, including Diehl, Dick Broholm, and Loren Mead, issued the charge of clericalism against this genre of writings. Of course, not all theologians and clergy were guilty of clericalism. Many understood the different roles of the gathered and the scattered church but simply lacked the theoretical framework, practical experience, or education and training to introduce and support authentic lay ministry outside the church walls.

The other way of thinking about lay ministry understood its focus on the secular world but was affected by aspects of liberation theology and exhibited a de facto bias against those who participated in the mainstream economic sphere and corporate world. Liberation theology's "preferential option for the poor" has sometimes been interpreted as an indictment of business professionals and all who engage in the marketplace. Labeling business-people as "oppressors" leads to the not so subtle inference that their lives run counter to the kingdom of God. Thus, many do not feel welcome in the church. Yet in its more constructive forms, liberation theology raises vital questions of social and economic justice that those called to the marketplace can participate in answering. Unfortunately, in its less constructive forms, it becomes a theological rationale for clergy and theologians who adopt an implied, if not direct, "preferential hostility toward the corporate world" and those who work in it.

A notable exception to these two ways of understanding lay ministry arose during wave two. A small group of theologians and clergy wrote books that sought to understand the plight of people in the workplace, to meet them where they were, and to offer practical guidance for daily living and work.[88] For instance, Lutheran theologian Frederick Wentz wrote texts that accented specific ideas and ways for parishioners to do lay ministry in the weekday world. And pastors James Anderson and Ezra Jones wrote a helpful book, *Ministry of the Laity*, about how work was ministry and the way that faith might inform people in their place of work. A more popular pastoral (and commercial) version was Norman Vincent Peale's *The Power of Positive Thinking* (1952) and subsequent publications by *Guideposts*. Yet despite this development, the other two modes of understanding lay ministry—as increased participation in interior church committees and functions, or as a liberation theology critique of those engaged in the marketplace—generally held sway in the latter part of wave two. For these and other reasons, many theologians and clergy writing on lay ministry misunderstood its underlying theology, mistook its ecclesial aim, and misappropriated its use.

Books intended to popularize the practice of lay ministry were mostly written by and for laypeople themselves, particularly those active in the business world. This category was very diverse, often reflecting the sociological orientations and theological accents of the individual authors. For example, one type of writing was biographical or autobiographical, telling the story of how God worked in the businessman's life to help him achieve commercial fame and success. Some books of this type are sincerely and humbly written.[89] In contrast, others were only thinly veiled hagiographies or promotional books casting the author as a hero deserving of God's financial blessings.[90] Still other lay-authored books were more textured and nuanced, focusing on the how-to of the struggle to integrate the claims of their faith with the demands of the commercial world.[91] Some theologians and clergy might be tempted to dismiss such writings as theologically simplistic or even flawed. However, such a reductionist and sweepingly pejorative view obscures the insights, popularity, and influence these books have had on laity. The authors wrote out of a particular context of the daily challenge of integrating faith and business and, in essence, created a biblical hermeneutic of the business world. Indeed, their work is not inconsistent with the methodologies of black, feminist, womanist, and liberationist theologies, which taught the importance of context and experience in the hermeneutics and application of faith. In a similar vein, the academy might recall the warning of Kraemer, who criticized most discourse by theologians as understandable only to them and as failing to integrate the "counsel and co-operation" of laypeople.[92] Indeed, Kraemer was of the view that books written by lay authors such as C. S. Lewis and others "reach far more people than the books of a great number of theologians together."[93] The bestseller status of popularized wave three authors, such as Rick Warren (*The Purpose Driven Life*, 2002) and Ken Blanchard (*Leadership by the Book*, 1999), would seem to bear out Kraemer's opinion.

The ministry of the laity era did not come to an abrupt halt as the Social Gospel era did. Indeed, it seemed to have a lingering decline that is hard to correlate with any particular societal event or theological issue. Rather, several societal forces in the 1960s and 1970s demanded fresh theological engagement and thus diverted ecclesiastical attention from lay ministry concerns. For instance, the Civil Rights movement, the women's liberation movement, legalized abortion, and the Vietnam War with the related peace movement were all competing for the church's focus. In addition, the threat of nuclear war, the arms race, and heightened environmental concerns moved to the top of the church's agenda.

In addition to these societal factors extrinsic to the institutional church, evidence suggests that the church essentially coopted the energy of the lay ministry movement, directing it to the internal life of the gathered church instead of equipping the laity and unleashing lay ministers into the external life of the scattered church. As evidence of this theory, Kraemer, Weber, and Gibbs each reflected toward the ends of their lives about the hopes and disappointments of the lay ministry movement. Kraemer, writing in 1958, lamented that even in "a book rich in mature wisdom," such as H. R. Niebuhr's *The Purpose of the Church and Its Ministry*, the "laity and its crucial significance . . . is hardly, if at all, mentioned."[94] Gibbs, reflecting in 1982 on thirty-five years encouraging lay ministry, acknowledged the great improvement from the early twentieth century but still lamented the work that still lay ahead for authentic lay ministry to take hold. Gibbs cited four reasons for the failure to make more progress: not enough serious engagement of the topic, either by theologians or laity; tensions between laity and clergy; improper understanding of the church as an institution; and a lack of long-term financial commitment to help new ventures get under way.[95] Weber, writing in 1996 about a lifetime of involvement in the lay ministry movement, wrote:

> The early movements of Life and Work and Faith and Order appeared
> like army officers without troops. Church leaders and theologians were
> present, but the large majority of Christians involved in secular profes-
> sions and attempting to be present as Christ's witnesses in the structures

of society were hardly represented. The Geneva seminars had served the officers and not the laity.[96]

Notwithstanding their observations, I find there are several additional reasons that wave two's interest in lay ministry was sidetracked and receded. First, as I have noted above, the ministry of the laity movement was largely led by, constituted by, and aimed at clergy and theologians. Laypeople—the very people the movement was supposed to be for and about—were, for the most part, excluded from the agenda, structure, and dialogue. Moreover, when laity were involved, they were usually white males, reflecting the leadership patterns of society, with few women or people from racial or ethnic minorities. Not surprisingly, the final product was of little interest to the laypeople most interested in integrating faith and work, nor did it meet their needs. Indeed, as Shoemaker astutely observed decades ago, clergy should be involved, but laypeople should lead the FAW groups. Second, although perhaps unintentionally, Weber's image of officers and troops raises the issue of clericalism, or a two-tiered church citizenship of lay and ordained, which the Protestant Reformation fought hard to eliminate.[97] Although the church's representatives might talk about lay ministry, its actual structure and actions did not empower that ministry to flourish.

A third reason that wave two's interest in lay ministry receded involves the theological academy. The academy operated mainly at the theoretical level and did not make a sustained effort to connect that theory to daily work life. Also, the academy was interested foremost in training clergy, not laity. As Gibbs wrote, "[T]he bulk of money in theological education still goes to the training of ordained clergy," and "almost all new ventures in the theological education of the laity are organized and funded outside the normal church budgets and structures."[98] To the extent that denominational judicatories sought to create lay ministry programs, these staff jobs were the first to be eliminated as declining membership translated into challenging financial times.[99]

The fourth reason for the waning interest in ministry of the laity occurred at the level of the church. As noted, clergy and church professionals often redirected the movement's energy and purpose, redefining lay ministry as more active involvement in church committees and the internal life of the gathered church. Whether church professionals never fully absorbed that, by definition, the location of lay ministry was extrinsic to the gathered church or whether they were threatened by a loss of power and control is open to debate. In any event, as Weber wrote, "I fear that to a great extent our whole discussion on the laity has become just a matter of slogans. . . . if you look at the budgets of almost all the churches, you see that practically nothing has changed."[100]

A fifth reason for the decline of wave two, as noted earlier, pertains to the influence of liberation theology on a generation of mainstream preachers and theologians. In the wake of the societal challenges and issues the church faced during the latter two decades of wave two, liberation theology's "preferential option for the poor" and its critique of oppressive multinational business practices gained a popular following in the mainstream academy. With vestiges of Marxist social analysis still operative in many denominational policy papers, people in the workplace, particularly in for-profit businesses, were led to conclude that participation in the marketplace was unpleasing to God, making money was evil, and life in the economic sphere was somehow intrinsically tainted. Conversely, the opposite reaction occurred in the more conservative churches in response to the social activism of the 1960s and 1970s. True to their premillennial roots, these churches focused on a life of personal piety and salvation, which allowed businesspeople not to feel disenfranchised from the church. These churches encouraged lay ministry to occur outside the gathered church and in the workplace. As we shall see later, their understanding of lay ministry was often narrow, with an accent on evangelizing and personal piety, but it did at least retain aspects of the outward oriented character of lay ministry in and to the world.

Sixth, and finally, returning to Wuthnow and Bosch's frameworks, church teachings on the spiritual and the material—that is, on faith and work—were often misguided. Churches that taught orientations of harmony, compartmentalization, or conflict—rather than integration—tended to be unsupportive of the ministry of the laity. Moreover, often as unwitting heirs of the postmillennialist and premillennialist traditions, congregations were given a false choice between personal salvation and piety or organizational transformation and social justice in the economic sphere, as if God were interested in just one and not the other.

In light of how both the early twentieth-century Social Gospel era and the midcentury Ministry of the Laity era receded, it is tempting to conclude that these two waves of FAW failed. If the criterion for success is never to ebb and only to flow then, in a sense, they did fail. Indeed, in many ways, these waves of FAW activity left little visible imprint on the shoreline of daily church life and academic focus. On the other hand, these two waves kept alive a tradition of lay initiative and engagement—in other words, ministry—in the daily Monday-through-Friday life of church members. Lay ministry is arguably a classic interpretation of Christian discipleship, a tradition faithful to the New Testament teachings and the first three hundred years of the life of the church, before formal lay-clergy distinctions took hold.

Thus, despite the inability of waves one and two to sustain new attitudes in the church and the academy regarding the centrality of lay ministry and the quest to integrate faith and work, the FAW activity succeeded in furthering the theological awareness of and dialogue surrounding faith at work. Nor did it disappear from the Christian landscape, as many people and organizations that were active during the Ministry of the Laity era retained their vitality and continued their efforts in the current wave three of the FAW movement, in which we find ourselves now.[101] Work-related questions about meaning, purpose, ethics, and how to express one's faith at work begin to drive the movement. And there appears to be an irrepressible urge in laity to live an integrated life. This manifests itself in a deep desire to connect faith and work, while hoping for both personal and societal transformation.

FOUR

The Faith at Work Era (c. 1985–Present)

In the summer of 1995, I sent out a letter to some four hundred executive contacts and business acquaintances around the world to advise them that I was leaving my partnership to return to the United States to study theology. I was leaving my dream job in London as a partner in a private equity firm to follow a new calling I had discerned. Having been raised in the northeastern United States, where faith is a personal and private matter, I was rather embarrassed to say why I was leaving or what I was going to study, but in the spirit of full disclosure, I told the truth: at age thirty-eight, I was going to seminary to study theology and see what it had to do with the business world and the people in workplace. Expecting mostly snickering and derisive responses, I was stunned to receive back more than 150 faxes, letters, and phone calls. What surprised me even more was that my letter seemed to strike a deep chord with the recipients. Despite external measurements of career and financial success many of these executives were feeling a deep emptiness and a disconnect from the beliefs, people, and things they valued most in life. I still remember one phone call vividly, and it portrays well a composite view of many of the responses:

> I have worked hard to reach the pinnacle of my profession. I have more money than God, yet I am unfulfilled. My marriage is a shambles, I hardly know my kids, and when I look in the mirror, I wonder where the man went who so idealistically graduated from college 30 years ago and was ready to make his mark on the world. I'd like to talk to my pastor, but he has no clue about my world and the pressures I face. Let me know what you find at seminary. I'd like to talk with you.

This interest by others in my study of theology might never have happened had it not been for an unusual constellation of social and economic variables that emerged and coalesced in the mid-1980s. Although the Ministry of the Laity era had gradually receded by then as social and ecclesiastical conditions sapped the movement of its energy and purpose, these new circumstances helped to create the conditions that gave rise to the third wave of the movement called the Faith at Work era. This era is evident as early as 1985, built momentum and size through the 1990s, and still continues today with no sign of receding. And the social and economic conditions that helped to spawn, sustain, and drive this newest version of the FAW movement are, if anything, intensifying.

Societal Context of FAW: Why Again and Why Now?

There are no broad studies or scholarly theories offered by theologians as to why the FAW movement was spawned, what caused its ebb and flow over the past century, why this third phase of the movement emerged, and why it remains active today with little sign of receding. To gain such an understanding, I turn first to the social sciences for possible theoretical underpinnings for the movement and socioeconomic research that illuminates it, which I then interpret theologically. University of Chicago Nobel Prize–winning economist Robert William Fogel offers a sound theoretical framework upon which to build. Second, I bring in my own observations about the new social conditions that are key contributors to the rise of the Faith at Work movement in wave three and draw on some of the insights of Harvard Business School researcher and ethicist Laura Nash.

Fogel is not writing specifically about the Faith at Work movement, yet his findings in *The Fourth Great Awakening and the Future of Egalitarianism* help to frame the overall social economic context in which the FAW movement emerged, and he offers specific reasons as to why such a movement might continue to flourish.[1] Fogel combines five main themes—technological change, economic growth, cultural crisis, religious crisis, and political crisis—in a detailed historical economic analysis that sees American history as periodized into four great awakenings. He views these great awakenings as "reform movements with an ethical/programmatic phase followed by a legislative/political phase."[2] Notably, he suggests that faith, in particular evangelical Christian faith, has played a crucial role in American history and public policy during these four major great awakenings. His Fourth Great Awakening roughly correlates in time to wave three of the FAW movement.[3]

Fogel's second major finding, and more pertinent for the purposes of this study, pertains to the relative importance of material assets versus immaterial (or spiritual) assets. In contrast to prior periods, historical economic evidence suggests that now it is no longer access to or the distribution of material resources that is essential to an egalitarian future. Rather, the essential issue facing America now is access to and the distribution of spiritual resources. Fogel asserts:

> [T]he future of egalitarianism in America turns on the nation's ability to combine continued economic growth with an entirely new set of egalitarian reforms that address the urgent spiritual needs of our age, secular as well as sacred. Spiritual (or immaterial) inequity is now as great a problem as material inequity, perhaps even greater.[4]

Among such spiritual or immaterial assets, he includes some seventeen attributes, including a sense of purpose, a strong family ethic, self-esteem, and spiritual enrichment. In an interview I conducted with him (February 8, 2002), he more expressly mentioned "organized religion and its ethical moral teachings" as a spiritual asset. Critics of Fogel's theory of great awakenings challenge his interpretation of history, theology, and politics.[5] Less challenged, however, are his assertions that religion and spiritual assets have played an important role in economic development and the shaping of an egalitarian society and that today they play an even more important role than they did the past. In effect, Fogel suggests a strong link can and should exist between the corporate world of materiality and the religious world of spirituality. If Fogel is right, it seems that a corporation's bottom line can and maybe even should include Faith at Work initiatives. That is, if access to and distribution of spiritual resources are now the most important factors upon which the egalitarian health and wealth of the American people depend, then the Faith at Work movement's aim of integrating spirituality and work is all the more significant. Indeed, the hypothesis that religion does have consequences in the presumptively material realm of economics, which Max Weber gave as a sociologist of religion in the early twentieth century (see *The Protestant Ethic and the Spirit of Capitalism* and *Economy and Society*), is now supported in new forms by Robert William Fogel and several other major writers in new forms in the early twenty-first century.[6]

Within this macroeconomic-historical context, Nash and McLennan's study of the Sunday-Monday is informative.[7] They surveyed church members, pastors, and seminaries to see what support, if any, the ecclesiastical community was providing to the laity in their daily work.[8] Arguably, the mere existence of this study serves as evidence of Fogel's suggested Fourth Great Awakening. Nash and McLennan do not offer a specific theory as to the origin of the FAW movement. However, they suggest that "six major realities have particularly influenced the shape of new spirituality programs," including the impact of the baby boomer generation, the new global economy, increasing work-related stress, new scientific concepts, postmodern paradigms, and the rise of the business guru.[9] These and other factors are addressed below.

Nash and McLennan have a different focus than does Fogel, but combined, their research offers complementary evidence of the conditions that have created and are sustaining the Faith at Work movement. While helpful, neither sought to offer a theological or ethical analysis of the movement's social and economic factors. Further, neither sought to examine the shape and form of the Faith at Work movement, nor to offer theologically based suggestions for its continued unfolding. To better understand the societal and theological context of wave three, I examine here three interconnected areas of importance—changes in geopolitics, the law, and demographics; changes in workplace patterns; and changes in faith patterns—that gave rise to and continue to sustain the Faith at Work movement.

The political landscape underwent a dramatic change in the 1980s and 1990s, and the increased role of public religious discourse was unmistakable. On an international scale, the Berlin Wall came down in 1989, and within a short time, the world observed the peaceful dismantling of the USSR. While many factors contributed to that fall, it was due at least in part to religious ideas, such as papal encyclicals critical of the human rights abuses of communism and its rejection of private property, and Pope John Paul II's public and private interventions. In parallel, there was a general global move away from state-controlled, collectivist political and economic ideologies, and a general move toward some form of democratic governance and deregulated free-market economies. While democratic capitalism is certainly not without shortcomings, communism and Marxism were generally seen to have been flawed experiments: inefficient economically, fraught with corruption, harmful environmentally, stifling of human creativity, abusive of individual human rights, and void of spiritual guidance and moral authority. Another major event with international ramifications was the nonviolent removal of apartheid in South Africa in the 1990s. Like the other events, this also catapulted issues of human dignity and moral authority into the public consciousness, with an added overlay of the role of international business in helping to support or bring about the demise of apartheid. Religious organizations around the world challenged business leaders to align their faith teachings with their marketplace practices and to challenge the injustices of apartheid.

Closer to home, in the 1980s the United States saw the reengagement of conservative religious voices in American public policy debates. The Moral Majority and other well-organized grassroots campaigns challenged social policies and cultural directions (particularly as regards school prayer, family values, marriage, and abortion), in much the same way that liberal religious groups challenged the social policies and cultural directions of the 1960s and 1970s (particularly as regards racism, women's rights, the Vietnam War, and poverty). While perhaps not their primary aim, Jerry Falwell's Moral Majority and its heirs (such as the Christian Coalition, Pat Robertson's 700 Club, Dr. James Dobson's Focus on the Family, and numerous other conservative Christian entities with political activism and aims) had the unintended consequence of reintroducing religious discourse into the public square. This trend has only increased during President George W. Bush's two terms and his administration's open policy to include, if not privilege, religious discourse and reasoning. In new ways, however, this revived a tradition of theologically informed public discourse in America,[10] exemplified in earlier decades by Walter Rauschenbusch, Reinhold Niebuhr, and Martin Luther King, Jr., and still practiced in wave three by some leading international figures.[11] A common thread among these geopolitical events—from the dismantling of the USSR to the fall of apartheid in South Africa to the rise of conservative Republican politics in America—is the role that religious discourse played, both publicly and behind the scenes.

In parallel to and connected with the religiously infused geopolitical changes, a mixture of legal and demographic changes contributed to an increase in religious expression in the U.S. workplace during the 1980s and 1990s. A national study by human resources managers on "religion in the workplace" attributed this to several concomitant factors, including judicial findings, legislative action, greater employee awareness of legal rights, and new immigration patterns with workers requesting accommodation to practice their religion while at work.[12] Many people had incorrectly assumed that it was illegal to practice any form of religious expression in the workplace. Almost reflexively, people cited the constitutional "separation of church and state" as the rationale for such a view. However, as constitutional scholar Stephen Carter[13] and others[14] have pointed out, this is an inaccurate reading of the First Amendment to the U.S. Constitution.[15] Religion in the workplace is regulated by a variety of laws, including several different federal laws and regulations, state laws, and the U.S. Constitution.[16] In particular, Title VII of the Civil Rights Act of 1964 "bars discrimination in the workplace on the basis of religion."[17] The Title VII definition of *religion* was amended in 1972 to "require employers to 'reasonably accommodate' an individual's sincerely held religious observances or religious practices. The employer can avoid making an accommodation only if to do so would constitute an 'undue hardship' on the employer's business."[18]

In short, private-sector employers are gradually learning that expressions of faith in the workplace are not illegal per se. Moreover, they are also

learning that failure to understand this and to accommodate reasonable requests may subject them to charges of discrimination and EEOC lawsuits.[19]
Thus, employees do have legal rights and a fair degree of latitude for religious
expression, even including proselytizing, so long as it is not considered harassment. At the same time, general legal principles regarding harassment and
hostile work environments also pertained to those who express and practice
their religion at work. This patchwork of laws regarding freedom of expression, discrimination, harassment, and equal opportunity evolved significantly
since wave two. The result of these legal rights and greater awareness of these
rights are key societal factors contributing to creating the conditions for
wave three of the Faith at Work movement to commence and flourish. Indeed,
in the wake of the 9/11 terrorist attacks, questions of religious expression and
discrimination in the workplace have only increased, particularly with the
influx of Muslim workers, often political refugees, to the United States.

In conjunction with the geopolitical and legal changes, the demographic
impact of the baby-boomer generation emerged as another key factor. Due to
the size of the group and its economic purchasing power, the baby boomers
(i.e., the generation born after World War II, between 1946 and 1964) were
dominant trendsetters in the 1980s and 1990s. In the 1990s and 2000s, this
generation has become the primary influence in the workforce, assuming
the mantle of corporate and governmental leadership. While some charge this
generation with being narcissistic and self-centered,[20] others see it as more
complex and perhaps naïvely idealistic. For instance, David Brooks's at times
satirical *Bobos in Paradise* observes the boomer-aged consumers' shift from
social righteousness (being anti-establishment and anti–Vietnam War) to
righteous materialism (purchasing environmentally friendly products).[21]
Brooks contends that baby boomers are growing up and looking for an alternative to the midcentury work ethic of "the man in the gray flannel suit."
Wave three boomers want to have successful careers and material pleasures,
but they also want to do it in a way that is environmentally friendly, socially
conscious, and self-fulfilling. While not always successful, this is a generation
that seeks balance and integration. The result is a renewed interest in developing strategies that offer insights into a holistic life, including a return to
religion and spiritual resources.

The economic context of the mid-1980s, when wave three began, was a
time of great upheaval and change in the corporate world. In the early 1980s,
many pundits had predicted the end of U.S. global economic dominance.
Crippled by the Organization of Petroleum Exporting Countries (OPEC) and
the oil embargos of the late 1970s, the Dow Jones industrial average sank to a
modern low of 777 in 1982, some 20 percent lower than in 1966. Inflation and
interest rates were at historic highs, the U.S. economy was in a recession, and

a sense of doom and gloom pervaded U.S. business.[22] The so-called tiger countries of the Asian Pacific rim and "Japan Inc." were heralded as the new economic forces to be reckoned with, providing innovative and desirable consumer products with superior quality and lower prices. West Germany was also held up as a superior marketplace model in the way that its interconnected relationships among banks, corporations, and labor unions seemed to create the conditions for its postwar economic miracle.

However, by the middle of the 1980s, the U.S. economic climate improved dramatically as a result of renewed emphases on quality, service, and technology, as well as the development of innovative financial instruments, restructurings, and other corporate strategies. For instance, the merger mania of the 1980s was fueled by creative new financial instruments such as leveraged buyouts (LBOs), management buyouts (MBOs), and junk bonds (high-yield but speculative lowest-grade corporate bonds). In addition, brash new banking and investment organizations, such as New York–based Kohlberg Kravis Roberts & Co. (KKR), specialized in management and leveraged buyouts, often buying large public firms and taking them private.[23] They also broke up, formed, and merged various enterprises. Corporate law firms, such as New York–based Skadden, Arps, Slate, Meagher, and Flom, specialized in mergers and acquisitions, creating new legal strategies for both hostile takeovers and defense work.[24] Michael Milken, Ivan Boesky, KKR, and others had recognized the economic malaise of American corporations, and they awoke corporate management out of its "dogmatic slumber" (to borrow from Kant) and underperforming ways. Indeed, the *Harvard Business Review* noted that shareholders benefited immensely, as "hostile takeovers and LBOs became the primary vehicle to close the value gap."[25] As a result of these and other factors, there emerged a heightened management accent on short-term financial gains and results. While this was good for shareholder value and the long-term health of some operating divisions, the break-up of big conglomerates (e.g., Beatrice Companies, RJR Nabisco) caused huge short-term social and human costs, such as layoffs, plant closings, the elimination of middle-management layers, the break-up of lifelong-employment concepts, and evaporating employee loyalty. Unlike traditional economic down cycles, which affected just blue-collar manufacturing jobs, these changes also affected middle-and upper-middle-class white-collar workers. Indeed, in the wake of the recession and corporate accounting scandals of the early 2000s, many pundits charge that the excessive accent on short-term financial results, earnings per share, and stock price has also negatively affected the longer-term health of corporations.

Some refer to the 1980s as "the greed decade"[26] while others call it "the golden age of buyouts."[27] All of the turmoil that resulted from the merger mania had a significant human cost, resulting in widespread restructuring and layoffs, whose reach was not limited to white-collar elites in Wall Street and corporate boardrooms, but was felt across the United States. Moreover, the stock market crash of October 1987 caused further uncertainty and dislocation to blue- and white-collar workers alike, as companies quickly responded with deep layoffs, and an air of anxiety permeated American workplaces. The old covenant between employer and employee, particularly in middle-management and white-collar jobs, with expectations of loyalty and lifelong employment, was forever over.

Only toward the end of the decade did business scholars begin to question the ethical concerns of the boom in mergers and acquisitions. In an article entitled "The Often Overlooked Ethical Aspect of Mergers," the *Journal of Business Ethics* observed, "Several recent surveys have indicated that based on past experience, more than half of these mergers won't work out. It appears that many times the last consideration . . . are the human resources matters of the merged corporation."[28] Looking back on this decade, the *Harvard Business Review* concluded that the 1980s were a curious mixture of crime, greed, value creation, new ideas, and great social dislocation.[29] And as art often imitates life, the brash dismantling and restructuring of America's corporate world in the 1980s was captured in several critically acclaimed books and popular movies.[30] Finally, as William Taylor notes in the *Harvard Business Review*, "A true reckoning with the 1980s must analyze both the economics and the illegalities, both the value creation and the social costs."[31] Taylor concludes:

> Takeovers and LBOs had a profound effect on the fabric and psyche of American economic life. They also recast the distribution of rewards and sacrifice within companies, usually with little regard for responsibility or need. The undeniable reality is that the people who experienced most of the suffering—those who lost their jobs, those who kept their jobs but lost their sense of loyalty and security, those whose communities were turned upside down—played no role in creating the original problems.[32]

Closely related to the economic climate, as both cause and effect, were the rapid wave three developments in technology. In the 1980s and beyond, advanced new information technologies and manufacturing techniques changed the operational infrastructure of the corporate world much in the same way that the new financial engineering methods changed the balance sheets of corporate America. The technological changes were many, including telecommunications (satellites, cable, fiber optics, and broadband), computers (mainframe processing power, silicon chip advances, and the personal computer), software (systems and applications), transportation (container

ships), robotics, and offshore manufacturing. In the 1990s the Internet revolution occurred, introducing the World Wide Web, e-mail, dot.com businesses, "clicks and mortar," business-to-business (B2B) applications, and a
host of so-called new economy models. The results of these technological
changes, which continue today, are immense and yet to be fully understood.
Large portions of the workforce became "free agents," preferring part-time
and consulting assignments over the constraints and binding nature of
full-time employment.[33] To a significant extent, it is possible that America's
history of individualism created the conditions for this free agent–fueled
technological boom period. Prior to the burst of the dot.com bubble in 2001,
an entrepreneurial culture was born, such that in 1999 more M.B.A. graduates
went into start-ups than into investment banking or consulting for the first
time ever.[34] After the bubble burst, Federal Reserve Board chairman Alan
Greenspan chided the market for the "irrational exuberance" of investors in
the 1990s.[35] In light of all these factors, the U.S. workplace and the workforce
will never be the same.

Positively, for many, these innovations led to increased opportunities,
lower barriers to entry, reduced costs, revolutionized global import-export
possibilities, decreased product design and manufacturing time, reduced
controls over foreign currency exchanges, less restricted movement of capital
across borders, and lower labor costs. These and other technological changes
combined to create both possibility and promise for blue- and white-collar
workers in the United States. For many, it created new job options and career
paths. Unprecedented numbers of employees became paper millionaires from
stock options and grants, initial public offerings (IPOs), stock appreciation,
and cash bonuses. Despite this financial success, or perhaps because of it,
increasing numbers of affluent professionals also felt that their lives were out
of balance and spiritually impoverished.

But for many, these innovations had significantly negative economic
and social costs, such as layoffs, plant closures, elimination of middle-
management layers, career uncertainty, longer work hours, skill- and job-
retraining needs, and general insecurity. Those without access to the skills of
the new technologies risked being left behind economically. Moreover, the
lines between home and work became blurred as people began working longer
hours.[36] As a result of these profound changes in work patterns and other
factors, business newspapers and journals began to feature stories of businesspeople who were no longer satisfied with their career ambitions and
making money, who felt spiritually empty and unfulfilled from their work,
who were tired of living compartmentalized and bifurcated lives, whose
health and well-being were suffering from workplace anxiety, reengineering,
downsizing, long hours, and little sense of meaning or purpose.

Paralleling these broad changes in religiously influenced geopolitics, demographics, economics, and technology, a noticeable change occurred in the 1980s in the way that religion and spirituality were perceived and practiced. This can best be understood by observing the changing patterns in religious beliefs and practices. Robert Wuthnow and George Gallup have gathered evidence concerning these changes and have interpreted the beliefs and practices that began early in wave three and continue today. As for practices, in his 1998 study *After Heaven: Spirituality in America since the 1950s*, Wuthnow suggests that "a profound change in our spirituality practices has indeed taken place during the last half of the twentieth century."[37] Wuthnow is not referring to public forms of religion and religious expression per se, but to the "more subtle reordering that has taken place in how Americans understand the sacred itself."[38] His thesis is that Americans have shifted from a spirituality of dwelling to a spirituality of seeking, where a "spirituality of dwelling emphasizes habitation," whereas "a spirituality of seeking emphasizes negotiation."[39] Of course, "one form is not entirely new, nor is the other completely out of vogue."[40] Further, Wuthnow observes:

> [D]espite the fact that dwelling and seeking are familiar aspects of human life, the circumstances in which people live typically reinforce one or the other type of these orientations to a greater extent in different historical periods. With relative stability, a spirituality of dwelling can be a compelling way of thinking about the universe, whereas times of uncertainty and change are more conducive to seeking.[41]

These conditions of uncertainty, change, and lack of stability are precisely those that many workers face today and are consistent with the seeker orientation of those engaged in the Faith at Work movement. These conditions existed prior to 9/11 and have only increased since then, particularly in light of the fear of further domestic terrorist acts and the war in Iraq. Reinforcing these findings is the earlier observation that people increasingly prefer to view themselves as spiritual instead of religious (see chapter 1). Moreover, spirituality's accent on seeking, discovering, and applying faith in practical ways to daily life correlates well with the Faith at Work movement.

Regarding practices, Gallup observes that the decline in the mainstream denominations since their peak church attendance in the 1950s has been offset by an increase in Catholic, Southern Baptist, and Pentecostal churches, while membership in other independent and free-standing evangelical churches "held steady."[42] Data from Barna Research Group and others confirm this pattern. Consistent with Wuthnow's concept of seeking, Gallup observes the move away from denominational loyalty. Believers no longer expect to join the church of their parents. Not content to accept the full range of church teachings and doctrine of their own tradition, baby boomers have become "grazers at the spiritual smorgasbord," sometimes even attending more than one house of worship.[43] Many boomers in the Christian tradition have become cafeteria Christians, choosing the beliefs and practices they like and rejecting those that they find disagreeable, outdated, or unimportant.

As for beliefs, North Americans still report an overwhelming belief in God and view themselves as spiritual. Gallup says, "Americans today appear to be just as attracted to religion as they were a half century ago," with 95 percent of the public in 1947 saying they believed in God and 96 percent of the public in 1997 saying they believed in God.[44] Indeed, there has been a marked surge in those who say they "feel the need in their lives to experience spiritual growth" (surging 24 points in just four years, from 58 percent in 1994 to 82 percent in 1998).[45] The result of such a felt need to experience spiritual growth, coupled with Wuthnow's concept of the new spirituality of seeking helps to explain the explosion of interest in Faith at Work groups as a new means of manifesting this search.

The result of applying these beliefs and practices to life in the marketplace may help to explain the marked increase in late twentieth- and early twenty-first-century Faith at Work activity. Significantly, the evidence confirms a new workplace search for meaning and value, as "the percentage that says they have thought a lot about 'the basic meaning and value of their lives' has swelled eleven points—from 58% in 1985 to 69%" in 1999.[46] Further, the "rejection of materialism" is given as one of the key reasons for this new quest for meaning.[47] Gallup observes a "mounting body of surveys, findings, and data" that identify the powerful role of the "faith factor" as an essential internal motivating force for how Americans choose to live their lives.[48] He concludes, "Two of the underlying desires of the American people at this time are to find deeper meaning in life and to build deeper, more trusting relations with other people in our often impersonal and fragmented society."[49] The result, for many, is to find this deeper meaning, trust, and overcoming of fragmentation through participation in FAW groups. Moreover, there appears to be a utilitarian benefit, as well, as "the deeply spiritual or religiously committed among the American population have fewer drug and alcohol problems, less depression, and lower rates of suicide. They enjoy their lives and marriages more than do the less religious in society."[50]

In view of this constellation of societal changes, I cannot identify a specific date or a single variable that alone accounts for wave three's emergence in the 1980s and continuation through today. Rather, a rich compendium of significantly altered and still-changing geopolitical, legal, demographic, economic, technological, and religious factors, within a historical context, converged to create fertile soil for the Faith at Work movement to emerge and flourish.

Wave Three: A Quest for Integration

In light of this context and the prevailing socioeconomic conditions of constant change, the types of issues and needs driving those in the Faith at Work movement become clearer. Men and women in large corporations are no longer content to be "the organization man" of the 1950s and 1960s or "the organization woman" of the 1970s.[51] Toward the end of wave two, people began to seek an alternative to the unsatisfactory options of harmonization, conflict, or compartmentalization and found that alternative in integration.

If there is one overriding theme or organizing principle that appears to be a commonly held view by virtually all participants in the movement and that drives interest in Faith at Work, it is: a quest for integration. There is a shared view that faith and work are not meant to be separated or isolated from each other. Businesspeople want the ability to bring their whole selves to work—mind, body, and soul—and are no longer satisfied with sacrificing their core identities or being mere cogs in the machine, nor do they want a disconnected spirituality. People in the workplace of all levels and types no longer seem willing to leave their soul with the car in the parking lot. They reject a dualist or Manichaean view of the world where religion is held distant from and seen as unrelated to the materiality of daily work. Indeed, just as they seek spirituality in their work, they want to bring the issues of their work into their worship. Christian businesspeople and other professionals find common agreement that living a bifurcated life, where faith and work are compartmentalized, is neither true to the Gospel nor a healthy way to work.

Integration acknowledges the distinctive natures of faith and work, as well as other different spheres of life, while also bringing them together in a reconstructive, dialectical, and holistic fashion. The quest for integration avoids the naïveté of expecting the kingdom of God to be realized here on earth, but it also rejects the alternative extreme of despair and cynicism. The quest for integration seeks to approximate wholeness and balance while recognizing the difficulty of attaining it.[52] It knows the reality of sin, yet it hopes for sanctification and transformation in light of salvation promises, even if these can only be fully realized in an eschatological horizon beyond our present capacities.

The quest for integration, as the organizing principle for the demand side—to borrow a term from the business world—of FAW, can be analyzed typologically. Within each type, there are also varying degrees of how faith is manifested at work. That is, FAW participants and groups exhibit differing types of integration of faith and work, both in conceptual and practical terms across the three arenas of workplace identity. People identify with their own work or position, the organization that employs them, and the numerous stakeholders they impact in society at large. Further, there are several ways in which participants understand and manifest their need to integrate faith and work.

The issues that men and women face in wave three constitute the demand side of the equation just as the various groups, conferences, and newsletters constitute the supply side of the movement (see chapters 6–7). The demand for the FAW movement also offers yet more evidence for one of Diani's components of what comprises a social movement.

Formal evidence of the demand emerges from research into the Faith at Work movement, including surveys and studies that reveal a consistent pattern of issues that seem to drive or motivate those participating in the movement.[53] More informal and anecdotal evidence emerges from a review of the media, the business academy, the growth in "spirituality and work" nonprofit organizations, personal stories of businesspeople, and conferences, newsletters, and Web sites all dedicated to faith at work (see chapter 6 and the bibliography).

The demand for faith at work may best be understood by identifying and analyzing the needs that businesspeople and other workers feel. These needs and issues are found in and across three arenas in which most businesspeople are located. Conceptually perceived as three concentric circles, most businesspeople operate within the arena of their own immediate work and job description, within the larger corporate arena of their organization, and finally within the even broader arena of society at large. Some of the demand-side issues are located in just one arena, while others can be found in all three. That is, sometimes an FAW issue is largely personal, yet that same issue might also have organizational relevance or even societal ramifications. Some participants in the FAW movement focus on personal faith and work concerns, while for others the reference point is organizational or even societal concerns. Many in the Faith at Work movement have a focus on addressing questions of social justice, economic justice, and the underlying structural conditions that impact these topics. In this sphere of interest, businesspeople and Faith at Work groups with postmillennialist roots are often found. As noted in chapter 2, the postmillennialist theology emphasizes the importance of saving society and improving the conditions that cause social injustice.

The research for this book suggests that, broadly speaking, the manifestation of this quest for integration of faith and work can be seen in four major types of faith issues: ethics, evangelism, experience, and enrichment, or the Four E's. In practice, these manifestations are often interrelated and overlapping. Some participants in the movement are motivated by all four areas of concern, whereas for others, involvement in the FAW movement may be driven exclusively by one issue or category. I elaborate on the Four E's in more detail in chapters 6 and 7, as part of an extended discussion of a proposed analytical framework called the Integration Box.

Just as individual people in the marketplace manifest their quest to integrate faith and work through these Four E's types, FAW groups and organizations display these same tendencies. The first mode of integrating faith and work is the *ethics* type. For many businesspeople in the movement, ethics is the primary way their faith manifests itself at work, by connecting biblical ethics to concrete applications in marketplace settings. They seek to discern and culturally transpose biblical teachings or principles to the complex ethical dilemmas faced at work in contemporary society. To this type, ethics can range from personal behavior to more public social or corporate ethics. Conflict can emerge in cases where personal ethical standards come into conflict with or challenge the larger business ethos of the company for which they work or, indeed, the industry sector in which they operate.

The second manifestation of faith and work is called the *evangelism* (or expression) type. This group focuses on the expression of faith at work, which often, though not always, is verbal. The evangelism type is both straightforward and complex. Based on several factors, people have different understandings of and comfort with the Great Commission (Matt. 28:19–20), which teaches Christians are to spread the Gospel to all ends of the earth. Those coming out of the premillennialist traditions see this as central to defining "faith at work," indeed maybe even one of the primary purposes of the workplace. Others, coming largely out of the postmillennialist tradition, resist evangelizing coworkers, finding it to be a misuse of marketplace relationships and purposes. Thus, some view work primarily as a mission field with the main purpose of evangelizing others, while others view work itself as mission, part of fulfilling one's vocation.[54] Indeed, the issue of evangelizing in the workplace can cause conflict even between Christians in the FAW movement. Moreover, many who are outside the movement, but hear of it, often incorrectly presume that Faith at Work is a homogeneous movement and merely a euphemism for evangelizing coworkers.

A third manifestation of integrating faith and work is the *experience* type. People and groups with this accent focus on how they experience their work in theological or spiritual terms. Businesspeople of this type increasingly look for meaning and purpose in their work. People expect work itself to be more than an instrumental activity as a mere means to pay the mortgage or a duty as a member of civil society. Indeed, employees want their work to be more than just a job. They seek intrinsic meaning and teleological purpose in their work. They may even express it theologically in terms of wanting to view their work as a vocation or spiritual calling. These existential questions of meaning, purpose, and calling can be found in the individual job arena, in the corporate arena, and even at the societal level as employees question the role their organizations play in the other domains such as politics and the environment.

A final and very broad manifestation of integrating faith and work is the *enrichment* type. This is an expansive type, often inward focused in nature, and including many related issues, such as spiritual disciplines, therapeutic healing, and transformation. For instance, many express renewed interest in spiritual nurturing and growth. This covers a range of personal spiritual disciplines, including development of prayer and meditation practices, Scripture study, spiritual discernment skills, and greater self-awareness and consciousness. Further, some people become active in the Faith at Work movement with therapeutic goals in mind, seeking personal healing from emotional, physical, or psychological damage suffered in the workplace, incurred from events such as downsizing, poor management, prolonged stress, competitive pressures, extended time away from home, and skill obsolescence. This inner healing and enrichment often take place in isolation but also in community by virtue of membership or participation in an FAW group. Such group involvement, in turn, leads to an accent on collective solidarity, fellowship, and broader growth as a community. Another very important attribute of people of the enrichment type is a desire for transformation. At the personal level, some express this by involvement in the human potential movement and the reading of self-help books. For others, particularly in the Christian tradition, transformation is understood in ontological and religious terms where the self is reborn and transformed in the image of Christ. The issue of transformation can also shift its reference point from the personal arena to the corporate arena, seeking, for instance, to help one's company change its corporate culture, or even to the arena of society at large. Thus, the enrichment type can range from the very personal to the very public with far-reaching effects.

The organizing principle of integration, combined with the Four E's just described and placed in the setting of the broader social, political, and cultural context that emerged in the 1980s, gave birth to wave three of the FAW movement. Indeed, nationwide clusters of FAW activity, as seen more fully in chapters 6 and 7, help to provide further evidence of this as a bona fide social movement. Indeed, the third component of Diani's three-part framework of what constitutes a movement[55] emphasizes that movements respond to "conflictual issues." Diani broadens the conception of *conflict* to include "areas previously considered typical of the private sphere, involving problems of self-definition and challenges to the dominant life-styles, for example."[56] Further, he distinguishes between political and cultural conflict at both the systemic and nonsystemic levels, whether dealing with power, material goods, or socially shared meanings. Indeed, he notes that many social movements of a cultural nature (versus a political nature) "tend to focus more and more on self-transformation."[57]

This understanding of conflictual issues correlates well with the FAW movement of wave three; political issues are seldom the focus, whereas personal and organizational transformation is often central. The conflictual issues motivating many in the FAW movement are grounded in a desire to resolve the moral and ethical conflict experienced between the claims of their faith and the demands of their work. The faith teachings of participants often seem to stand in opposition to workplace norms and rules, resulting in a sense of bifurcation and ethical conflict. Further, this conflict can manifest itself in a desire to transform oneself, often involving therapeutic and spiritual healing, as in the enrichment type above. In addition to personal conflict and a desire for transformation of the self, evidence also suggests that many in the FAW movement find their religiously grounded values in conflict with company norms and practices. They find conflict at the individual, organizational, and societal levels, and they participate in the FAW movement as a way to resolve some or all of these areas of cultural conflict between religious teachings and economic reality. They seek transformation of themselves, their company, and sometimes even society itself.

FIVE

Response of the Church and the Theological Academy to FAW

A 1998 *Wall Street Journal* article noted, "Successful professionals are trying to return to church or synagogue. But they don't always know how to start again, nor do religious institutions know how to reach out to them. 'We have no way to talk to them,' a church official says. 'You don't ask a CEO to stuff envelopes.'"[1] Thus, there exists a mutual problem. Like two nervous teenagers who are attracted to one another and want to date, no one knows how to make the first move. And besides, why not ask a CEO to stuff envelopes?

Among the many roles and functions of both the church and the theological academy is to think theologically about the nature and purpose of humanity. So it would seem that those institutions would be deeply involved with any major issue involving daily life, including engagement in the economic sphere. It would seem that the church would be interested in providing theological reflection and ethical guidance to laypeople on all topics of social importance, including life in the marketplace and the nature and purpose of work. Similarly, it would seem that the academy would want to train pastors to help laypeople on those same topics. We might think the church would be interested in being present in the whole of life, including the workplace where most parishioners spend the majority of their waking hours, and that the academy through research would support such a view. We might think the church would be interested in helping the laity in matters of vocational discernment and spiritual nurturing to sustain themselves in their particular callings and daily ministry. Yet, in these matters, the anecdotal and empirical evidence suggest just the opposite.

It would seem that the church could be one of the best resources to help people live balanced and meaningful lives at work. The church could offer theological and ethical resources to help transform corporate life and its impact on society. The church could provide spiritual insights into our humanity and the purpose of human work that could revolutionize our approach to business life. Yet, in most cases, it does not. Why?

The Silence of the Church

Unlike many European countries today, the church is not a marginalized factor in American society. The National Council of Churches (NCC) reports that its "36 Protestant, Anglican and Orthodox member denominations include more than 50 million persons in 140,000 local congregations in communities across the nation."[2] Add to this the nation's non-NCC evangelical, Pentecostal, free-standing, and Roman Catholic churches, and that number could probably double.[3] Individually and collectively, these estimated 280,000 churches could exert a major influence on society in general and the business world in particular. Yet broadly speaking, the empirical evidence suggests that these churches retain a Sunday-centered and institutional orientation that does not meet the growing needs and concerns of workers, especially businesspeople. They are left to fend for themselves theologically or to turn to secular sources for ethical guidance and spiritual nurturance about matters pertaining to their daily ministry and the environment in which they work.

While the empirical evidence and felt experience of many businesspeople demonstrate an ecclesiastical neglect and apathy toward honoring and equipping those who work in the marketplace, there are some notable exceptions to this general finding. Some churches have recognized the demand for a theological, ecclesiastical, ethical, and pastoral response, and they have developed Faith at Work programs.[4] These initiatives, usually local in nature, often result in a specialized ministry, complete with weekday-oriented small groups and programmatic initiatives, as well as inclusion in Sunday's liturgical life in the form of sermons, prayers, and commissioning.

Notably, according to a study by Stephen Hart and David A. Krueger, the churches that display a positive response to the needs of the workplace and those called to the marketplace often tend to come out of evangelically oriented churches and, to some extent, Pentecostal churches.[5] Indeed, the same study suggests that evangelicals "show a consistently higher level of integration between faith and work than do other religious groups. This is true not only with regard to discussing religious matters at work but across the board, including use of faith as a basis for decision making."[6] In addition, the evidence suggests that, generally speaking, the black church has a longer tradition of holistic thinking that views all of human life as coming under the influence of Christ and the earthly guidance of the church.[7] That is, the black church experience is traditionally less inclined to compartmentalize the

Sunday and Monday worlds in the way that the white church historically has done. As such, the black church may be more effectively ministering to workplace-related needs and issues faced by congregants. Further, the evidence suggests that black church clergy do not tend to have the antimaterialism and anticapitalism tendencies evident in the mainline white church. Indeed, many black churches stress the importance of entering into and succeeding in the business world and in the professions. This is an often overlooked but important dimension of Martin Luther King, Jr.'s message during the Civil Rights era,[8] and it is a theme continued today by many black church leaders.[9] Notably, as one black pastor surveyed said, "What's wrong with wanting to help your congregation improve their income?"[10] However, this accent in the black church on financial and workplace success can also include theologically problematic "health and wealth" prosperity gospel preaching. Moreover, anecdotal evidence suggests that, as black churchgoers attain more workplace success, they increasingly face many of the same Sunday-Monday gap tensions outlined in this book.

Thus, despite some exceptions,[11] the evidence strongly suggests that the church in general seems uninterested in, unaware of, or unsure of how to help the laity integrate their faith identities and teachings with their workplace occupations, problems, and possibilities. One prestigious business magazine, Across the Board, expressed the problem in 2001 with a cover story entitled "How the Church Has Failed Business."[12] It substantiated the claim that there is a gaping chasm between what is heard on Sunday in one's place of worship and what is experienced on Monday in one's place of work. This Sunday-Monday gap between clergy and businesspersons, between ecclesiastical and business life, and between worship and work has been documented in individual narratives, anecdotal evidence, and empirical studies.[13] The evidence is derived from the church's actions (both form and substance) and also from the church's inaction or silence. This pattern is apparent at all levels of the ecclesiastical hierarchy, from the local church to the various judicatory levels of the denomination, and includes ecumenical bodies such as the NCC and the World Council of Churches (WCC). Indeed, the higher up the church hierarchy one climbs, the less interest—let alone awareness—there is in speaking to the Sunday-Monday gap.

Bill Diehl, as noted earlier, is a former sales manager with Bethlehem Steel, active Lutheran layperson, author, and leader in the FAW movement. Diehl has been sharply critical of what the church professes about lay ministry and Christian vocation versus what it actually does to affirm and equip those called to live out their vocation in the marketplace. In a comment that could easily have come from a typical FAW participant of today, in 1976 Diehl expressed his sense of abandonment from the church (note that a careful reading of his words also reveals concern about all of the Four E's of ethics, evangelism, experience, and enrichment):

> In the almost 30 years of my professional career, my church has never once suggested that there be any type of accounting of my on-the-job ministry to others. My church has never offered to improve those skills which could make me a better minister, nor has it ever asked if I needed any kind of support in what I was doing. There has never been an inquiry into the types of ethical decisions I must face, or whether I seek to communicate the faith to my co-workers. I have never been in a congregation where there was any type of public affirmation of a ministry in my career[as a sales manager]. In short, I must conclude that my church really doesn't have the least interest in whether or how I minister in my daily work.[14]

While Diehl's words were written thirty years ago, the evidence suggests that these words still ring true for a majority of churchgoers in the United States. Wave three surveys and anecdotal evidence consistently suggest that Diehl's experience is not an isolated one. Pastors, generally speaking, do not connect the Gospel message to the issues and concerns of those operating in the business world.[15] For instance, sociologist Stephen Hart and business professor David Krueger conducted an interdenominational and interfaith survey in 1989–1990 through the Center for Ethics and Public Policy to find out what church members expect of their clergy to support and strengthen them at work, and whether they received the support they needed or wanted.[16] Their findings captured the great distance or gap that businesspeople feel between themselves and church professionals.[17] Significantly, "most members of religious communities believe it is good to connect faith to work life" and desire clergy guidance.[18] Although "members affirm the idea of an integrated faith," most parishioners fail to receive pastoral support to attain this integration.[19] While Hart and Krueger report that most respondents want to connect faith and work, "most connect faith to work less than [to] other spheres of life, some have trouble making connections in concrete situations, and a significant minority (except the Evangelical Covenant Church) do not even affirm connecting faith to work."[20] Nash and McLennan report that this lack of pastoral support has "created a significant gap between our life at church and our life at work."[21] Notably, there is also "a strong and widespread desire for congregational support and guidance in integrating faith and work, but not many receive such support."[22]

Despite this clear demand for clergy engagement with work related issues, it appears that most clergy "are not providing much relevant and useful support or members are not taking advantage of it."[23] Indeed, religious professionals and clergy seem to avoid the topic. For instance, "only about one tenth of the respondents report that their clergy often address work issues in their sermons."[24] By contrast, half or more report that clergy often address other areas of life, such as family matters and community outreach. Moreover, although "organized religion continues to play a major, pivotal role in U.S. society," Gallup and Lindsay also find that faith communities "sometimes fail to challenge believers to their calling."[25] They suggest, consistent with Wuthnow's findings, that faith communities are good at comforting people but not as good at challenging them to change their lives and empowering them to do more social outreach.[26]

Viewing this issue from the perspective of pastoral care is also instructive. Somewhat surprisingly, pastoral care ranked low in Hart and Krueger's survey despite being "a very important resource for members in other contexts."[27] This response was interpreted to mean that "perhaps members perceive clergy as unsympathetic or lacking sufficient knowledge and experience of the work world to be of much help, or perhaps they feel these dilemmas are not 'religious' enough to bring to clergy."[28] That is, congregants do not willingly turn to clergy or view them as a resource in times of work-related trouble or problems. Indeed, "only 6 percent frequently talk over work problems or conflicts with their clergy, only 10 percent with friends in the congregation and only 4 percent with support groups in the congregation."[29] People experiencing problems or issues at work tend to avoid their church family, turning instead to family, coworkers, and secular workplace-related resources. Wuthnow's research concurs with these basic findings, noting "only 20 percent of church members say they have talked about their work with a member of the clergy during the past year."[30] Similarly, Nash and McLennan find that "most business people report less-than-satisfactory connections between religion and business in their lives. Yet they are not at all certain that they want to go to the church for an answer."[31]

Viewing this issue from the perspective of Christian ethics in business and financial affairs is also instructive. One Presbyterian Church (USA) survey of congregations and clergy observed

> the lack of attention given to work ethics and personal financial issues within congregations. When asked how frequently they counsel members about such matters, few pastors indicated that such discussions had occurred "often" in the past year. In fact, only 11% reported that they had often counseled parishioners on "the social values and business ethics of where they work," only 19% on "the relationship between faith and personal finances," and only 23% on "personal pressures, conflicts, achievements, and values related to their work."[32]

When clergy were asked how many counseled parishioners "occasionally" on these three areas, not surprisingly the responses increased (46 percent, 43 percent, and 55 percent), though notably still not a majority. Moreover, "only 5% of pastors reported that they had 'often' counseled members of their congregation over, 'how their faith might guide their investment decisions,' and only 18% responded 'occasionally.' "[33]

Further evidence of the church's contribution to the Sunday-Monday gap comes from Nash and McLennan,[34] who observe, "The most disturbing finding in our study was the degree to which the ecclesiastic community appears unconscious of the distancing and its role in contributing to the underlying causes."[35] Moreover, consistent with other research, they found that most businesspeople feel that clergy do not understand their world.[36] The issue is exacerbated by the suggestion that clergy disagree with that lay opinion. For instance, the Social Issues in Investing survey concludes that in comparison to lay elders and members, "around 15% more pastors and clergy disagreed with the statement, 'members of clergy have very little understanding of what it is like in the real workaday world.' "[37] Pastors often rightly claim to have good personal relationships with businesspeople. However, for most, these relationships seldom go beyond the social level to understanding the work lives of businesspeople, helping them frame their work in terms of calling, or offering guidance or nurturance related to the Four E's: ethics, evangelism, experience, and enrichment.

To assess the relative ecclesiastical importance of FAW at the denominational "headquarters" level, one can apply three simple tests. First, as a matter of operational focus, in comparison to other departments, how much staffing and what amount of budget resources does the FAW ministry receive (presuming there even is an FAW-focused department)? Second, how frequently are FAW issues addressed theologically, and what is the content of this expression, as seen in denominational policy statements and discussion papers?[38] The third way is to study the WCC's own self-analysis in this regard. As to the first test of staffing, during wave two, most major denominations developed some form of lay ministry staffperson or resource office.[39] By early in wave three, most major denominational judicatory offices, including the Southern Baptist Convention, the Evangelical Lutheran Church of America (ELCA), the Presbyterian Church USA (PCUSA), the United Methodist Church, and the Episcopal Church (ECUSA), had staff personnel responsible for this area. In some cases, such as the ELCA, they adopted the departmental name "ministry in daily life." However, due to declining membership and contributions during wave three, most denominational headquarters and judicatory staff faced personnel and program cuts. Areas such as lay ministry and ministry in daily life were often seen as nonessential and noncore to the

work of the church. Accordingly, these positions were eliminated or consolidated into other jobs, such that organizational focus on FAW was lost. For
instance, in 2003, the ELCA abandoned its lengthy commitment and eliminated the one full-time position that had been dedicated to this area, and in
the PCUSA, responsibility for ministry in daily life has been subordinated and
subsumed into other staff functions.

As to expression through theological statements on public policy issues,
there is significant commentary on macroeconomic issues at the denominational level, particularly by those denominations inclined toward social activism. For instance, in the case of the PCUSA, there is a tradition of social
activism and analysis of and commentary on economic matters and vocation,
resulting in a steady stream of position papers and policy statements. A useful
reference point is the *Presbyterian Social Witness Policy Compilation*, which
covers some fifty years of Presbyterian policy statements.[40] This compilation
offers several insights into the pattern that the PCUSA has developed, both
in form and substance, in its attitude toward the business community and
those called to work in it. In terms of substance, the policy papers are largely
oriented to macro policy and structural questions, usually pertaining to issues
of economic justice, sustainable development, offshore manufacturing, and
third world debt forgiveness.[41] However, they seldom speak to the level of
individual vocation, accountability, and responsibility in the marketplace.
Even the statements that attempt to move to the micro or personal level
seldom apply to the average businessperson or worker in the pew. Notably,
little attention is paid to individual accountability, or guidance for those
whose economic reality or sense of vocation leads them to work for the very
businesses which are the object of the theological critique. Further, these
policy statements tend to assume a pejorative attitude toward the fallen, if
not unchristian, nature of business itself, at least in its capitalist form. Finally,
in terms of substance, they presume the righteousness of certain economic
decisions (e.g., consumer boycotts, individual and institutional divestment of
certain stock holdings, minimum income levels, and other forms of governmental and regulatory intervention) without making the theological case for
these actions, or allowing for other legitimate Christian approaches to social
and economic problems.

In terms of tone, the statements are also unhelpful. From the perspective
of persons engaged in the business community who seek to reform the system from within and to lead their companies in accordance with biblical
teachings, these statements often have a patronizing and platitudinous tone
that turns away the very people the church should be finding as allies.
Statements "calling on U.S. corporations to be responsible and just to workers
and the environment" seem to suggest that U.S. corporations prefer to be

irresponsible and unjust.[42] This consistent pattern of negativity, in both substance and form, apparently caught the eye of the editor of the *Presbyterian Social Witness Policy Compilation*, who at one point felt compelled to note, "The Assembly isn't exclusively a gloomy messenger of prophetic insight. It does not chide corporate society to the exclusion of celebrating significant accomplishments."[43] While the comment was perhaps well intended, the evidence fails to support the claim.

The primary theological bright spot for this second test pertains to writings on vocation, which connect to what I call in the experience type of integrating faith and work. The Reformed churches in general, and the PCUSA in particular, have a rich theological tradition of recognizing and honoring the close link between Christian vocation and work. This is evidenced in the *Social Witness Policy Compilation*'s section on "work as vocation," which covers several decades of affirming statements of the vocational legitimacy, value, meaning, purpose, and dignity of work.[44] Regrettably, however, these papers seldom move from theory to praxis, or from the structural to the personal. For this reason, similar to most of the other macroeconomic position papers and proclamations, these vocation and work statements often do not deal with the practical issues faced by churchgoers in their daily work.

A notable exception to the macroeconomic policy orientation and the generally negative attitude toward business is the policy paper adopted by the 1995 PCUSA General Assembly entitled *God's Work in Our Hands: Employment, Community, and Vocation*. This monograph was designed to move from theory to practice and thereby lead the church to concrete action, implementation, and advocacy. In contrast to most of the other statements, this policy paper acknowledged the complexity of actual marketplace situations, noting, "it is understood that particular circumstances mean that faithful responses may vary."[45] It is constructive and affirming in tone and is a clear deviation from the antibusiness moralizing and chiding tone evident in the other statements. *God's Work in Our Hands* includes twelve principles of vocation and work designed to form a framework for practical decision making and action. Positive as this document is, however, it does not serve to change the direction or overall tone of PCUSA economic policy, as shown by subsequent papers that do not adopt this view. Moreover, the other examples of reasonably positive treatments of business as vocation and the issues faced by individuals in the marketplace were not included in the *Presbyterian Social Witness Policy Compilation*. For instance, consider the Presbyterian Church (USA)'s *Reformed Faith and Economics* (1989), a collection of thirteen essays developed over a three-year period of consultations by various Reformed scholars. It is a carefully compiled assemblage of essays on biblical perspectives, the Reformed tradition on economic justice, contemporary policy issues, and church responses. Like many denominational statements of its era, it was prepared in part in response to *Economic Justice for All* (1986). *Reformed Faith* seeks to frame modern workplace issues, largely structural in nature, in theological terms and to offer proposals for improvement. Another omitted text from the *Presbyterian Social Witness Policy Compilation* is *Challenges in the Workplace* (1990), a resource paper prepared by the PCUSA Task Force on Issues of Vocation and Problems of Work, addressing the practical dimensions of vocation. For the larger denominational picture, Wuthnow's findings are instructive. He notes:

> [C]hurches and religious leaders, more likely, say nothing at all about the material life except to voice an occasional jab at the worship of mammon, adding hastily that there is nothing wrong with money as long as we do not love it too much. Even those most concerned about such social issues as peace, poverty, inequality, and economic injustice have been surprisingly blind to the economic realm.[46]

When the church does tend to the economic realm, "An overwhelming share of [its] attention has been focused on government, wanting it to do more, wanting it to do less, lobbying, sending it petitions, and treating it as the way to get anything done. And yet, by comparison, the economy is by far a more powerful institution in our society than government."[47]

As regards the third way to analyze the ecclesiastical response to the Faith at Work movement, I now turn to the WCC's own self-analysis. The WCC commissioned a series of discussions and papers and a consultation in the 1990s, resulting in the collection of essays called *A Letter from Christ to the World: An Exploration of the Role of the Laity in the Church Today.*[48] Edited and compiled by Nicholas Apostola, this work offers evidence of the WCC's lack of focus on faith at work concerns. Apostola notes that the WCC's Department of the Laity was closed in 1971, with its functions subsumed into other WCC bodies that had different missions. Following the Canberra assembly in 1991, and subsequent reorganization of the WCC, "the issue of the laity re-emerged, but with an interesting new focus: Lay Participation towards Inclusive Community."[49] Thus, "lay ministry" as understood during wave two as referring to "the Christian and daily work," was redefined to meet the WCC's new emphasis on "participation in the struggle for justice and freedom of the poor, the marginalized and the socially degraded."[50]

Unless businesspeople adopted the political and economic views of this new theological ideology, they were essentially marginalized and excluded from the ecumenical debate, a development that earlier lay leaders, such as Hendrik Kraemer and Hans-Ruedi Weber, would have found inconceivable. Indeed, Apostola noted in 1998, "today when we gather in ecumenical gatherings, the preponderance of laity is no longer evident. Clergy are often the representatives in ecumenical meetings, regardless of the ecclesiastical self-understandings of particular churches. In fact, in these contexts, we sometimes talk about laity as objects to be trained rather than people in partnership."[51] Moreover, Konrad Raiser, general secretary of the WCC, spoke in 1998 of the "increasing specialization of ecumenical work" being "filled by specialists with theological training"; the laity, he said, "have almost disappeared from ecumenical discussion."[52]

These observations from the 1990s are still applicable today. Looking ahead, Raiser correctly predicted, "The point of reference for the laity issue is no longer the old distinction between the church and the world."[53] Instead, Raiser saw "newly emerging social movements" that "indicate the short-comings of the traditional social, political and economic structures and institutional forms for regulating society."[54] Raiser understood the social conditions and context of wave three that have given rise to many new social movements, such as Greenpeace and others, though he failed to identify the FAW movement. Indeed, his social and theological analysis contained a prima facie critique of capitalist economic structures. Moreover, Raiser's otherwise astute description and analysis of the move away from traditional under-standings of lay ministry missed, as did apparently the WCC itself, that these "newly emerging social movements" were not just indications of political and economic shortcomings. Rather, these movements also indicated the short-comings of the church, the ecumenical movement, and the WCC itself. Indeed, as I argue, the emergence of the Faith at Work movement in the mid-1980s reflects dissatisfaction with the church as a source of ethical guidance, spiritual nurturing, and inspiration for daily work life. According to Nash and McLennan, "As one religiously devout business school professor said to us, 'It's not really clear that the church has anything to say in this arena that's of any use.' "[55]

Another self-analysis at the ecumenical level is Mark Ellingsen's *The Cutting Edge: How Churches Speak on Social Issues*, commissioned by the Institute for Ecumenical Research and published by the WCC. *The Cutting Edge* is the result of extensive ecumenical research that offers "a descriptive analysis of the churches' official statements (i.e., those approved by the churches' highest governing authorities)," issued from the 1960s to the 1990s, concerning nine socioethical issues selected for study.[56] As further evidence of the theological presuppositions embodied by the mainstream church, only three official statements on economic issues during these thirty-plus years conceived of the modern corporation in a positive light, as a potential collaborator in and contributor to matters of theological concern, such as economic justice, human rights, and environmental stewardship. The preponderance of these statements sent the clear message that corporations and other for-profit organizations were the cause of socioethical problems. The WCC, blinded by its own theological ideology, failed to see any co-creative possibilities, contributions, or potential for moral or societal good coming from the marketplace.

An Insufficient Theology

There are several reasons why clergy and religious professionals do not perceive and therefore do not respond to the needs that are driving the FAW movement. One of the root causes for this failure seems to be theological in nature, and the theological traditions they were taught in seminary. Influenced by and as a result of theological orientations, several other factors create and foster the problem of the Sunday-Monday gap, including marketplace perceptions and awareness, liturgy, clericalism, language, and lack of clergy training to attend to workplace concerns. In addition, some businesspeople contribute to the Sunday-Monday gap, preferring to leave their work behind on Sunday and not think about it as part of their worship. This compartmentalizing of the two worlds only serves to exacerbate the situation.

Theologically, many clergy and religious professionals have not studied or developed a theology of work as part of their overall systematic theology.[57] As Miroslav Volf observes in *Work in the Spirit*, theologians spend more time researching the fine doctrinal points of ancient church debates than they do contemplating a contemporary theology of work:

> Amazingly little theological reflection has taken place in the past about an activity which takes up so much of our time. The number of pages theologians have devoted to transubstantiation—which does or does not take place on Sunday—for instance, would, I suspect far exceed the number of pages devoted to work that fills our lives Monday through Saturday.[58]

Of course, the Christian ethics tradition has paid attention to theology and business. Even in this branch of the academy, however, scholars who take a constructive view of capitalist and nonstate-controlled marketplace economies have been in a minority for much of the twentieth century.[59] Many of today's leading senior theologians, ethicists, and clergy are deeply influenced by Christian Socialism, branches of Barthianism (that accent the action of God, the finitude of the person, and Barth's early theological support of socialism), liberation theology (emphasizing state-controlled economic structures, rejecting free markets, and viewing capitalist businesses as oppressors), and even some Franciscan and monastic strands that glorify poverty and simplicity. In particular, many of today's religious professionals were trained in liberation theology as a normative way of thinking that was fashionable in mainstream seminaries and divinity schools during the latter three decades of the twentieth century (and that remains so in many programs). Liberation theology's preferential option for the poor is often interpreted in material terms (not spiritual) and has resulted in a de facto bias against the theological and human possibilities of the marketplace and those involved in the business world. In similar fashion, many of today's leading systematic theologians, ethicists, and clergy are heirs of Christian socialism, which was popular among many leading mainstream theologians, including to varying degrees Rauschenbusch, Tillich, Barth, and Reinhold Niebuhr, during the first two-thirds of the twentieth century. Both Christian socialism and liberation theology rely heavily on Marxist categories of analysis, historical interpretation, and methodology, which presuppose a prima facie rejection of: capitalism, nonstate-controlled forms of economic organization, ownership of private property, and the role of religion. Influenced by Marxist categories of analysis and economic presuppositions, the problems of industrialization and automation, and the deconstructive methods of postmodernism, many clergy and theologians failed to find and articulate a constructive doctrine of vocation or theology of work.

Another theological way to frame the problem draws on the earlier discussions of premillennialism and postmillennialism, where a false either-or choice gave Christians in the workplace limited views of work, the marketplace, individual salvation, and societal transformation. As a result, many clergy have a limited biblical hermeneutic of work, lying either at one extreme, which views that the material world, wealth, the marketplace, and work in largely negative terms, or at the other extreme, which maligns the Puritan work ethic and preaches the so-called prosperity gospel that promises riches to all who are faithful.

The church's theological understanding of itself, the laity, and daily work also explains why the church is not meeting the demand side of the FAW movement. Hans-Ruedi Weber, contributing to the WCC's 1998 consultation on treatment of the laity, notes that the church and the ecumenical movement typically understand the clergy-laity relation in terms of the doctrine of the church. Weber argues that a better theological understanding is to locate the conversation in the doctrine of creation and the hope for a new heaven and earth.[60] He observes that for most laity, "in their experience, dialogue and collaboration with people of other faiths, especially secularists, are more urgent than interconfessional dialogue. They also tend to have a less church-centered understanding of the ecumenical move-ment."[61] Expressed differently, the church too often has an internal focus on its own institutional life and existence, at the expense of an external focus on living out the mission and purpose of the church as the body of Christ.

As an outgrowth of the church's theology, clergy perceptions of the mar-ketplace further contribute to why the church is failing to meet the demands of the FAW movement. These perceptions often impede clergy's ability to give ethical guidance to those who seek to integrate faith and work. In general, clergy appear to focus on criticizing the obvious problems in the marketplace, without appreciating the complexities or even the theological possibilities of the marketplace. Moreover, Wuthnow argues, modern theological literature and scholarly research have not acknowledged the important role that religious commitment can and should play in guiding work and ethical behavior at work. He faults the clergy for deemphasizing religion's teachings on work-related ethics, observing that, instead, "We have come to think of religion—at least implicitly—as a way of making ourselves feel better and have largely aban-doned the idea that religion can guide our behavior, except to discourage activities considered blatantly immoral."[62] In addition to the increasingly therapeutic role the church has assumed, Wuthnow also observes that in many cases the church has acculturated itself to the world, thereby losing its unique insights into humanity and ability to contribute to society.[63]

In general, it is fair to say, and as noted several studies concur, that many clergy perceptions of the marketplace and businesspeople are grounded in a suspicion of capitalist structures and those who engage in them. While clergy may retain strong personal relationships with businesspeople at a personal level, socializing and indeed, courting their financial pledges to the church, many unwittingly perhaps continue to transmit anticapitalist messages to their congregation. The perception being sent from the pulpit is that busi-nesspeople are greedy, captive to the values of an oppressive system, and insensitive to the plight of the poor. While certainly true in some cases, this sweeping portrait of people in the marketplace does gross injustice to the average person's workplace experience. Moreover, few clergy consider that businesspeople themselves may be objects of oppression. For example, many businesspeople feel powerless against the negative forces of corporate life. Corporate downsizings have left many feeling betrayed and helpless, while increasing workloads and various forms of discrimination (age, gender, race) create oppressive environments for many who feel trapped in jobs of mean-inglessness, pain, and emotional anguish. Indeed, many business people might agree with the church's social justice agenda but differ on the means to accomplish it.

Theological attitudes toward the marketplace and those active in it are also often reflected in church liturgy, contributing further to the gap between Sunday worship and Monday work. This liturgical indifference to the Sunday-Monday gap is promulgated, as noted earlier, by the paucity of sermons that deal with work, the worker, and the workplace. Indeed, as Hart and Krueger and others demonstrate, one can sit through a year's worth of worship services and seldom hear a connection (let alone a constructive connection) between one's faith claims and one's workplace reality. Wuthnow observes that one "informal poll of church members revealed that 90 percent claimed to have never heard any sermons or lessons on relating their faith to their work."[64] Other research, according to Wuthnow, paints an only slightly less gloomy picture. Research shows that "most respondents desire more congregational emphasis on work issues," but fail to receive it despite the finding that "the more frequently their clergy deal with work issues in sermons, the more satisfied members are with the current degree of attention to work in their congregation."[65] While sermons are often the most visible form of liturgical indifference to the workplace, other aspects of worship (including prayer, confession, pardon, music, commissioning, and benediction) contribute as well.[66]

The theology behind church polity and governance, as it relates to the role of clergy and the clergy's sense of identity, also contributes to the church's response to FAW. In particular, drawing on insights from Loren Mead, writer, teacher, and founder of the Alban Institute, he and many others see clericalism itself as significant contributor to the Sunday-Monday gap and another reason that the church is not meeting the Four E's demand for ethics, evangelism, experience, and enrichment. Mead defines *clericalism* as the church being owned by its clergy, noting, "Clericalism—like sin—is carrying a good thing too far."[67] He argues that it is about "a pattern of action" and an "all-embracing assumption that shapes how we think about churches and how we think about the roles each of us plays in the life of the church."[68] The roles of clergy and laity are clearly defined, and the spheres of life in which they each have authority are also defined. Clericalism may not have been consciously intended, but it often becomes a de facto reality. The result is two classes of citizenship in Christian life, where many laypeople feel relegated to second-class status in the kingdom of God. Moreover, related to clericalism is an ecclesiology that focuses on the life of the gathered church, often at the expense of (or in opposition to) the scattered church. In such churches, increased lay ministry is often defined as serving on more church committees.

The language that the church uses to preach, teach, and speak to congregants can serve as a bridge or a barrier to those seeking to connect faith and work. Theologically precise language is important and necessary to discuss and differentiate fine theological points and doctrines. Technical language also helps to refine our belief, describe things accurately, and clarify difficult concepts. Indeed, clergy and theologians, like lawyers, doctors, and engine mechanics, appropriately have specialized languages for their fields. Specialized language only becomes problematic when clergy do not transpose ecclesiastical and theological nomenclature into the vocabulary of their parishioners and seekers, just as a doctor must transpose complex medical terminology into the patient's language to be understood. Mead also points out the power dimension of theological discourse, identifying "the language of academic theology" as "the approved medium of conversation."[69] Mead is critical of the power imbalance this creates between clergy and laity, saying that clergy often use the power of theological discourse to "invalidate nonclergy input to the conversation."[70] Similarly, Nash and McLennan identify language as one of the main problems contributing to the clergy-businessperson divide, observing, "It is as if they speak two different languages."[71] They criticize clergy for using obtuse technical jargon and for moralizing in generalities when they engage the business world. In contrast, they observe, businesspeople use language that tends toward the simple, the concrete, and the pragmatic.[72]

As discussed above, theology as manifested in pejorative marketplace perceptions, liturgical narrowness, clericalism, and obstructing language all combine to serve as impediments to ministering to the needs of those in the workplace. However, for those whose theology allows for or even encourages support for faith at work, there is little seminary training to equip them in this endeavor. Indeed, my research shows that there are many clergy and religious professionals who want to respond to the needs expressed by the FAW movement but are unsure how to do so. Frequently, those pastors and theologians who are interested in addressing the needs and manifestations of the FAW movement—ethics, evangelism, experience, and enrichment—and other issues faced by those called into the commercial world, feel inadequate to the task. As obstacles, they cite a lack of direct business experience, an insufficient awareness of the issues, a lack of ministry models to emulate, and even a sense of intimidation by the business world.

The discussion thus far has focused on the ecclesiastical side of the problem of why the church is not responding to the needs of the FAW movement. However, in addition to clergy who misunderstand, miscommunicate, or dismiss the needs of the FAW movement, there are also businesspeople and others in the marketplace who contribute to and exacerbate this ecclesiastical tendency. They have contributed to the Sunday-Monday gap in several ways. For instance, though they appear to be a minority, some in the marketplace prefer to compartmentalize their Sunday and their Monday. As discussed in chapter 1, in its extreme, compartmentalization is the opposite of integration. Compartmentalizing is a way of avoiding the difficult ethical and moral situations that businesspeople often face at work. Robert Fuller refers to it as "compartmentalizing their 'churched' and 'unchurched' beliefs into separate categories."[73] The compartmentalizer prefers keeping faith and work separate to avoid the struggles that integration usually demands.[74] This is all the more challenging for businesspeople, as compartmentalization not only seems necessary but is often rewarded in other spheres of life.

In addition to compartmentalizing, lack of theological knowledge contributes to the problem. Many businesspeople and others in the marketplace, like the rest of the lay population, are not biblically literate and, on the whole, have become increasingly unfamiliar with the basic content of the Bible, its truth claims, classic narratives, moral lessons, ethical teachings, and spiritual insights. This biblical illiteracy places the laity in a position of reliance on the clergy, at the same time that it perpetuates distinctions and stereotypes of religion and the marketplace as being two unrelated worlds. Further, lack of biblical literacy also exacerbates the clericalism and language problems noted above. Moreover, some businesspeople resent what they perceive as external meddling and moralizing from clergy. This is particularly true when clergy are not familiar with basic business issues and moral tradeoffs, and offer simple bromides and generic critiques against obviously unethical practices. For example, a clergyperson might be quick to criticize a businessperson caught offering a bribe to gain a contract (and rightly so). But is that same clergyperson engaged enough to offer theological guidance if that businessperson were not to offer the bribe, thereby losing the contract and having to lay off a hundred workers due to lack of orders? Perhaps because people in the workplace crave theological guidance and pastoral support on such difficult challenges, they dismiss clergy critique even when it is deserved. Thus, frustrated by the apparent lack of interest or uneducated response to the challenges they face in the marketplace, many workers and professionals simply give up on the church and turn instead to secular therapists, consultants, and self-help guides for ethical guidance and spiritual nurturing.

The Failure of the Theological Academy

I have suggested that the primary cause of the Sunday-Monday gap is theological and ecclesial in nature and that the closely related issues of pejorative marketplace perceptions, liturgical narrowness, clericalism, language, and inexperience all combine to serve as impediments to ministering to the needs of workers and professionals in the FAW movement. If this is accurate, then the next step is to probe deeper, asking how and where the theology of clergy and religious professionals is formed.

The nation's seminaries and divinity schools are largely in the business of doing three things. They prepare men and women to become pastors; they train and certify the next generation of theologians and religious scholars; and they reflect theologically on issues of the church, doctrine, and practice. Each seminary and divinity school has its own denominational (or interdenominational) roots, confessional emphases, methodological preferences, theological specialties, and other identifying features. In addition to family, childhood church, and personal experience, someone's theology is deeply influenced and shaped by the faculty and curriculum to which he or she is exposed in seminary. For that reason, the pertinent question here is the extent and content of theological education that addresses faith at work concerns.[75] This can be measured through empirical research into curricula, attitudes toward economic matters, American Academy of Religion (AAR) papers, and texts written by theologians.[76]

There are several likely reasons that the academy has exhibited an indifferent to pejorative stance toward the workplace and those in the corporate world, including a lack of business expertise among theologians; doctrinal and ideological differences; the residual effects of Christian socialism and liberation theology; WCC and other ecumenical moves away from lay ministry to a new interest in social justice, community, and inclusiveness of the other (and a lack of seeing the business community as a place for that to occur); a reluctance of faculty and administrators to embrace interdisciplinary topics; and the absence of a departmental location or discipline in AAR for FAW. Indeed, this final point may be a major contributing factor. The issues driving the FAW movement do not all fit neatly into one seminary department or discipline and tend typically to span the areas of theology, ethics, biblical studies, ecclesiology, church history, mission, pastoral care, homiletics, and practical theology. The most logical place may well be ethics or practical theology, but then the workplace issues tend to be reduced solely to questions of ethics.

Theological schools that are generally considered to be evangelical or conservative are increasingly more inclined to see the relevance of theology to the workplace and, in various ways, are trying to teach and think theologically about the issues surrounding the Faith at Work movement.[77] In contrast, institutions typically considered to be mainstream or liberal range from being silent to being negative about FAW issues.[78] A few exceptions to the latter point are emerging. For example, in the mid- to late 1990s, Harvard Divinity School experimented with the idea of a faith at work research specialty in the Center for Public Policy and Values, but the idea lost support and was dropped. However, encouraging developments are beginning to take place at several seminaries and divinity schools. For instance, in the late 1990s, Yale Divinity School (YDS) entered this field with two conferences called Bridging the Gap, inviting a mixture of businesspeople and theologians to dialogue. Paul Minus, a YDS graduate and retired church historian, taught an adjunct course at YDS on faith at work in 2001 and 2002. These efforts, spurred by an earlier internal assessment called the Kelsey Report, led Dean Harold Attridge and the faculty to consider new ways to look outward, and to engage and shape the great social issues of the day. With this support, in 2003 Miroslav Volf, long interested in a theology of work, ecclesiology, economic matters, and broader questions of faith as a way of life, conceived of and founded the Yale Center for Faith & Culture. One of its primary areas of attention is a specific focus on the economic sphere, conducted through it Ethics and Spirituality in the Workplace program.[79] As part of my role as the center's executive director, I teach an interdisciplinary course comprised of MBA students from Yale School of Management and MDiv/MAR students from YDS. Interfaith in nature, it is entitled, "Business Ethics: Succeeding Without Selling Your Soul." Luther Seminary (Minnesota), under the leadership of Jack Fortin, has established the Center for Lifelong Learning, which seeks to assist the church in supporting lay ministry, and help bridge the gap between communities of faith and communities of work. Princeton Theological Seminary under the guidance of Max Stackhouse founded the Kuyper Center, yet FAW has not been broadly embraced by the faculty as being theologically central to a Master of Divinity (MDiv) education. Other exploratory or related initiatives are under way at Columbia Theological Seminary (Virginia), Methodist Theological School and Trinity Lutheran Seminary (a joint initiative of these two schools in Ohio), Notre Dame, and Pittsburgh Theological Seminary, though the long-term institutional commitment remains to be seen.[80]

Even in light of these strong efforts, one can scarcely say that FAW has been embraced by the mainstream theological academy, and evidence suggests that the teaching at most divinity schools and seminaries still does not address the needs of the movement, as manifested in the Four E's of ethics, evangelism, experience, and enrichment. One survey of the nation's top twenty seminaries concludes that "few divinity schools or congregations have taken a serious note" of the issues driving the Faith at Work movement.[81] In addition to ignoring the issues faced by businesspeople, seminaries offer little analysis of or appreciation for the moral roots of the modern corporation, the concept of business as a calling, or the multiple tasks that business performs for society and the common good.

Not surprisingly, perhaps, few seminarians surveyed were familiar with their denomination's theology toward marketplace matters or had tried to use Scripture passages pertaining to business in their studies or preaching.[82] Only a minority of those surveyed responded positively with constructive, practical ideas pertaining to sermons and guidance on workplace integration, and "almost a third of seminarians had no reason to believe that business-people needed any special ministry."[83] For many, there is "even the refusal to differentiate business as a legitimate topic for theological inquiry."[84]

The result of the absence of teaching on FAW issues is that future clergy are given little to no training on how to minister to the pains and possibilities that people in the marketplace confront daily. While seminaries recognize and even ordain clergy to specialized ministries as chaplains in hospitals, retirement homes, the military, and prisons, few consider the workplace as a theologically valid venue for ordained ministry. Further, most seminaries do not equip pastors in the local church to reform their marketplace perceptions or shape their liturgy, vocabulary, and other theological presuppositions with a view toward intentionally ministering to the needs of the business community. Even courses that should logically address these issues (e.g., pastoral care and counseling, clinical pastoral education, and field education) seldom include ministry to the workplace. At best, courses on ethics, vocation, and lay ministry occasionally touch on the issues and needs that drive the FAW movement.

Closely related to the absence of seminary teaching on FAW issues, the evidence suggests that the overarching presuppositions among theological faculty about capitalism, business, and marketplace issues range from indifferent to negative. The evidence suggests that seminary faculty tend to portray the business community and its underlying dynamics as simplistic (ignoring the moral and ethical complexities); sinful (as if capitalism and its participants were prima facie theologically incorrect); unsympathetic to social justice concerns (wanting merely to maximize profits with no sense of social responsibility); harmful to and exploitative of people (where people become disposable assets); interested exclusively in profits (and not how the profits are earned); and disinterested in the common good of society (leaving that to government and others to address). Moreover, in the few instances when professors have taught business and religion courses, the content and syllabus descriptions were often weighted toward economic theories hostile to capitalism, laden with imbalanced critiques of global corporations, and containing romanticized celebrations of church mission work, political activism, and organized labor.[85]

Thus influenced by their faculty, the result is that seminary students' attitudes toward business and religion, as well as to FAW, are "overwhelmingly negative."[86] Students are often left with a one-note song, "lecturing, not listening," concluding that the best way to address business and FAW issues is by proclaiming a prophetic voice.[87] Notably, only one student surveyed by Nash and McLennan, an evangelical seminarian, had a more constructive view. The danger, in the end, is that seminary education biases future pastors against the structural and contextual world of business, without any appreciation of its constructive and co-creative possibilities to help society and promote the common good.

An additional source for understanding seminary attitudes toward economic matters and their relation to social justice is an extensive study, *The State of Economic Education in United States Seminaries*,[88] which surveyed the economic education of religious leaders.[89] The study sought to understand the place of social justice issues in theological curricula and the "views of economics and social justice held by the faculty."[90] *Economic Education*, conducted by Green and Schmiesing, found that social justice is an important part of seminary education at many institutions, but that "at a significant number of schools, teaching about social issues is not a key part of seminary training."[91] The researchers found that there was "considerable variation in how social justice appeared in the curriculum, with one-third reporting considerable emphasis; two-fifths, some emphasis; and more than one-quarter, less emphasis."[92] They observed three basic types of social justice curricula: incidental, extensive, and intensive. For those institutions where social justice is considered theologically important, the study found that "economics, as a discipline distinct from social ethics, receives scant attention in the curricula of most seminaries."[93] However, "while it is only reasonable to expect that seminary training would involve an emphasis on moral principles in any treatment of social issues, it is significant that economic analysis of social problems seems to play only a marginal role in addressing those issues."[94] Notably, this survey observed that there is considerable agreement on the importance of and need for socially active churches but that "there has been deep division—even within the churches—as to the precise manner in which this social obligation is discharged."[95] The Acton Institute argues that this dilemma is "often based on differing ideas about the relationship between economics and theology."[96] The question of how seminaries define social justice, and the related role of economics,[97] is instructive in that few of the twenty topics covered under the rubric of social justice pertained to economic matters, and of those that did, most "appeared near the bottom of the list."[98] Further, "the respondents reported negative views toward multinational corporations, with most disagreeing that corporations are a force for genuine human development (30 to 8 percent) and agreeing that multinational corporations are a cause of poverty and injustice (29 to 19 percent)."[99]

Moreover, the study found that liberal-leaning schools were more likely to have a mix of moral and economic principles in their programs, while the conservative programs were more likely to stress only moral principles.[100]

A strong correlation between the three types of social justice curricula and the religious traditions of the institutions was observed. For instance, 59 percent of the programs where social justice curricula were incidental were evangelical; 52 percent of the extensive programs were mainline or ecumenical; and 49 percent of the intensive programs were Catholic or Orthodox. Moreover, the study findings suggest:

> [I]n those places where there is the most interest in social and economic issues and where they are being most comprehensively addressed, there is also the most skepticism toward market activity and the most advocacy of governmental regulation and other limits on that activity. In those places where there is more skepticism about governmental regulation and more advocacy of market activity, there is also less interest in social issues and less focus on them as part of theological training.[101]

As one of the coauthors noted, "[T]he study illustrates that seminary faculty—the teachers of the next generation of religious leaders—are still highly suspicious of the market."[102]

Another way to measure the failure of the academy to address FAW issues is to consider the way in which the American Academy of Religion treats the question of faith and work, seeing this as indicative of the level of theological interest in and influence on the movement. For instance, a review of AAR meetings over the past decade reveals little theological awareness of or attention to the FAW movement.[103] The few times that business and marketplace issues were addressed at AAR tended to be in a critical fashion. Business was generally portrayed as a source of oppression and inequality; critiques included sweeping generalizations about, for example, the negative aspects of globalization while seldom considering the creative and positive potentialities of the modern marketplace.

In stark contrast, and ironically perhaps, the Academy of Management (AOM) has a special-interest group called Management, Spirituality, and Religion (MSR), which brings scholarly attention to management questions pertaining to faith and work (see chapter 6). While often lacking theological insights and ignoring questions of truth claims, AOM's MSR group of scholars nevertheless recognizes the important role that religion and spirituality play in corporations and in the lives of individual businesspeople.

Further, whether through AAR or AOM members, there is a paucity of theological research and discourse that seeks to describe and explain the

Faith at Work movement as a whole or to offer critical reflection and pre-scriptive frameworks to help shape and inform the movement itself, the academy, or the church. The few constructive theological writings that do exist are rare and provide only partial glimpses into the movement and its issues.[104] These writings tend to be organized around specific questions, including sociological issues, work as a vocation, wealth and poverty, theology of work, globalism and economics, ethics of work and business, social issues, and pastoral care. Some contemporary scholars provide partial research into FAW issues, providing analytical and theological resources and serving as a point of departure for the current study's findings and proposals. For instance, Robert Wuthnow's sociological research offers helpful empirical evidence of the disconnection people feel between their Sunday worship and their Monday work, and he partially documents the movement's growth (*God and Mammon in America*, 1994; *Poor Richard's Principle*, 1996; and *Crisis in the Church*, 1997). However, his project does not seek to offer theologically or ethically informed solutions. Researcher Laura Nash offers helpful descriptive data on the role of faith for evangelical business leaders, but does not offer a theological analysis or prescriptive ethical response (*Believers in Business*, 1994; and with Scotty McLennan, *Church on Sunday, Work on Monday*, 2001). Miroslav Volf offers an original and groundbreaking contribution toward a new theology of work building on biblical conceptions of charisms as an alternative to traditional Lutheran conceptions of vocation (*Work in the Spirit: Toward a Theology of Work*, 1991). Volf's intent, however, is not to explore the FAW movement or how it relates to itself and the church. Douglas Meeks argues for an economic model that sees the triune God helping to create, redeem, and sustain the economy of the household, yet does not link this theory to praxis in a pluralistic society (*God the Economist*, 1989).

Donald Shriver's interest in economic issues is acute, addressing specific ethical questions, such as sustainable development, and limiting himself largely to political solutions (with James W. Kuhn, *Beyond Success: Corporations and Their Critics in the 1990s*, 1991). German Ulrich Duchrow sees globalism as intrinsically wrong and seeks to raise it to the level of status confessionis (*Global Economy: A Confessional Issue for the Churches?* 1986). Stanley Hauerwas argues for disengagement from society and refuge in Christian communities, and thus offers little constructive ethical guidance (*Character and the Christian Life*, 1985; and with William H. Willimon, *Resident Aliens*, 1989). In contrast, Ronald Sider helpfully argues for engagement in society, but his analysis of the economic issues is often flawed and his solutions are overly simplistic (*Rich Christians in an Age of Hunger*, 1990; *Just Generosity*, 1999). In a similar vein, evangelical scholar Craig Blomberg argues that greater financial generosity will solve most social problems, while ignoring the root or structural causes of such injustices (*Heart, Soul, and Money*, 2000; *Neither Poverty nor Riches*, 1999). Swiss scholar Lukas Vischer wants to move away from traditional church teachings on work and replace them with a more idealistic view that excites but fails to recognize the role of sin in any economic structure (*Arbeit in der Krise*, 1996). Thomas Naylor, Rolf Österberg, and William Willimon address questions of meaning and purpose but ignore other FAW issues (*The Search for Meaning in the Workplace*, 1996). Pastoral theologian James Dittes studies the human experiences of people in the work world but is burdened by pejorative theological presuppositions about work (*When Work Goes Sour*, 1987; *Driven by Hope*, 1996). A promising book by business scholar Douglas Hicks (*Religion and the Workplace: Pluralism, Spirituality, and Leadership*, 2003) proposes a leadership model of "respectful pluralism" for companies to deal with religious diversity in a majority Christian culture, though he does not seek to understand the FAW movement qua movement nor interpret it theologically.

In light of the theological academy's lack of awareness of or focus on the Faith at Work movement or the underlying issues driving the movement, it is not surprising that related theological writings are limited and insufficient. Moreover, with a few notable exceptions, most theologians do not develop interdisciplinary competence nor seek to understand the complexities of modern global economies and develop a constructive theology of work. Some of these exceptions include homiletician Barbara Brown Taylor, pastoral care theologian Don Browning, theologians Miroslav Volf, James Childs, and Richard Mouw, and social ethicist Max Stackhouse, to name a few. Taylor accents the theological importance of the daily vocation of all baptized believers and the necessity of preaching to that context. She observes that "those in the pulpit may know where they belong, but the people in the pews hold dual citizenship" and often are left to fend for themselves between Sundays with little guidance from clergy.[105] Browning is one of the few doing interdisciplinary work to integrate pastoral care and social ethics (*Religious Ethics and Pastoral Care*, 1983). Volf's earlier work was, among other things, a constructive move to introduce gifts of the spirit to complement if not replace traditional Lutheran conceptions of calling (*Work in the Spirit*, 1991), and his more recent theological reflection considers the relationship of work in light of the relationship between humanity and God, with both current and eschatological considerations in mind. Childs seeks to modify Luther's two-kingdom theology, saying that the orders of creation should be divided into two parts: orders of vocation, in which people carry out their call to service in worldly arrangements; and orders of anticipation, in which people strive for the common good though business activity as an anticipation of

God's coming kingdom (*Ethics in Business*, 1995). Mouw argues that daily life and work, even in the corporate world, can be holy (*Called to Holy Worldliness*, 1980). Stackhouse argues for business as a profession, the creative potential of corporations for social change, and he says that corporations are no more nor less fallen than other human creations and institutions (with Dennis McCann and Shirley Roels, *On Moral Business*, 1995; with Browning, *God and Globalization*, 2001). Stackhouse has also introduced curricular innovations to engage seminary students on topics concerning ethics and the professions.

Despite the findings of the surveys mentioned earlier in this chapter, the above theologians and other factors offer a glimmer of hope in the theological academy regarding new initiatives to constructively engage the issues facing today's businessperson. For instance, as noted earlier, the Ethics and Spirituality in the Workplace program at Yale Divinity School's Center for Faith and Culture and Luther Seminary's Center for Lifelong Learning might be the harbingers of new pedagogical models and attitudes in the academy. However, these two efforts notwithstanding, to a large extent, it appears that the more evangelically oriented seminaries are more engaged in FAW questions than their mainstream counterparts. Seminaries such as Fuller and Gordon-Conwell have developed centers and even doctor of ministry (DMin) programs to focus on FAW questions and, in many cases, to serve as bridges among the church, the academy, and the business world.[106] For instance, Fuller Seminary president Richard Mouw proposes a new hermeneutic that is a living reflection of the laity, not the church (*Consulting with the Faithful*, 1994). Mouw has been arguing for the centrality of a Monday-centered faith for years (*Called to Holy Worldliness*, 1980), accenting the theme of Christian discipleship in the world. In 1996, Fuller Seminary founded the De Pree Leadership Center (named after former Herman Miller, Inc., business executive and author Max De Pree). The center was established "as a resource to leaders and exists to promote values-based relational leadership that nurtures effective organizational community in business, in the church and in the academy."[107] The original director was noted lay author Rob Banks;[108] in 2001, he was succeeded by Walter Wright, former president of Regent College in Vancouver, one of the few theological schools known for an accent on faith and work.

Another example of evangelically rooted curricular interest in FAW is Gordon-Conwell Theological Seminary. In 1994, it created the Mockler Center for Faith and Ethics in the Workplace with the mission to equip "the church and its members to bring the work of Christ into the activities of daily life, especially life in the workplace."[109] The center works to prepare future clergy to minister to the needs of those in the business world and to teach DMin candidates similar awareness and skills. In addition to its own faculty and courses, it invites outside scholars and Christian executives, such as Tom Phillips, retired chair and CEO of Raytheon Corporation, to design and teach courses. For instance, Phillips teaches a course called "Practical Faith in the Marketplace," which "brings together business people, pastors, and students to examine real-world topics of faith and the workplace."[110] Notably, both the De Pree Center and the Mockler Center were initiated and founded by committed Christian business leaders, who felt the church was not supporting them in their vocation in the business world. Colman M. Mockler, former chairman of Gillette, "was very interested in exploring how faith impacted his work as an executive and leader in industry and spent many an hour probing the issues of faith, values and ethics in business."[111] He once observed, "I wish pastors had a clue. I want to be equipped on Sunday for what I face on Monday."[112]

In addition, evangelically oriented Regent College in Vancouver is essentially dedicated to the question of faith in the workplace, with a particular focus on educating and equipping lay businesspeople to see their work as ministry. It describes itself as an international graduate school of Christian studies with "a mission of seeking to educate, nurture, and equip men and women from around the world to live and work as servant leaders."[113] Notably, Dr. R. Paul Stevens carries the title of professor of marketplace theology and leadership.[114]

Despite these encouraging developments, the evidence is clear. Generally speaking, neither the church nor the theological academy has had an intentional ministry or theological focus to help and equip laity, particularly those who work in the marketplace, in their daily work. This, despite the Hart and Krueger finding that "many Christians and Jews hunger for more support from their religious communities in relating their faith to their work lives."[115] The all-to-frequent reality is they do not receive it there, so they turn elsewhere. Many people in the marketplace turn to pop-culture solutions, self-help books, New Age spirituality, private piety, or Gnostic back-to-nature movements to find meaning and purpose in their lives.[116] In the meantime, the church who has so much to offer sits on the sidelines with half-empty pews.

SIX

Faith at Work as a Social Movement

André Delbecq, university professor and former dean of the Leavey School of Business at Santa Clara University, located in the heart of Silicon Valley, has long been interested in matters of spirituality and its impact on work and leadership, particularly for senior executives. Yet even he is surprised at the surging interest in FAW, noting, "There were two things I thought I'd never see in my life, the fall of the Russian empire and God being spoken about at a business school."[1]

Compiling empirical evidence of movements that are dynamic, decentralized, loosely networked, informal, and unstructured can be methodologically challenging. Movements such as Faith at Work have no single umbrella membership organization, definitive survey, or government study to provide quantitative data of their size, form, or substance. Moreover, to date, the FAW movement as a movement has not been systematically studied nor definitively described.[2] To overcome this lack of readily available information, the variety of sources offered here can, when taken together, begin to paint a comprehensive profile of the movement. In particular, my research draws on a wide range of primary sources, including the 2003 *International Faith & Work Directory*,[3] media coverage, books, newsletters, magazines, Internet sites, conferences, interviews, firsthand experiences, and on the emerging body of research in the business academy.[4]

The Evidence Abounds

The most exhaustive quantitative and qualitative research to date on FAW groups, undertaken primarily by general editor Michael McLoughlin of YWAM Marketplace Mission and his Scruples organization[5] (with help from collaborators Os Hillman of Marketplace Leaders, Neal Johnson of Institute for Marketplace Ministries, and myself, the then president of the Avodah Institute), is called the 2003 *International Faith & Work Directory*.[6] This is the third edition of what was originally called *The Scruples Directory of Marketplace Ministry*.[7] The second edition, *The Scruples Directory: Millennium 2000 Edition* contained more than 750 listings,[8] whereas the 2003 *International Faith & Work Directory* (hereafter *Faith & Work Directory*) contains listings for more than 1,200 groups, institutions, and organizations that in some capacity are part of the FAW movement. Our research reveals that the number of new organizations has at least doubled every decade since the 1960s.[9] This empirical evidence helps to substantiate the theory presented here that wave three of the FAW movement took hold in the mid-1980s and has grown exponentially ever since. The *Scruples Directory* and its successor, the *Faith & Work Directory*, focus mostly on North America and Europe, though our study also gives indications that this movement is having a worldwide impact. Thus, while the focus of this book has been the North American manifestations of the FAW movement, the evidence in the *Faith & Work Directory* also supports the thesis that the FAW movement is not only active in North American Protestant and Catholic circles but is growing on an international basis, as well. For instance, the *Faith & Work Directory* notes that the International Christian Chamber of Commerce, founded in 1985 in Belgium, now has members in eighty countries. Our research found that the Full Gospel Business Men's Fellowship International is approaching its goal of having members in two hundred countries. The Christian Business Men's Committee now has members in fifty countries, and the newer Europartners is growing in Europe.

As the *Faith & Work Directory* demonstrates, one of the primary forms of expression of the FAW movement is groups. For readers seeking names and more information on these FAW groups, I provide many examples in the endnotes to this volume. These groups range in size in terms of both staff and membership. At the smallest end of the spectrum, we find informal and loosely organized groups. They are usually led by volunteers and may only have one to two dozen members. The groups are often locally oriented without Web sites or promotional material, and tend not to be have any legal status, and thus remain largely uncounted by our research. Moving up in size and complexity, some groups are staffed by one part-time person with a regional membership following, while other organizations have dozens of staff and measure their membership in the thousands.[10] Most of these larger groups are structured as nonprofits, although increasingly many are for-profit business ventures offering a range of consulting, publishing, and other services.[11] Some groups are formally structured with dues, attendance expectations, and other membership requirements.[12] Some include specific confessional or doctrinal statements to which members must ascribe.[13] However, it appears that most groups are not formal membership associations in the traditional sense; rather, they are loosely structured with minimal expectations or demands of participants. Most groups desire to be welcoming to all, regardless of theological orientation, although in practice, many groups have implicit theological positions on various ethical or social issues that gradually evolve and are subsequently maintained by a self-selecting membership.

Groups are one of the more visible and helpful means of measuring and assessing evidence of the FAW movement. However, individual expressions of FAW are also important. These individual expressions are difficult to measure, but they manifest themselves in the large quantity of people who attend conferences, buy books and magazines, subscribe to newsletters, visit Web sites, and utilize other modes of expression that pertain to FAW. These individuals form, in many ways, the backbone of the movement.

Another way to show evidence of the FAW movement is to review the media to discover if and how the movement is covered by the press. Newspapers, magazines, and journals have been reporting on the "faith at work story" since the late 1980s, coinciding with the commencement of wave three. The bibliography contains a representative sampling of many of these articles on the FAW movement. Notably, it is primarily the secular general and business presses that are reporting on the movement, and not the religious presses. The development and growth of the FAW movement has been closely observed and covered by the secular media, including TV, radio, and print outlets. Television and radio have covered some aspects of the movement,[14] however, the movement seems to lend itself to and be particularly evident in print media. The business and general presses provide extensive evidence of the unmet needs and conditions giving rise to the movement and profiles of a wide range of groups, members, and modes of expression.

Demonstrating that the FAW movement is not limited to the "Bible Belt" or other regional biases, data indicate the breadth of the media coverage across local papers throughout the country, as well as regional, national, and international outlets. For instance, internationally recognized business newspapers, such as the *Wall Street Journal* and the *Financial Times*, have had feature series and multiple articles on the issues surrounding spirituality at work. Other nationally read newspapers, such as the *New York Times*, the *Christian Science Monitor*, the *Los Angeles Times*, and *USA Today*, have all had stories, in many cases feature articles and supplement sections, on the FAW movement. Similarly, regional and local papers, such as the *Dallas Morning News*, the *Santa Fe* (New Mexico) *Chronicle*, and the *Lancaster* (Pennsylvania) *Era*, have also covered the movement. Moreover, the majority of these stories are in the business or general interest sections of the newspaper, and not in the religion section.

Magazines and periodicals have also recognized the increasing interest in religion and spirituality in the workplace. The venerable business publication *Fortune* magazine ran a July 2001 cover story entitled "God and Business: The Surprising Quest for Spiritual Renewal in the Workplace,"[15] and more recently in 2006 *Fortune Small Business* had a cover story, "Jesus at Work."[16] Another well-regarded business magazine, *BusinessWeek*, ran a 1999 cover story on faith in the workplace entitled "Religion in the Workplace: The Growing Presence of Spirituality in Corporate America."[17] Even *Newsweek Japan* had an article reporting on the American phenomenon.[18] In addition to business newspapers and journals, further evidence of this movement can be found in general newspapers and periodicals, ranging from local papers to airline magazines.[19]

One thing that is notable about all of these stories in the business and general press is that they are written with a respectful and generally approving tone. Of the more than 150 sample articles on these topics in the bibliography, only two concluded that the quest to integrate faith and work was a bad thing in itself for workers and the business community.[20] Most articles recognize that there are serious and valid concerns over how to introduce faith or spirituality into the workplace in responsible, appropriate, and legal ways, but seldom is the concept itself outright rejected. The main concerns have to do with proselytizing, harassment, and accommodation of religious practices that disrupt normal work flows or environments. Perhaps the generally favorable review reflects that most people in the workplace want to be treated holistically, and for the majority of people that includes their spiritual dimension. A quick review of some article titles is indicative of the themes and issues around which the movement is organized and to which the journalists are responding, including "When Business Gets Religion," "Exploring Spiritual Approach to Business-World Challenges," "New Spirit in the Workplace," "Serving the Ultimate Boss," "Souls Restored in the Workplace: Spirituality in Business," "Instilling Spiritual Values in the Workplace," "Bible in the Boardroom?" and "Regulating Religious Life in the Office."[21]

As the media coverage and my review of the movement show, most FAW initiatives and special-purpose groups[22] have formed outside the authority, involvement, or impetus of the institutional church. The articles confirm that, in general, the FAW movement has been launched and led largely by lay leaders who find the church unaware of, unresponsive to, unfamiliar with, or systematically critical of the problems and possibilities they face as Christians with vocations in the marketplace. Few religious professionals are involved in the day-to-day leadership of these organizations.[23] In the absence of consistent or broadly sustained interest by ecclesiastics and theologians, the business community is itself responding to the problem of the Sunday-Monday gap. Not surprisingly, the FAW movement has an entrepreneurial orientation, as business leaders, consultants, and various voluntary associations have launched a variety of initiatives to help businesspeople integrate faith and work. Thus, the movement could be called the supply-side response to the unmet needs, or demand side, of the modern workplace. Further, the various groups and people in the movement tend to segment themselves in order to target the driving concerns of ethics, evangelization, experience, and enrichment.

As further evidence of the movement, a number of books have been written over the past decade or so, mostly by lay businesspeople—not pastors or academics—on spirituality and work.[24] Some books are expressly from the Christian tradition, while others are more generically spiritual and pluralistic, avoiding specific religious identities. The growth in the quantity and quality of books on FAW is staggering, as even a casual review of bestseller lists and the shelves at Barnes & Noble demonstrates.[25] To quantify the FAW books from the Christian tradition, a new resource compiled by Hammond, Stevens, and Svanoe entitled *The Marketplace Annotated Bibliography: A Christian Guide to Books on Work, Business & Vocation* is especially helpful.[26] This volume, compiled from a Christian perspective, contains an annotated review of more than seven hundred selected texts and publications.[27] Hammond et al. focus on what some in the movement call "ministry in daily life," a rubric that includes all nonordained activities from the household to leisure to the office. The *Marketplace Annotated Bibliography* is organized around a thematic index that helps to profile the topical contours and target audience of the movement. Yet even *The Marketplace Annotated Bibliography* is incomplete, as its evangelical Christian orientation tends to omit texts representing different theological perspectives on FAW, such as those from liberal Christianity, New Age and more generically spiritual approaches, and from other religions. Despite its limitations it is an excellent resource providing extensive and representative evidence of books written about faith and work during waves two and three of the movement.

A glance at the titles of a sampling of the books written by Christian businesspeople during wave three, many included in Hammond et al.'s volume, indicates the range of FAW topics and issues of concern: *Balancing Your Faith, Family, and Work* (Gelsinger, 2003), *God Is My CEO: Following God's Principles in a Bottom-Line World* (Julian, 2001), *Spirituality @ Work: 10 Ways to Balance Your Life On-the-Job* (Pierce, 2001), *The Fourth Frontier: Exploring the New World of Work* (Graves and Addington, 2000), *The Soul of a Firm* (Pollard,

1996), *God on the Job: Finding God Who Waits at Work* (Smith, 1995), *Jesus, Inc.* (Jones, 2001), *Jesus CEO: Using Ancient Wisdom for Visionary Leadership* (Jones, 1995), *Roaring Lambs: A Gentle Plan to Radically Change Our World* (Briner, 1993), *Thank God It's Monday: Ministry in the Workplace* (Greene, 1994), *The Soul of a Business: Managing for Profit and the Common Good* (Chappell, 1994), and *Loving Monday: Succeeding in Business without Selling Your Soul* (Beckett, 1998).[28]

Further evidence of the movement is the growing body of research, curricula, and texts emerging from the Academy of Management on issues pertaining to management, spirituality, and religion. As Judi Neal, executive director of Spirit at Work, recently retired business professor, and one of AOM's pioneers in the field, observes, what began on the fringes of the academic world is now a "global phenomenon."[29] Further, Delbecq, another leader in the business academy's research into spirituality, religion, and work, has commented that "the intersection of spirituality with business is currently the most published new topic in business school literature."[30] Indeed, the title of one academic conference at a state university, Going Public with Spirituality in Work and Higher Education, is indicative of the new intellectual receptivity to spirituality and religion.[31] As University of Massachusetts chancellor David K. Scott, the conference host, commented, "a powerful movement" is under way to transform how we think about education, the workplace, and organizational life through "integrative approaches that overcome fragmentation, specialization, and isolation in life and learning."[32] As evidence of this, a recent news story on spirituality in business reported, "Indeed, 30 MBA programs now offer courses on the issue" of spirituality in the workplace,[33] and FAW was also the focus of a recent *Harvard Business School Bulletin*.[34] One of the leading management scholars and authors is Oliver Williams, whose book *Business, Religion, and Spirituality: A New Synthesis* (2003) continues a distinguished career of teaching and writing that links business ethics and religious teachings, not only out of his own Catholic tradition but others as well.[35]

In her paper, "Spirituality in the Workplace in Higher Education: A Global Phenomenon,"[36] Neal notes that the movement is no longer limited to practitioners, but has been embraced by the management academy. While not exhaustive, I have given examples in the notes of this volume of an ever-growing range of conferences, courses, and programs in business schools,[37] research journals (including special issues),[38] centers,[39] and professional associations.[40] While no hard data are available, leaders in the field agree that starting around 1990 conferences on integrating spirituality and work began to appear in the United States and Canada. By 2000, more than twenty large-scale formal conferences had been held, and the number continues to grow, with increasing reach beyond North America to countries including Australia, England, India, Ireland, New Zealand, the Philippines, Switzerland, and Wales. In many ways, estimates by Neal and others are low, as they tend to focus on academic conference or gatherings largely in the New Age genre. Thus, these estimates miss the very large number of conferences that are specifically Christian in content and attendance.[41]

A Diverse Movement

Describing the FAW groups and participants and how the quest for integration manifests itself reveals a variety of attributes and characteristics. The evidence suggests that it is misleading to presume that any single variable or characteristic of one group is representative of the whole movement. Indeed, there are several demographic and theological characteristics that influence the shape and content of the movement, in terms of member profiles (e.g., male-female, black-white, liberal-conservative, etc.) and modes of expression (e.g., small-group gatherings, conferences, Web sites, eNewsletters, blogs, books, etc.). Thus, while the FAW movement in general is organized around a quest for integration, it is not monolithic. Indeed, sociologists generally agree that while social movements do have a collective identity and organizing principle, this need not imply homogeneity of either form or substance.[42] There are several possible ways to describe, understand, and analyze the diversity of FAW in wave three,[43] yet thus far a theologically and sociologically sufficient approach has not emerged.[44] Mentioned earlier and discussed in more detail in chapter 7, I propose a typology called the Integration Box and the Four E's that might help begin to fill that void.

The participants and groups that comprise the FAW movement might best be understood by describing their member profiles (including demographic, theological, and academic descriptors), their modes of expression (including print, electronic, and face-to-face communications media), and the emerging peripheral influencers of the movement, including academics and advisors. These descriptors of participants in the FAW movement cover several factors. They include, for instance, geography, industry sector, company, employee group, professional level, and gender. Geographically, the movement exhibits a broad range of diversity, in terms of both location and target audience. Geography is often the defining characteristic in terms of limiting the target audience and focus of a group, or alternatively it can serve as a motivator for groups with larger visions. Some groups are city- or region-focused.[45] Others, while perhaps based in a particular city, have a national reach with a city-based strategy replicating their presence and impact through local chapters or representative groups around the country.[46] Many of the groups with national demographic bases also have expanded internationally.[47]

Industry sectors and related professional guilds and gatherings, as another FAW demographic profile descriptor, are increasingly popular. Many FAW participants find it preferable to convene with others in the same profession or line of work, finding ready bonding in common professional language and issues. Often a trade or profession has particular issues, as well as general manifestations of the Four E's of ethics, evangelization, enrichment, and experience. The particular issues often serve as galvanizing and motivating factors for gathering. Being among friends or colleagues familiar with such shared problems often makes it easier to find ethical guidance, spiritual nurturance, and professional support. Indeed, as shown by the *Faith & Work Directory*, the range of industries and professions that has developed FAW groups is extensive and growing.[48] In addition to formalized groups, sometimes Christian FAW groups gather informally within or alongside an industry guild or professional association. By definition, most are difficult to identify and measure.[49]

Related to professional groups and guilds are Christian business networks. These groups seek to combine normal business networking and marketing (as might be found in a chamber of commerce or Rotary Club) with Christian principles, perspectives, and fellowship.[50] In contrast, there also exist special-purpose FAW business groups that seek not to increase their own network but to help less-privileged people to start their own. This part of the FAW movement is focused on issues of social and economic justice, often with the aim of helping others to become economically self-sufficient. These groups offer Christian-based business expertise, capital, and networking services to entrepreneurs in the United States and internationally in underdeveloped and developing regions. One strand of this is the Christian micro-enterprise movement, which offers Christian versions of secular micro-enterprise lending and investing.[51]

Another demographic item in the member profile in the FAW movement is the specific companies themselves. I have introduced the term "faith-friendly" companies as a new way to think about faith in the workplace (see chapter 8). Faith-friendly companies actively embrace and welcome the spiritual nature of their employees at work, deeming it positive and beneficial for both employees and the company. Yet, faith-friendly companies are very different from "faith-based" companies. Faith-friendly companies respect equally the variety of spiritual identities and religious traditions represented by employees. In contrast, a faith-based organization is grounded in and privileges one religious tradition over others. While some family-owned and privately held companies have long been known to be faith-friendly,[52] there is also increasing evidence that the movement is taking hold in publicly traded Fortune 500 companies.[53] Indeed, many such companies have established and authorized both formal (often under the banner of diversity initiatives and affinity groups) and informal employee groups that meet regularly on company premises to discuss issues pertaining to faith and work.[54] Some FAW affinity groups revolve around prayer and Bible study. While often Christian, there are also groups from other religions. For instance, the management at Bear Stearns, a venerable finance house on Wall Street, formally endorses and pays for a weekly Torah class and a biweekly Mishnah class, taught by two different rabbis and held in company conference rooms. Other FAW groups focus on business ethics and how to improve within their job functions and workplace; and yet others consider how to reach out to and serve fellow employees. Many of the formally sanctioned groups have been authorized under the corporate trend of encouraging diversity training and supporting affinity groups. Affinity groups, generally speaking, are organized around common interests, hobbies, or employee characteristics, such as race, ethnicity, gender, and sexual orientation. Initially meant to help support minority and historically disenfranchised populations and serve as a source of networking, today diversity and affinity groups are more about attracting and retaining the best talent, and helping to create a corporate culture that mirrors one's customers. Leaders of religious affinity groups and GLBT (Gay Lesbian Bisexual Transgender) groups often express initial concern or even hostility toward each other. Management is often reluctant to endorse the formation of religious affinity groups (e.g., General Motors) for fear that these two groups will cause division and conflict. But over time many of the harshest critics have become the biggest advocates, such as at American Express.[55] Moreover, Ford Motor Company's "Ford Interfaith Network" group was essential in helping to defuse fears of retaliatory violence against Ford's large Muslim workforce in Detroit after the 9/11 terrorist attacks. While FAW affinity groups may vary in mission and purpose, the one from Coca-Cola may be seen as a representative example. Its literature notes: "The Coca-Cola Company's Christian Fellowship exists to bring together a community of Christians who support each other and The Company's values and goals by integrating our Christian Faith and our work."[56] Further, Coca-Cola's Christian Fellowship's formal statement of purpose[57] includes the cornerstones of integrity, accountability, building relationships, respect, diversity, morality, and service, as grounded in biblical teachings and manifested in Jesus Christ.[58]

Related to the member profile demographic of company is the arena of corporate chaplains. Industrial and corporate chaplaincy is not new, though the concept fell largely out of practice for much of the twentieth century, before enjoying a brief surge of experimental interest in the 1950s in England and France through worker-priests (see chapter 3). Corporate chaplaincy in America has made a comeback over the past two decades.[59] One chaplaincy agency estimates that there are now more than two thousand workplace chaplains nationwide.[60] Some are directly employed by the company as part of its human resources staff, whereas others are outsourced through chaplaincy agencies. Through agencies, companies hire both part- and full-time workplace chaplains. The largest workplace chaplain agency is the Dallas-based Marketplace Chaplains USA, founded in 1984 by a retired military chaplain, Gil Stricklin. At last count, Marketplace Chaplains USA had more than 1,900 chaplains providing services to more than 400,000 employees and their families, covering 325 companies in 44 states and more than 560 cities.

The functions of corporate chaplains generally include "walking the floor" and being a listening ear and comforting voice for employees, many of whom have spiritual needs but are not members of a particular congregation and do not know where to turn in times of personal or professional crisis. Corporate chaplains often perform hospital visits, grief counseling, and occasionally even funerals for family members of employees who are not members of a particular congregation or worship community. Employers are increasingly aware that employee well-being and company performance are negatively affected by a variety of personal and professional tensions, fears, dilemmas, addictions, and other problems experienced as a part of daily life. Thus, most corporate chaplain providers justify the cost of their chaplains under the umbrella of corporate wellness programs or EAPs (employee assistance programs). But corporate chaplaincy programs are not without their critics. Those opposed assert that corporate chaplains are apologists for management and not critical enough of structural issues; have a hidden agenda of evangelizing workers; are not uniformly trained or held to a professional code of ethics; and are difficult to implement in diverse interfaith environments.

A further indication of the growing academic and practical interest in this field came in 2005 when the Yale Center for Faith & Culture at Yale Divinity School hosted a national conference called Workplace Chaplaincy: Hot Issues and Best Practices. More than 120 people attended this unprecedented event, representing a diversity of theological views (Christians, Jews, and Muslims), occupations (businesspeople, chaplains, clergy, academics, and service providers), and perspectives (liberal, conservative, and mainstream). One Fortune 75 company, Tyson Foods, Inc., employs more than 125 corporate chaplains across dozens of plants and offices around the country. While it is hard to quantify the benefits financially, chairman and CEO John Tyson told the conference attendees that he had "no doubt," based on story after story, as to the program's human and bottom-line value. One Tyson Foods plant manager, for instance, was originally deeply skeptical of the concept and did not want his already thin profit margins to have to absorb the "nonproductive" costs of a workplace chaplain. That same manager today will jokingly say that only over his dead body will he allow you to remove his chaplain. Another vivid example came from Robert Pettus, vice chairman of Coca-Cola Bottling Company Consolidated, who spoke at the conference. Pettus has studied the costs and benefits of a workplace chaplaincy program and concluded that they more than pay for themselves in terms of lower turnover, higher morale, and healthier staff. By way of example, Pettus shared that some union employees—who happened to be a group of single mothers—approached him and said that, if tough economic conditions meant the workplace chaplaincy program might have to get cut, they were willing to give up other benefits instead so as to keep that one. In thirty years of work in human relations, he had never heard such an offer. To be sure, corporate chaplaincy is not for all companies, based on a variety of factors, including geography, culture, and history. There are several themes that emerged from the conference that deserve further scholarly research and practical consideration.[61] Yet what is clear is that appropriately introduced and managed, in certain corporate settings a workplace chaplain can significantly and uniquely enhance a company's well-being.

Workplace chaplains largely although not exclusively attend to the spiritual needs and problems of hourly and lower- to middle-management employees. In contrast, the FAW movement also has solo practitioners, similar to consultants or executive coaches, who work with a select group of business leaders. Indeed, there is an association called the Spiritual Coaches Network composed of consultants, largely with a New Age or generic spirituality orientation, who specialize in coaching executives on their spiritual journeys.[62] Unlike formally trained workplace chaplains who tend to be grounded in and certified by a particular religious tradition, most of these spiritual coaches are not ordained, formally trained, or certified by a governing body. There are also distinctly Christian forms of such spiritual advisors, chaplains of a sort, who convene regular gatherings, discussions, and one-on-one meetings with CEOs and other senior executives. They function in a variety of ways, often serving in a private or off-the-record capacity as a chaplain, spiritual director, discipling mentor, accountability partner, coach, or counselor.[63]

Another demographic factor that sometimes determines the membership profile of FAW groups is the level of participants within an organization. That is, some groups form around issues unique to certain hierarchical levels of the company, such as senior management, middle management, clerical, or blue collar. For example, several groups have emerged whose members or participants are primarily CEOs and senior executives.[64] In contrast to intracompany affinity groups, these FAW organizations are composed of people from different companies. Attendees and members of these groups discuss issues that are unique to their level of responsibility, such as earnings pressures, litigation threats, succession planning, relocating manufacturing sites, downsizing, dealing with sycophants, use of power, wealth, and pride. Many find great value in having a confidential place to share such issues and concerns with a peer group, discussing topics that may not be understood by others with different responsibilities or that are inappropriate for public disclosure. Some of these groups meet at a hosting executive's office, while others prefer to meet off-premises in a restaurant or hotel conference room or on a conference call. Privacy is central to these FAW members. Most of these kinds of groups seek to cultivate values and the virtue of integrity in the personal and business decisions of the member executives. It is not uncommon for executives to share deeply personal or professional dilemmas, asking for prayer, support, and guidance.

Gender is another demographic differentiator of FAW membership profiles. While most FAW groups and organizations welcome both men and women, some particularly aim at one or the other. As with many other areas of society and other voluntary associations, some groups prefer to be men-only or women-only, recognizing that sometimes this provides greater intimacy and safety when discussing certain topics. Some FAW groups limit membership to men largely on theological grounds and gender role expectations of the members.[65] FAW groups that are only for women are an emerging sector of the FAW movement that is addressing what appears to be a growing demand of many professional women for a confidential, sympathetic forum.[66] Several groups, organizations, conferences, radio shows, and publications particularly target professional women.[67]

Theological Factors and Group Profiles

FAW groups have a range of theological emphases that influence not only their formation but also their function. These emphases include traditional categories of fundamentalist, evangelical, Pentecostal, mainstream, and liberal orientations, as well as New Age and mixed spiritualities that draw on a variety of religious traditions and practices, including forms of Buddhism and Hinduism. Understanding FAW groups and participants is aided by an awareness of their theological emphasis. For instance, there are several significant FAW organizations sponsored by so-called para-church entities (ministries such as Campus Crusade for Christ, InterVarsity, and Navigators). These para-ministry-sponsored FAW groups typically fall under the evangelical theological umbrella.[68] As is more fully explained in the next section, evangelizing is a central theological motivator and accent for these kinds of FAW groups,[69] while other FAW groups actively eschew evangelization.[70] In like fashion, still other groups are motivated theologically to focus primarily on ethical and structural economic justice issues.[71]

Another theological factor that is sometimes operative in FAW groups is a denominational or confessional orientation. While membership in most organizations transcends denominational ties or identity, some groups have explicit restrictions. This is most evident in the Roman Catholic tradition, where certain FAW groups have been formed that are exclusively for Catholic members.[72] Moving further away from formal Roman Catholic church affiliation and influence, there are some Catholic lay organizations that are more ecumenical in nature. While not denying or ignoring their Roman Catholicity, they welcome participation by and with Protestants and others.[73]

Within Protestantism, only two denominations stand out as having theological attributes that have shaped specific groups and parts of the FAW movement. The Evangelical Lutheran Church in America has supported and been part of the Faith at Work movement. Until a 2004 staff downsizing, ELCA had a department in its Division of Ministry that focused on ministry in daily life throughout much of wave three of the movement. Headed by lay leader Sally Simmel for more than a decade until the department was eliminated, ELCA published helpful pamphlets, produced congregational aids and resources, hosted conferences, and experimented with electronic means of practicing and supporting ministry in daily life. Another model example is the Mennonite church through its MEDA (Mennonite Economic Development Associates) organization. MEDA far outstrips most denominations in terms of both commitment and content, particularly relative to its proportionally small overall membership. While most of what MEDA does is open to all faiths, it usually draws its members from its own ranks. MEDA hosts annual conferences on FAW-related topics, publishes a magazine and books, and provides many other resources.[74] In addition, MEDA is a leader in Christian-based micro-lending and economic development.

An emerging theological and ecclesiastical factor, in terms of target audience, location, and delivery channels is the local church. Despite the general pattern of most churches not being formally involved in the FAW movement (see chapter 5), there is increasing evidence that this is changing in some local congregations and in some of the megachurches. This is most evident in larger churches and those with an orientation toward evangelization, which have hired part-time laypeople[75] and, in some cases, ordained clergy[76] to build and lead local church-based FAW programs. These programs are aimed at existing church members, as well as used for outreach to seekers and the so-called unchurched.

The New Age, or "secular spirituality," part of the movement does not lend itself to location in a Christian framework per se, although as discussed later in this chapter, it deals with many issues found under the enrichment aspect of the Four E's. Moreover, many baptized but nonchurchgoing Christians are drawn to the New Age movement, while retaining loose connections to their Christian roots or self-image.[77] Broadly speaking, FAW groups of this nature are spiritual hybrids and tend toward relativism or individual choice in matters of doctrine or epistemology.

In contrast to the theological academy, as noted earlier, the business academy is bursting with interest in the subject of spirituality and religion in the workplace.[78] While the business academy is not, strictly speaking, an FAW group of practitioners, it does represent an emerging force of influence for the movement, and hence is worthy of comment and inclusion as an aspect of member profiles. The Academy of Management locates its interest in the FAW movement largely through the subdisciplines of organizational development, behavioral management, human relations, and leadership. In 2000, the AOM approved a new special-interest group called Management, Spirituality, and Religion (MSR). In 2002, MSR attained standing as an approved interest group within the AOM. The group has matured to such an extent that at the 2002 annual AOM meeting in Denver, there were more than two dozen sessions sponsored by MSR, including a doctoral consortium, professional development workshops, paper sessions, and a keynote all-academy session on how religious traditions connect to the lived experience of the contemporary CEO. At the 2006 AOM annual meeting in Atlanta, MSR's growth and improved quality of scholarship impressed even the toughest of skeptics. MSR membership today exceeds 700 scholars and practitioners.

AOM's interest in management, religion, and spirituality developed gradually, and the creation of the MSR group is a result of progressive academic interest in a series of intertwined topics. Notably, much MSR interest and scholarship have been driven by secular academics, who typically avoid mention of whether and how personal confessional beliefs shape their research. In parallel to these scholars, there is a growing group of business scholars who intentionally combine confessional beliefs with scholarly research into marketplace issues.[79] This wave three rediscovery of the role of religion in business may have first started with the academy's focus on business ethics, which in a formal sense was "largely a creation of the twentieth century, with a quickening of interest and activity in the period 1970–1986."[80]

Although some scholars, such as management guru Peter Drucker,[81] have long argued that "there is no such thing as 'Business Ethics,' there is only ethics,"[82] nevertheless, an academic specialty in business ethics began to flourish in American M.B.A. programs, along with a parallel and often related interest in corporate social responsibility.[83] Progressively, the study of business ethics led to inquiry into corporate values, mission statements, professional codes of conduct,[84] stakeholder theory, the "softer" nonempirical side of managing people, and nondiscrimination statements as part of hiring practices. In conjunction with corporate diversity initiatives, EAPs, and the late 1990s' so-called dot.com or New Economy accent on creativity and holistic being came the hesitant first steps toward overt mention of religion and spirituality.

Some leading business scholars of this emerging field of spirituality and work reviewed the earlier literature on spirituality and work and concluded that most authors and practitioners focus on only one of four possible levels of analysis: 1) individual, 2) group, 3) organizational, and 4) societal.[85] The authors contend, "Researchers and practitioners will be more effective if they simultaneously consider these four levels rather than only one at a time in their analysis."[86] The authors note that the preponderance of literature and interest is at the individual and group level, with less research going into the organizational and societal levels. By the time of the 2002 AOM meeting, MSR research interests were maturing from the earlier accents on theoretical development, clarifying definitions of key concepts, and "creating justification for the importance and validity of the inclusion of spirituality and religion into the management field," to a new stage of development concentrating on developing research methodologies for the material and nonmaterial and documenting organizational experiences with spirituality in the workplace.[87]

Related to the business academy is the burgeoning field of consulting services to business organizations and executives, focusing explicitly on issues pertaining to spirituality, religion, and faith in the workplace. A new "conflation between business and spirituality" is happening where many of the most reputable management gurus now include spirituality in their writings.[88] These mainstream consultants focus on spirituality as a factor in employee creativity, personal growth, leadership, finding meaning and purpose in work, and holistic living and as a resource for empowerment.[89] The consulting field now has specialists in spirituality, who offer classes in meditation, yoga, relaxation techniques, and work-life balance. As noted earlier, even the specialized field of executive coaching now has a subspecialty called "spiritual coaches." With the exception of some authors like Ken Blanchard, most secular business writers, consultants, and coaches avoid raising consideration of truth claims of various religions, preferring to deal with spirituality in general and to draw on its largely utilitarian benefit to businesspeople and corporations.

As noted earlier, there are thousands of special-purpose groups in existence, manifesting themselves in a variety of ways. For instance, some FAW groups are structured around a particular style or mode of interaction favored by members. Some groups employ the rubric of Bible study, seeking to find links between scriptural lessons and workplace experiences, while others prefer to discuss pressing personal situations being faced in the workplace. Some groups are teaching- and lecture-oriented, with members or outside speakers sharing their experiences or knowledge on a particular theme. Some are oriented toward case studies, seeking to answer real-world or hypothetical business problems. Yet other groups have more of a therapeutic tone, with members sharing each other's pains and burdens, either in small groups or through accountability partners. One general factor is the frequency of meetings. Some groups meet regularly before work (in a restaurant, train station, country club, or someone's office), some meet over lunch (in a restaurant or an office conference room), and some meet on Saturday mornings. Most meetings last no more than sixty to ninety minutes. The convener usually leads meetings, presenting a topic or message and guiding the discussing, although some groups share this responsibility with rotating leaders. Some FAW gatherings, usually smaller and more intimate in nature, are covenant groups where accountability partners check in with each other, often sharing deep pains, problems, and confessions.

Communication with and among FAW Participants

In addition to these groups, which physically gather and meet to discuss issues of common concern, there are also other forms of expression and communication. One of the most prolific modes of expression of the FAW movement is via the Internet. FAW Web sites abound, making the launch of an FAW group relatively simple, inexpensive, and far reaching. As with all Web sites, some are merely informational or promotional, essentially taking their printed literature and placing it online. Others are innovative and interactive, seeking regular contact and relationship with their audiences and providing relevant news and helpful information. Many include electronic newsletters, e-mail prayer networks, Internet chat rooms, blogs, streaming videos, and downloads. Most groups and individuals in the movement employ communications strategies that combine new and old technologies (e.g., magazines, circulars, books, videos, and CDs), as well as special gatherings for conferences or retreats.

As with many other contemporary special-purpose groups and voluntary associations, FAW groups publish, as noted, written and electronic newsletters as a primary mode of expression to communicate with their constituent base. Newsletters are particularly helpful for geographically diverse group members. Some newsletters are still printed, but gradually most are being replaced by electronic versions. They vary in industry and thematic focus, as well as theological perspective. Broadly speaking, these newsletters typically contain a mixture of biblical reflections on various thematic aspects of integrating faith and work, practical tips and resources, and profiles of Christians in the workplace.[90] Some of the Web-based newsletters have membership lists in the tens of thousands.[91] Some are very sophisticated in both technology and content, while others are basic and simplistic. Some are sent out as daily devotionals, while others are weekly or monthly in nature.[92] Moreover, many FAW groups have developed topic-specific e-mail chat rooms designed to bring people together to discuss specific FAW issues and interests.[93] One example of a successful interactive newsletter is Greg Pierce's Faith and Work in Cyberspace. Pierce poses questions to his subscribers having to do with practices and spiritual disciplines in the workplace. He gathers, consolidates, and publishes the responses from his readership.[94] However, as with secular Web sites, the user traffic on the threaded discussions ebbs and flows, and they seem less popular as the novelty wears off. As with other Internet communities, blogs seem to be gaining in popularity, and are replacing the earlier chat rooms.

Magazines and journals are another popular and effective mode of expression for FAW groups and participants. Increasingly, many of these magazines and journals rival secular magazines in terms of the quality of writing, appearance, and subscription levels.[95] While each FAW periodical has its own style and content, what is common across all is the desire to help readers in their quest to integrate faith and work. For instance, one well-regarded FAW periodical, *Marketplace* magazine, published by MEDA, was one of the first FAW publications to emerge in wave three and still remains in operation.[96] *Marketplace* blends a mixture of practical and informational stories about real Christians in business, the challenges of being called to business, and helpful tips on how to live out that calling. *Marketplace* also reports frequently on the Christian-based micro-lending and micro-investing movement. Over the years, topics have included business as calling, the high cost of dissent, saying no to bribery, and the busyness trap. Other popular FAW magazines include *Life @ Work Journal*, which is no longer published,[97] and *Business Reform* magazine, in some ways a successor to *Life @ Work Journal*. *Business Reform* has a different editorial design but also deals with practical business issues, drawing on Christian teachings for guidance. It has included feature articles on topics such as doing business in tough times: the Bible and bankruptcy, motivation and compensation, the sabbath, business and culture: bringing business culture into his light, business ethics, banking and finance, management, and wealth.

In addition to quality writing and production, the circulation levels of some FAW magazines exceed those of many other Christian journals and popular magazines, and even rival some secular periodicals. At its peak, *Life @ Work* had a circulation of 120,000. *Business Reform* had 30,000 paid subscribers as of 2002 and, as a result of a marketing arrangement, increased its base of paid subscribers to 200,000 in 2003. As a relatively new journal, this compares favorably with other Christian periodicals, such as *Christianity Today* (155,000 subscribers) and *Christian Century* (30,000 paid subscribers and 52,000 readership).[98]

FAW as a Social Movement

There is overwhelming evidence that faith at work activity meets the three sociological criteria I established earlier to be a bona fide social movement. Its many modes of expression involve a "plurality of individuals, groups, and/or organizations" and often involve a loose "network of relations," thus meeting the first criterion of being a social movement.[99] As noted, participants span a broad range of industry sectors, geographic areas, job descriptions and levels, and ages. Individuals and groups involved in the FAW movement convene in local chapters, in national gatherings, and increasingly between and among groups that have no formal affiliation. Moreover, the networks of groups that have formed in wave three range from loosely related in some cases to more tightly clustered or affiliated in others. In addition, there is a plethora of informal, unaffiliated, stand-alone groups that have formed in local communities and regions. This is consistent another observation about movements that "while informality and looseness are essential properties of the system of interaction, the same is not necessarily true of single units of the system."[100]

Participants in FAW activity also meet the second criterion of having a "collective identity." Here, *collective identity* is defined as a "shared set of beliefs and a sense of belongingness."[101] However, diversity can still exist, as having a collective identity does "not imply homogeneity of ideas and orientations within social movement networks."[102] The collective identity of the FAW movement can be understood in three ways. First, the collective identity finds commonality in the participants' theological identification and confessional claims as, say, Christians; they want to know how their Christian identities should affect their view of and behavior in the business world. While the particular theological tenets and emphases may differ from group to group, participants in the FAW movement are generally bound by a deep sense of spiritual belief and identity. Christians often speak of a strong belief in God as revealed in Jesus Christ and sustained by the Holy Spirit. Christian participants in the movement span a full theological range from conservative (e.g., CEO Forum and Legatus) to liberal (Shalem Institute and the Institute for Servant Leadership). The movement also includes people of other religious traditions, as well as those who reject organized religion altogether, preferring to pick and choose from various religious traditions and maintain a loosely defined conception of spirituality (e.g., Martin Rutte's Livelihood). They, too, have the quest for integration, or holistic living, as an organizing principle.

The second part of FAW's collective identity comes from the common shared experience of being workers in the workplace. While individual jobs, workplace situations, and contexts vary, there are several connecting themes that enable, for instance, a sales representative and a pharmaceutical researcher to find common ground. Last, participants in the Faith at Work movement find a collective identity in the generally shared experience that the church is not aware of their plight, does not assist them to overcome the Sunday-Monday gap, and may even send condemnatory messages about their participation in the for-profit world, which is portrayed as sinful, fallen, and to be avoided.

As shown here and in chapter 4, the movement also meets the third criterion of emerging in response to "conflictual issues." The demand side of the movement amply demonstrates the conflicts and struggles that businesspeople experience as part of the Sunday-Monday gap and the lack of help provided by the church (see chapters 4 and 5). Moreover, there are often conflictual issues between FAW needs and legal, social, and family demands. In short, there is overwhelming evidence that the various types and forms of Faith at Work collective activity constitute a bona fide social movement. And history teaches that social movements—consider the civil rights or feminist movements—make deep and far-reaching changes to society's customs, laws, attitudes, and institutions.

SEVEN

Analyzing and Understanding the Faith at Work Movement

In 2003, I attended a conference in Santa Fe called the International Conference on Business and Consciousness. This conference attracted people who comfortably assumed the label of "spiritual" but eschewed any identity with organized religion. Most of the attendees preferred individual expressions and formulations of spirituality, often drawing on and mixing together a variety of religious traditions and teachings to arrive at their own sense of the sacred. At a coffee break, one of the keynote speakers and leaders in this part of the FAW movement quietly took me aside and with kindly intent told me that I should be more careful with my word choice and the kinds of questions I was asking. "Some of the other attendees might be turned off by your mention of religion and business; organized religion is really frowned upon here," he said.

I also recently attended a dinner banquet of a prominent publicly traded company where one of the executives led the management team in a prayer before dinner, a prayer which ended with the words "In Jesus' name we pray." For many in the room, that was a comforting if not required ending to the prayer, while for others—some Christians included—the ending of the prayer took away from its otherwise positive intent and disturbed their sense of inclusivity and respect for the feelings of any non-Christian people in the room.

Each of these vignettes illustrate the power of language and word choice—particularly as regards the deeply personal topic of faith—either to shut down or open up conversation. Indeed, one of the commonly voiced obstacles to both the theoretical and practical discussion of the issues surrounding FAW is language: the words and expressions we use to talk about integrating faith and work. As noted, there are often linguistic and communication barriers between people of different faith traditions, as well as within the same faith tradition. These barriers also exist between theologians and business scholars, and between religious professionals and workplace professionals.

Moreover, even if a new language were developed, the lack of a good conceptual framework in which to locate this dialogue would impede discourse and analysis of the issues identified here as the Four E's under the categories of ethics, evangelism, experience, and enrichment, which together form the key elements of how FAW is understood and manifested. Today, participants in the movement have few alternatives to the failed frameworks and terminology of religion, which often operate in linear spectrums with mutually exclusive either-or poles. Such poles are limiting and not representative of the diversity of the movement or of the desire by most who are on a quest for integration. Most people in the FAW movement want to transcend the old labels of liberal or conservative, evangelical or mainstream, Right or Left, soul savers or society savers, premillennialist or postmillennialist, religious or spiritual, immanent or transcendent, inwardly or outwardly oriented, and so on. While such polarities are helpful in some contexts to highlight particular perspectives, they fail to offer an overarching framework for discussion that can be inclusive of diverse viewpoints. Indeed, participants in the FAW movement exhibit a variety of attributes, as seen in the Four E's, that cannot be reduced or stereotyped into merely one category of expression or identity. It is with these issues in mind that I propose a new framework called the Integration Box to facilitate ethical, theological, and social analyses of the movement.

Needed: A Common Framework and Language for FAW

The Integration Box builds on and utilizes this volume's findings about the demand side, supply side, and evidence of the FAW movement qua movement. It is clear that a quest for integration is the organizing principle of the FAW movement. Moreover, participants in the movement tend to experience and express the quest for the integration of faith and work through one or more of the modalities of ethics, evangelism, experience, and enrichment. When transposed into a new nonlinear theoretical framework, these Four E's result in what can be called the Integration Box (see figure 7.1), a model containing these four quadrants, or types, of FAW orientations and associated language. This conceptual framework facilitates critical analysis, discourse, and understanding the movement and its participants. Each quadrant represents one of the Four E's as the primary manifestation of the quest for integration.[1] Within certain boundaries, all Four E's are legitimate and valid

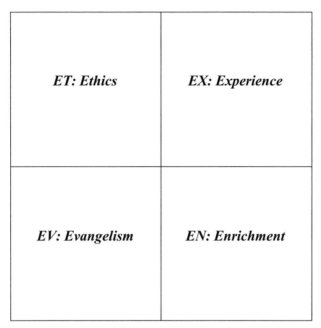

FIGURE 7.1.   The Integration Box: The Four E's

expressions of integrating faith and work. That is, anything inside the Integration Box is an attempt to integrate faith and work, however flawed or insufficient it may be. To be outside the box is effectively to adopt a strategy that believes that faith and work cannot or should not be integrated.

Some businesspeople, whether religious or not, feel that integrating faith and work is problematic and should be avoided, thus consciously choosing to live outside the box, so to speak. Others seek integration but do not have the skills or resources to know how to integrate faith and work in meaningful and appropriate ways, thus finding themselves outside the box by default, not by choice. Thus, whether consciously or unconsciously, many people of faith live bifurcated lives, compartmentalizing their faith teachings apart from workplace demands.

While this framework was designed as a result of studying the largely Christian dimension of the Faith at Work movement, it also functions well with other religious and philosophical traditions. The manifestations of ethics, experience, and enrichment can be found in virtually all religions. The accent on evangelism is, of course, most prominent in Christianity and Islam, though it can be found in some forms of Buddhism. While Hinduism and Judaism are not evangelizing religions in the way that Islam and Christianity are, nevertheless these two traditions are attentive to questions of expression of faith. How one expresses, communicates, and lives out one's faith matters. Thus, "expression" can serve as a functional equivalent to evangelism for the purposes of transposing the Integration Box theory into the wider global study of FAW, including other religious or faith traditions.

The Integration Box offers a viable theoretical and practical framework and language for all four manifestations, thereby enabling constructive analysis and critique of the key variables driving the movement and its participants. The Integration Box has the capacity to reflect the movement's diverse range of motivations, member profiles, and modes of expression, while still recognizing the common organizing principle of a quest for integration. Moreover, it gives linguistic and ideational specificity without being agenda driven or theologically limiting.

Significantly, my early findings suggest that people in the workplace have a natural orientation or predisposition to one or another of the Four E's as they seek to integrate faith and work. This natural inclination toward, say, ethics or evangelism may be a result of many variables, including church upbringing and reinforcement, personality type,[2] theological teachings, societal conditioning, gender, geography, and corporate culture. Most likely, it is a function of several of these factors. For some, these manifestations are conscious and intentional. For others, they are preconscious; and for yet others, a conversion, an awakening, a sensitizing, or a cognitive decision must occur for them to move intentionally into and among the quadrants. For these reasons, the Integration Box offers an effective means to identify the primary integration mode or type that someone employs in his or her expression of faith at work. Moreover, it can serve as a constructive tool not only to engender greater self-awareness of particular faith and work integration tendencies, but it can help people to become more aware and respectful of other types of faith at work expression.[3]

The flexibility of the Integration Box allows people and groups to be located in one or more types, thus avoiding the common problem of rigid typologies that often place individual types into strict opposition or incompatibility. The Integration Box reflects the reality that participants in the FAW movement exhibit varying and often multiple understandings and expressions of integrating faith and work. That is, some may exhibit the characteristics of and be located in primarily a single type, while others may exhibit characteristics of and be located in more than one type.[4] Indeed, some, albeit a minority, move among all four types based on context and other factors. Moreover, this integrated framework allows conceptual and practical space for seemingly unrelated member profiles and modes of expression to find common ground. This sometimes brings together strange bedfellows, such as theological liberals and conservatives, in the same quadrant, in cases where initial presuppositions would suggest an oppositional or even conflictual relationship. What follows is a deeper analysis that recognizes both the positive and problematic dimensions of each type.

Solution: The Integration Box and Its Four Modes

THE ETHICS TYPE

People and groups located in the ethics (ET) quadrant are those whose primary mode of integrating faith at work is through attention to personal virtue, business ethics, and to broader questions of social and economic justice. Their understanding of faith instructs them to accent ethics and righteous living as informed by religious principles and teachings. Their view of work is that it is part of God's created order, and accordingly it must be conducted in ethical, moral, and just ways. The ET type thus has an emphasis on discerning right action and ethical behavior in the marketplace; it also includes a focus on developing business practices and leadership styles that are modeled on biblical principles and figures.[5] As such, the participants and groups in the ET type form a broad tent and address a variety of issues, including personal ethics and behavior, corporate ethics, social and economic justice, and leadership. These ET issues are treated at many levels: micro (personal), mezzo (corporate), and macro (societal). While some general tendencies exist (such as a reliance on biblical principles and teachings as the foundation, motivation, and interpretation of ethics), this quadrant contains a theologically diverse collection of participants and groups. Moreover, expression for the ET type takes many forms, including nonprofits, for-profits, journals, conferences, Web sites, and the use of secular moral philosophy entities and teachings.

Though most businesspeople in the ET quadrant strive to be ethical and to make ethical decisions, few have formal training in philosophical or theological ethics as a discipline. Most would say that "ethics" is simply understood as doing what is right and avoiding what is wrong, as interpreted through some vague conception of religious principles, teachings, and themes. More than one person in the marketplace might equate Christian ethics, for instance, with the question "What would Jesus do?" But more formally understood, the discipline of Christian social ethics can be schematized in several ways, for which this book employs Stackhousian language and the three categories of deontology, teleology, and ethology,[6] and the three analogous Niebuhrian terms of the right, the good, and the fitting.[7] Both schemas argues that all three approaches or categories of ethics, while schools in their own right, are necessary to develop a more balanced and integrated theological understanding of ethics leading to biblical conceptions of justice. These schemas have their analogues in the corporate world and can be placed in conversation with the laws and regulations governing business behavior, corporate objectives and policies, and general marketplace ethos and best practices. Indeed, the parallels between these business concepts and the classic schools of ethics (deontology, teleology, and ethological ethics) are helpful to connect theory to praxis. That is, businesspeople turn to civil laws and regulatory bodies that provide deontological rules or guidelines to determine right action. They also turn to corporate mission statements that provide ethical guidance based on teleological aims to determine the good. Finally, people in the marketplace turn to company policies to provide ethological guidance on best practices to determine the fitting or most appropriate action in particular situations.

Generally speaking, those who are Christians and in the ET type find ultimate ethical authority not in human constructs but in biblical teachings and motifs. Yet the ethical choices that businesspeople face are often highly complicated and laden with tradeoffs, where even biblical teachings seem to clash. And even among the faithful, interpretations of how to apply biblical teachings can vary. The challenges become even more complex when moving from one industry or country to another. Some participants and groups in this type acknowledge the complexity and difficulty of applying theological principles to modern ethical dilemmas, noting that many decisions occur in the ethical gray zone. In contrast, others have a more black-and-white view of the world and find little ethical struggle. Most would agree, however, that applying spiritual principles and teachings to modern business dilemmas can at times be costly, at least in the short term, sacrificing corporate profits, personal careers, and jobs.[8] Indeed, as theologian Dietrich Bonhoeffer observed, doing ethics "is not to decide simply between right and wrong and between good and evil, but between right and right and between wrong and wrong."[9]

As noted, the groups and participants in the ET type manifest their ethical response to workplace issues at three levels: the micro (the personal), the mezzo (the corporate), and the macro (the societal). Historically, evangelical and theologically more conservative groups were associated with ethical issues at the personal level, while theologically more liberal groups were associated with the social activism and societal issues found at the mezzo and macro levels (see chapters 2 and 3). However, in wave three, that tendency changes. The evidence suggests that evangelical and theologically conservative groups in the ET type often move among the personal, the corporate, and the societal levels of business ethics (e.g., Evangelicals for Action and FaithWorks are groups that focus on macro ethical issues on the societal level). Curiously, the evidence does not seem to suggest the reverse trend, where theologically liberal groups are more engaged with business ethics at the personal level.

Many ET-oriented FAW groups, while recognizing the distinctions among micro, mezzo, and macro business ethics, do not privilege one and thus move freely among all three.[10] At the micro level, the ethical focus is primarily on issues surrounding personal ethics and behavior.[11] Participants in these FAW groups accent highly ethical personal business standards and stress the virtues of character, honesty, and respect for others. They deal with ethical issues such as peer or marketplace pressure to cheat on expense reports, to misrepresent a product to increase sales, and to put corporate interests above human relationships. Further, these groups seldom differentiate between the public and the private personas. That is, they teach that personal ethical behavior must be congruent with public business behavior. These groups deal with personal issues such as inappropriate relationships, swearing, temper, substance abuse, and other personal concerns that can come with power, money, and long periods of travel away from family. As such, these groups often encourage accountability partners and other modes of support for personal morality.

Other FAW participants in the ET type, while not indifferent to personal ethics, focus more on business ethics and topics affecting the broader mezzo level of the corporation. The FAW participants with this accent address issues such as product selection, quality, safety, whistle blowing, loyalty, and advertising.[12] Others focus on macro ethical questions involving corporate responsibility to society at large and economic justice as it pertains to all stakeholders and beyond.[13] Typical business issues addressed by groups with a macro ethical orientation include environmental analyses of manufacturing and product decisions, offshore working conditions and wages, and executive compensation.

In addition to how ethics function at these three levels, another component of ET-oriented FAW people are groups that draw on Christian ethics and biblical principles to inform and influence their understanding of business leadership. Many of these groups are for-profit consultants and firms.[14] Much of both scholarly and popular writing on business leadership in the FAW movement draws on Jesus as a model for "servant leadership."[15]

Within the diversity of the ET quadrant, the Southern Institute for Business and Professional Ethics is a representative example of the ET type. The institute's mission is "to raise awareness and understanding of ethics in business and professional life, to stimulate a productive community dialogue about ethical issues, values and responsibilities, and, in so doing, to contribute to the betterment of business and society."[16] Founded and led by layperson and businessman John Knapp, the institute is an ecumenical and interfaith organization, whose board is composed of individuals with connections to some of the most prominent businesses in Georgia. Based in Atlanta and with a regional focus, the institute hosts quarterly breakfasts, luncheons, and roundtables dealing with a variety of topical ethical issues.[17] The institute also conducts market research with Georgia CEOs on ethical issues with attention to practical solutions. Notably, in contrast to broader seminary trends, the institute has formed a relationship with Columbia Theological Seminary and now offers faith-and-work courses for pastors, church leaders, and seminary students.

Of course, ethical behavior is an important part of the lived experience of one's religious or spiritual identity. Yet, those located exclusively in the ET quadrant miss out on the rich dimensions of a mature expression of faith identity as seen in the other three manifestations of integrating faith and work. Moreover, ethics is often a popular manifestation of integrating faith and work because its language is often secular and accessible to people of different faith backgrounds. However, a slide into secular norms and language might also represent a risk for those in the ET quadrant. Without a commonly agreed-upon source of ethics, phrases like "just do the right thing" become meaningless clichés that offer little guidance and that mean different things to different people. Indeed, the great peril of ethics—be it secular forms or religious-based ethics—is the pride that comes from believing that humans can without error discern God's will or rationally discern right from wrong, good from evil, and fitting from unfitting. Nevertheless, those in the ET type have the potential to gain helpful and creative insights from responsible use of religious instruction and inspiration, the voice of one's faith community, prayers, and other forms of transcendental guidance.

THE EVANGELISM TYPE

The evangelism, or EV, quadrant contains participants whose primary mode of integrating faith at work is through evangelization, and the expression of their faith. This is most commonly seen in Christians and Muslims. For example, Christians places a high premium on the importance of introducing others to Jesus Christ as Lord and Savior, and helping others to develop a personal relationship with Jesus. FAW groups and individuals in the EV type view work and the workplace primarily as a mission field for evangelizing or witnessing to coworkers and others with whom they come in contact, including customers and suppliers. While not normative, many EV occupants have premillennialist inclinations (conscious or otherwise). Many participants and groups coming out of the evangelical tradition are likely to have this understanding of faith at work, conceiving the quest for integrating faith and work largely in terms of living out the Great Commission (Matt. 28:19–20) in the workplace.

FAW participants and groups in the EV type address the issue of evangelism through a number of structural and programmatic means. The structural options for those in the EV type range from small unincorporated groups that meet informally to formal membership organizations incorporated as nonprofit entities. Of this latter kind, many have a national presence with local chapters around the country and, in some cases, around the world. These are well-resourced organizations that include headquarters and regional staff.[18] They employ various modes of expression, including meetings, conferences, mentoring programs, teaching materials, study guides, newsletters, and Web sites.[19] This quadrant also includes some members of corporate affinity groups and Bible study groups inside for-profit corporations. There exists both formally recognized employee groups entitled to funding and the use of company premises, as well as others that are informal and, in some cases, less explicit about their goal. The formally recognized affinity groups publicly tend to reject evangelizing as their main purpose, although for some members that is the primary issue. Typically, formally recognized company groups accent a broader "Judeo-Christian tradition" and stress ethics and good corporate citizenship, as taught by following biblical principles.

Christian-based FAW groups that use international commerce and the general trend toward more open markets as vehicles to spread the Gospel of Jesus Christ are also located in this quadrant. In missionary circles, business is often used as the mechanism through which to spread the Gospel in countries where proselytizing and the free practice of religion in general, or Christianity in particular, are suppressed or forbidden (e.g., many of the former USSR countries, China, and several Islamic states). As one such American expatriate businessman shared, "There are missionary businesses that *fake it, take it,* or *make it.*"[20] The *fakers* use business shells as their cover for evangelizing and missionary work; in practice, little real work is done. The *takers* actually take a valid and legitimate job and perform the work associated with that position, such as teaching English, but they use their position primarily as a vehicle to evangelize. They often still rely on money from supporters at home to underwrite their mission and do not view their actual work or job as necessarily needing to be economically viable. The *makers* also hold real jobs, like the takers, but these people participate in and often run viable, profitable businesses that create real jobs and offer necessary goods and services on a competitive basis with other local companies in that economy. While makers also view business as a vehicle for evangelizing, that is not the sole purpose of the business; the business has to make it on its own and serve a useful marketplace function in order to be used for evangelization. While this image of fake it, take it, and make it was expressed in the context of overseas "business missionaries," the same logic and analogues apply to some EV attitudes in the United States.

One of the most focused FAW groups that represents the EV type is Executive Ministries, a branch of Campus Crusade for Christ, founded by successful business executive Arthur S. DeMoss. Executive Ministries' mission is "helping influencers reach influencers for Christ."[21] DeMoss was "burdened that so little was being done to share Christ effectively with this 'neglected minority'" of senior executives and influencers.[22] The strategy is for an affluent couple to host formal "outreach dinner-parties" in their stately home, country club, or luxury hotel, accompanied by music and a dinner speaker. The "Outreach Dinner Parties follow a step-by-step formula."[23] The speaker, usually a well-known entertainment or business personality, gives a motivational talk, including his or her testimonial to becoming saved in Jesus Christ. Then, "the 150 or more guests are given the opportunity to respond to an invitation to receive Jesus Christ."[24] They are invited to fill out a card asking for follow-up, if interested, and to learn more about Jesus Christ. Literature from Executive Ministries claims that "30 to 40 percent of the guests indicate either that they received Christ that evening or that they would like more information."[25] The follow-up includes invitations to structured Bible studies, discipleship relationships, conferences, and international trips, with a view toward turning new Christians into new evangelizers.

Evangelism is an important part of some people's Christian identity, whether its form is gentle or aggressive. To the surprise of many, generally speaking, proselytizing is fully legal in the workplace, so long as it does not become harassment, discriminatory, quid pro quo, or cause undue hardship to the business operation.[26] Like many things that are legal, that does not necessarily mean that it is an appropriate or wise thing to do. People in this quadrant who allow their emphasis on evangelism to dominate their actions may find that it impedes them from doing their jobs well or disrupts the basic functions, purpose, and responsibilities of the work at hand. Another concern about those exclusively located in the EV quadrant is a tendency to minimize or neglect addressing other structural ethical issues and social injustices, which are also central to a full Christian identity. And, as with all types, someone located exclusively in any one type misses out on richer and more mature ways of integrating faith and work by not drawing on the other manifestations of the Integration Box. Finally, as noted earlier, in some corporate settings, I have found that this type might better be named "expression," as that term allows for verbal and nonverbal forms of communicating the tenets of one's faith.

THE EXPERIENCE TYPE

In the experience (EX) quadrant of the Integration Box lie FAW participants and groups whose primary means of integrating faith and work involves questions of vocation, calling, meaning, and purpose in and through their marketplace professions. Their view of work is that it has both intrinsic and extrinsic meaning and purpose. That is, the particular work someone does, in and of its own right, is of theological value. Work has the larger role of serving greater societal purposes and needs. Discovering that work can be a calling, and finding meaning and purpose in work are often significant motivators that draw businesspeople to the FAW movement. The modes of support for groups and participants in this profile typically include books, retreats/conferences, biblical reflection, and psychological resources.

Christians and non-Christians alike often question the greater meaning and purpose of their work. They ponder if it is possible to be a data entry clerk or an investment banker or a CEO and still serve God. They wonder if sacred purposes can be found as a sales representative or advertising executive. They question whether they must leave the for-profit sector to enter the so-called caring professions as the only way to do full-time ministry, to view their work as a calling, and to find meaning in what they do.

Such questions reveal that this search for existential meaning and purpose in daily work is often rooted in an incorrect or limited theology of work. Too often, work is framed exclusively in materialistic terms. Some religious professionals view work as a form of exploitation and a curse, something to be liberated from, thus ignoring the many rich theologically informed existential understandings of the nature, meaning, and purpose of work.[27] Many people in the workplace have been conditioned by church experiences to think that "real ministry" can only be done or is most perfectly manifested by becoming an ordained minister, an overseas missionary, or by going into nonprofit work. Businesspeople privately admit that their work and their careers, however interesting and stimulating at times, often do not feel like a spiritual calling. Many professionals, especially when in transition between major life stages and seasons, take stock of their careers and question the value of their work.[28] Many are good at their work but find little intrinsic meaning or purpose in their roles, or question how they contribute to society at large. Others realize that their work is not aligned with their God-given gifts or natural joys. Many feel emotions of guilt, entrapment, and confusion over material success and spiritual emptiness. For these and other reasons, many FAW groups have developed in this quadrant to respond to these issues.[29]

A representative group of the EX type is Listening Hearts Ministry, which grew out of a research project led by Episcopalian layperson Suzanne Farnham. The purpose of the project was "to sift through the accumulated wisdom and experience of Christians over the centuries that related to spiritual discernment in community—then distill it and present it in a clear simple way that contemporary people could integrate into their lives."[30] This resulted in the book, *Listening Hearts: Discerning Call in Community*, edited by Farnham.[31] Based on the extraordinary response to the book, she subsequently founded an independent nonprofit FAW group called Listening Hearts, whose mission is to provide "programs, materials, and training to encourage and facilitate hearing the voice of God" and to help people find their vocational callings.[32] Listening Hearts accents the ancient Christian wisdom traditions of contemplation and spiritual discernment and more recent Quaker teachings of hearing the community's voice. To help laypeople discern their vocations, Listening Hearts offers retreats, workshops, and quarterly newsletters. In addition, it provides vocational discernment training for church groups and teachers to transfer these skills to the parish level.

Finding meaning and purpose in work is a common theme among religious and nonreligious people alike, as what we do and for whom we work forms important parts of our self-esteem and public identity. Thus, the EX focus, as a manifestation of integrating faith and work, finds easy connection points and common language with spiritual seekers and people of all faith traditions. Yet, at the same time, the EX type can place so much emphasis on *what* we do and *whether* it is a calling that it can overshadow *how* we do it and *who* we are as people. Moreover, there is a risk that those who exclusively identify their work as a calling may be more likely to experience trauma and identity crises when faced with losing their jobs, whether through dismissal, retirement, or medical disability. Inevitably, they must ask the question, "If my work is my calling, and I've just lost my job, does that also mean I've lost my calling, my purpose in life?" Moreover, inordinate attention to calling, meaning, and purpose can lead in some cases to a form of elitism in which people are led to believe that only stimulating and rewarding work, fully utilizing people's gifts and talents, can be considered a calling. This view forgets that many in the workforce have limited career or occupational choices. Many EX groups remind members that jobs of a routine nature and even mundane tasks have the potential to be experienced as callings even if someone's potential is not being maximized. Finally, as with each of the Four E's, those located exclusively in the EX type without attention to the other three manifestations of integrating faith and work miss out on the richer dimensions of a mature expression of religious faith and identity.

THE ENRICHMENT TYPE

The enrichment (EN) type constitutes the final quadrant in the Integration Box framework. The primary understanding of integrating faith and work for FAW groups and people located in this type is often personal and inward in nature, focusing on issues like healing, prayer, meditation, consciousness, transformation, and self-actualization. The EN's understanding of faith accents the restorative nature of God's power as a resource for healing, spiritual nurturance, and personal transformation. Their view of work is often dialectical, seeing it in black or white terms, as good or bad, as a source of personal benefit and reward, or as a place of suffering and pain. As with the other types, there are various modes of expression, including small support groups, and conferences, but internal and often private acts such as prayer and meditation practices are common.

In addition to the many Christian FAW groups in this type, there are a plethora of religious hybrids (e.g., Christian Buddhists, Jewish Buddhists) and secular spirituality groups, including those that can be broadly referred to as New Age groups. These New Age groups and their participants shun the term *religion* and prefer instead words like *spirituality* and *consciousness*. While not usually stated explicitly in their public documents, there is often an operative suspicion and distrust of monotheistic religions, particularly Christianity. This is due largely to the exclusive truth claims of monotheistic religions and the evangelism aspect of Christianity, which run counter to postmodern relativism. It remains to be seen whether this discomfort with Christianity will also extend to Islam, as these two religions share some similar characteristics, at least as regards monotheism, truth claims, evangelism, and proselytizing. Ironically, while purporting a spirit of diversity, tolerance, and inclusiveness, some New Age and generic spirituality groups can be more intolerant of groups they disagree with than the very groups they criticize.[33]

The EN type addresses a variety of issues, including a need for therapeutic healing, contemplative practices, personal transformation, and human potential. For example, some who have experienced downsizing or been emotionally hurt by the sometimes heartless experience of business turn to spiritual sources for healing and restoration. Others find calm and peace amid the daily pressures of work by adhering to regular prayer or meditation periods. In addition, this FAW type also includes those seeking personal transformation and maximizing their potential, often with an accent on using spirituality as a means to greater business and financial success. In effect, they view religion and spirituality as means to greater health, wealth, and happiness. As such, the EN type includes some curious bedfellows, including Christian contemplative and relational-oriented groups,[34] prosperity gospel groups,[35] and New Age human potential and consciousness groups.[36] The prosperity gospel and New Age groups in the EN type often understand "enrichment" in the literal and financial sense, and they focus on the material benefits that come from alignment with God's will or increasing one's inner consciousness.

A representative example of the EN type from the generic spirituality or New Age orientation is an organization called Spirit in Business, Inc. (SiB). The founder of SiB, former business executive Andy Ferguson, was inspired by the teachings of the Dalai Lama and the influence of a three-month visit to a Taoist/Buddhist facility in the Himalayas. Founded in 2001, SiB's mission is "to integrate, serve, and assist individuals, and organizations intent on promoting spirit in business throughout the world."[37] Its inaugural conference in 2002 attracted to New York City more than five hundred people, each paying tuition of $1,200. More than a dozen corporate sponsors also endorsed the event. SiB has a stated desire to welcome all who share its vision, including those from traditional religions, such as Christianity and Judaism, though, somewhat curiously, the stage was adorned with Buddhist and Hindu objects of devotion, while symbols of Christianity, Judaism, or Islam were noticeably absent. The keynote inspirational speakers came out of Eastern or hybrid spiritual traditions. The keynote business leader speakers often promoted a New Age version of self-help and personal success that was hauntingly reminiscent of the Christian prosperity gospel. The focus was on inner awareness, discovering the wisdom within, personal fulfillment, happiness, success, and human potential. Conceptions of sin, evil, and the fallenness of the human condition were seldom mentioned. Occasional reference was made to issues of business ethics, social justice, and responsibility but that was not the core accent. Ferguson envisions a business plan of international leaders and country-based chapters to bring together the best institutes and organizations involved with ethics, mindfulness, and the bottom line. Subsequent events have been held in San Francisco and in Europe.[38]

Prayer, meditation, healing, transformation, and spiritual nurturance in the workplace are important parts of Christian identity, and most other traditions as well. These aspects become problematic when EN types focus exclusively on the micro, or personal, level at the expense of tending to broader structural ethical issues at the mezzo or macro levels of global society. In the extreme, some EN groups become narcissistic, stressing self-actualization not self-sacrifice, self-improvement not social justice, personal gain not community good, and an orientation toward relativism and a denial of universal goods or truths. Finally, as with each quadrant, those located exclusively in the EN type miss out on the richer dimensions of a mature expression of Christian identity as seen in the other three manifestations of integrating faith and work.

THE EVERYWHERE INTEGRATOR TYPE

As with any framework, certain groups and participants in the FAW movement resist easy placement into one of the Four E's. Indeed, many, FAW groups address several if not all of the four manifestations of integrating faith and work. While not a quadrant, strictly speaking, these can be called the *everywhere integrators* (EI), indicating that they view several if not all manifestations of integrating faith and work as part of a mature or aspirational state. Although often grounded in one primary type, many people and groups move among and address the issues found in other quadrants of the Integration Box.[39] Some groups even move among all four types.[40]

A representative example of an FAW group that operates in all four quadrants is the Texas-based organization called Laity Lodge, part of the H. E. Butt Foundation. Founded during wave two[41] but still thriving in wave three, Laity Lodge is an ecumenical Christian retreat center that today hosts more than 2,500 adult guests per year. While not all of the retreats are faith-and-work oriented, many are. As regards the ethics (ET) type, these interests have been addressed at the biannual Laity Lodge Leadership Forum, attended by some of the nation's top corporate and civic leaders to foster conversation among those "who care for the quality of ethical, moral, and spiritual life" and to consider questions of integrating faith and work in all professions.[42] As regards the evangelism (EV) type, Laity Lodge understands evangelism as a basic part of Christian identity that includes the workplace in part but not exclusively as a venue for sharing the Gospel. Typical of the experience (EX) type, the underlying and accented theology of Laity Lodge is that all the people of God (*laos*) have a calling and a ministry to be performed in and through daily work. Toward this end, Laity Lodge hosts conferences and retreats around this theme, sponsors commercial radio spots, and has launched a Web site built around the tag line "the high calling of our daily work." As regards the final quadrant, the enrichment (EN) type, attendees are invited to slow down, reflect, pray, and contemplate their relationships with God, neighbor, and self, placing particular accent on personal spiritual renewal, relationships, and healing.

Another representative group that moves among all four quadrants, with particular attention to the needs of senior business leaders, is the CEO Forum. This group was founded by David "Mac" McQuiston in late 1996 as a branch of Focus on the Family. The CEO Forum's mission is to "effectively serve senior executives in large corporations by helping them to live Godly lives and create excellence consistent with a biblically based approach; thereby extending the work of Christ into the marketplace (corporations) and society."[43] Coming largely from a conservative evangelical theological orientation, by 2004, it had a membership of 130 CEOs, and it continues to grow. In 2005, the group separated itself from the Focus on the Family organization and established its own legal and structural identity as an independent 501(c)3 nonprofit. The CEO Forum is predominantly, though not exclusively, male in membership. As regards ethics (ET), members turn to the Bible as the source and seek to use biblical principles to guide personal behavior and leadership. Based on requests by members, CEO Forum staff prepare position papers to "identify and support specific initiatives on key moral/ethical issues affecting families and [the] broader culture."[44] For instance, they have prepared papers on domestic partner benefits and on corporate influence in the media. As regards evangelism (EV), members view the workplace as an important vehicle to communicate the Gospel, both through word and deed. They discuss the boundaries of responsible evangelizing in light of their positions of power and influence. And regarding the experience (EX) type, the CEO Forum frames work, in general, and leadership in particular, as a calling. Like workers at all levels, the members seek meaning and purpose in the long hours, pressure, intense travel schedules, and time away from family. As regards enrichment (EN), the organization sponsors quarterly conference calls for small groups of CEOs, which include a devotional, check-in time to hear and pray for personal matters (e.g., dealing with illness, addictions, marital issues, and work-family balance), and opportunities to discuss and pray over significant business decisions and issues being faced. The cliché that it can be lonely at the top is true, and these members find spiritual nurturance, encouragement, and accountability with their peers. In addition to the conference calls, the CEO Forum also hosts two conferences per year organized around topical business issues and (unintentionally) around the Four E's of the Integration Box.

While all typologies have their limitations, the Integration Box is a useful first step toward the development of a scholarly framework and language to help theorize about, analyze, and discuss the Faith at Work movement. The model has the potential to help both scholars and practitioners alike move out of the often limiting and divisive ways of thinking about FAW that are typical of dialectical polarities, such as liberal versus conservative, ethics versus evangelism, or premillennialism versus postmillennialism. A question still open to further research is whether these various FAW manifestations and our predispositions toward certain quadrants are a function of personality type,

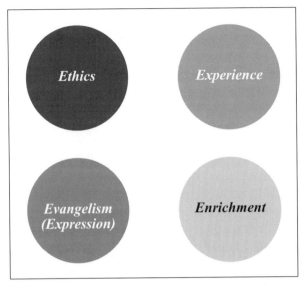

FIGURE 7.2 The Integration Box: The Four E's

family upbringing, church training, theological orientation, social conditioning, one's place of employment, personal choice, or some mixture of all
these variables. What is not disputed, however, is that integrating faith and
work takes many modes of expression and that these various manifestations
are reflected in the form and substance of FAW groups and participants.
Moreover, developing a self-awareness of one's natural quadrant is both
affirming to oneself as well as the key to enable respect for and even movement into other quadrants.[45]

Indeed, as I continue to reflect on and develop the Integration Box,
I increasingly find a more helpful image might be that of integration circles or
spheres. Each of the Four E's can be visually imagined as a circle, yet the
individual spheres might over time converge and overlap, like a Venn diagram
(see figures 7.2 and 7.3). And, as noted earlier, the manifestation of evangelism might more inclusively and constructively be labeled "expression."

If this book has a normative claim, it is that the integration of faith and
work, when done in healthy, respectful, and appropriate ways and with the
recognition that we live and work in a pluralistic culture, is a good thing.
Integration has the potential to enrich the individual worker—whether
secretary or CEO—the organization, and indeed society at large. It is also
true that unhealthy manifestations of faith and work can result in harassment, discrimination, and other dangers. Thus, it is important that the business community and other workplace settings find the appropriate language

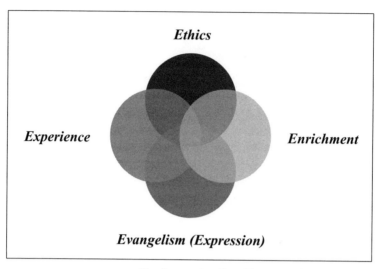

FIGURE 7.3 The Integration Box: The Four E's

and framework for faith at work. For this reason, the Integration Box makes an effective entry point for those who wish to integrate faith and work, given that no one of the Four E's is theologically superior to another. And for those who do not consider themselves spiritually oriented, this framework and language might enable them to better understand the significant portion of the workforce who are interested in faith questions and in living a holistic life that integrates mind, body, and spirit.

EIGHT

The Future of the Faith at Work Movement

As if on cue, a journalist will inevitably ask me toward the end of an interview, "Where do you think this Faith at Work movement is heading? Will it run out of steam, or will it continue to expand, perhaps in new shapes and forms?" This final chapter attempts to answer these questions. My response is that unless the desire for integration and a holistic life, and the other conditions that created this groundswell of activity, change—which seems highly unlikely given the static nature of the mainline church and the theological academy and the contrastingly mind-numbing speed of technological and social changes that bombard businesses, professionals, and workers of all kinds—I predict that the movement will continue to grow and develop in a variety of new ways and configurations. However, what remains to be seen is how the theological academy, the church, FAW participants, and companies respond? In light of this probability, it is appropriate to pause and critically reflect on the ramifications—positive and negative—of this direction and to propose fresh theological and marketplace resources to understand and engage the future of the FAW movement.

Implications and Proposals

In light of the FAW movement's growing social, economic, ethical, and theological significance, it should have major programmatic and pedagogical implications for the academy, the church, and corporate world. Indeed, the church and the academy could help to give new ethical shape to marketplace activity and business institutions and could provide spiritual nurturance and sustenance to participants in the FAW movement. In similar fashion, the church and the academy could benefit from the theological insights and ethical contributions that emerge from the world of practice by laypeople called to and engaged in the business world. The businesspeople involved in the FAW movement could positively affect the academy's theological agenda and reflections and could give fresh ecclesiastical attention to liturgical practices, church programs, and pastoral care. Following is a series of proposals, by no means exhaustive, to enable the church and the academy to engage the FAW movement, thereby contributing to and learning from it. Similarly, there follow proposals for participants in the movement itself, including how to draw more specifically on the rich ecclesiastical and theological resources of the church catholic.

A logical starting place for change is the place where clergy are trained. Seminaries and divinity schools should recognize anew the theological, practical, and pastoral importance of the workplace with a view toward training pastors to minister more intentionally and effectively to their parishioners in the business world and other workplaces. For some in the academy, this may require a theological paradigm shift to recognize that business, even operating under a marketplace system of democratic capitalism, can be a source of social justice. Toward this end, the American Academy of Religion should develop a faith at work track, creating a scholarly venue for research, publishing, career development, and conversation partners. This group would be encouraged to develop formal links to analogous organizations in other academic guilds (e.g., the Academy of Management). Further, curriculum committees and tenure committees at seminaries, divinity schools, and other graduate religious programs should encourage and acknowledge research, publishing, and teaching on the field of FAW and issues such as the Four E's. In addition, fellowships, stipends, tenure track positions, and chairs should be developed to motivate scholars to pursue this field, as has been done in other important new areas affecting society (e.g., African American, Latino, and feminist studies).

Research and creative affiliations would result in new pedagogical possibilities for M.Div. students, thus preparing future pastors to develop intentional FAW ministries in their own churches or places of calling. Even if students have no personal workplace background or experience, they can be educated to understand the issues that those in the workplace face. Indeed, students without a personal background involving serious illness or incarceration can be taught to minister to the sick and imprisoned. Thus, the issue appears to be one of training, not personal background experience.[1] One remedy would be to expand the conception of clinical pastoral education (CPE) and field education programs from the traditional realms of hospitals, prisons, and psychiatric wards to include internships in local businesses and workplaces. Through innovative CPE placements, seminarians would learn the language of the marketplace or other workplaces, as well as how to minister intentionally to the needs of those in the workplace. In addition, a rich array of new curriculum possibilities could accommodate a wide range of pertinent themes, whether under the rubric of ethics, evangelism, experience, or enrichment, as proposed in this book, or other frameworks.[2]

Following such developments, select schools should develop centers or institutes dedicated to theological, ethical, and pedagogical reflection on faith at work. Such centers could undertake joint ventures or selected research projects with scholars in other fields and professional schools (e.g., law, business, medicine), as well as denominational bodies. These centers should also consider affiliations with established FAW leaders and groups, as some have developed extensive curricula and course content, as well as offering access to networks of laypeople committed to integrating faith and work.[3] Indeed, some theologians might take "externships" and work for a business for a semester or a year, undertaking research and gaining firsthand familiarity with marketplace issues. Further, these FAW centers could develop education courses for people in the workplace, much as many M.B.A. schools offer executive education courses and continuing education programs. Similarly, these centers should consider hosting conferences for laity and scholars together (along the lines of the original vision for the Ecumenical Institute at Bossey) and offering consultations for academics looking to engage specific themes, issues, and topical matters.

In addition to changes in the academy, there are many ways in which denominations and judicatory bodies could facilitate local churches in engaging in and being part of the FAW movement as part of their ministries. For instance, denominational bodies could consider developing workplace-related Web sites with ideas, resources, curriculum suggestions, references to other successful church programs, books, articles, blogs, and topic-related chat rooms. Further, judicatory bodies could develop an FAW center of expertise, as the Mennonites have done with the Mennonite Economic Development Associates (MEDA). Such centers could sponsor research into the Four E's and other typologies, launch policy papers, start micro-lending organizations, develop adult education curricula, and support college ministry vocational discernment programs. Moreover, they could compile a database of church FAW programs, identifying best-practice models nationwide and sharing ideas and resources. Judicatory bodies should also sponsor, support, and participate in FAW groups, such as the interdenominational Coalition for Ministry in Daily Life, as a means to learn from, contribute to, and help shape the movement from within.

Pastors and churches that wish to respond seriously to the Sunday-Monday gap will need to develop new strategies of equipping laity for a ministry of integration that connects the Christian faith to the workplace in meaningful and constructive ways. The church is in a unique position to help as "greater involvement in one's congregation is strongly related to greater integration of faith and work."[4] In addition to equipping the laity in the quest to integrate faith and work, important and natural by-products are outreach and witness to others and the potential transformation of social and economic structures. Yet an intentional ministry to businesspersons and the workplace must be more than a laundry list of programs. Indeed, the church should not expect to make lasting inroads into the business community because of any single good program, adult education class, or sermon series. Rather, this attitude needs to be evident in all dimensions of ministry. As such, clergy need to have a consistent attitude toward ministry that seeks to engage and equip the businessperson in each of the areas of the Four E's.[5] Accordingly, a comprehensive strategy designed to equip the laity for a ministry of integration could identify all dimensions of a pastor's role that, if created with the needs of businesspeople and others in the workplace in mind, would help to bridge the Sunday-Monday gap.[6] While there are many ways to capture the essence of a clergyperson's job, I comment here on five core aspects of ordained ministry.

Clergy who wish to equip their people to integrate faith and work effectively will first need to develop a *ministry of presence and listening* in the work sphere. Clergy should go to their parishioners' places of work for short visits as regularly and naturally as they make hospital and home visits.[7] During such visits, good listening is the main skill required, just as during a hospital visit. A pastor does not need an M.B.A. nor to develop expertise in all fields of business to minister to people in the workplace, any more than a pastor needs an M.D. or to master all medical diseases and terminology to make effective hospital visits. However, just as most clergy develop a basic working vocabulary and knowledge of the medical world, so too should clergy develop that for the business world. My research leads me to the conclusion that "speaking different languages" is one of the chief obstacles to fruitful clergy-businessperson dialogue. A pastor lacking business experience or other workplace knowledge can readily gain it by turning to his or her congregation for informal help and guidance. If clergy make workplace visits, they will gain firsthand familiarity with the issues their people face, particularly as related to the Four E's, thereby enriching other parts of the ministry, including pastoral care, preaching, prayer, and teaching. Other ways that clergy can become better listeners and gain familiarity with basic workplace issues and vocabulary is to read the *Wall Street Journal*, participate in an FAW group, or receive an FAW magazine or eNewsletter. Through the ministry of presence and listening, the pastor will gain the trust and confidence of people in the workplace, thereby making it more likely that they will contact the pastor for theologically informed workplace-related guidance.

Clergy who wish to equip their people to integrate faith and work will also need to develop a *ministry of public preaching and prayer* that intentionally and constructively addresses all dimensions of the Four E's of ethics, evangelism, experience, and enrichment. Sermons and pastoral prayers play a vital theological role as part of a ministry of integration to those in the business world, helping people to discover their vocational identity, resist splitting the sacred from the secular, navigate difficult ethical questions, and gain comfort for personal needs and hurts. Notably, Hart and Krueger found, "most respondents desire more congregational emphasis on work issues [and] the more frequently clergy deal with work issues in sermons, the more satisfied members are with the current degree of attention to work in their congregations."[8] Indeed, "[i]t appears that respondents rate prayer, worship, and sermons very highly as a means to connect faith to work."[9] For instance, one pastor in New York City uses sermon titles like "What If St. Paul Worked for Goldman Sachs?" and "Your Monday Morning Pulpit" as a way to connect the Gospel message to the workplace lives of his congregation.[10] Thus, with careful crafting and intentional design, sermons and prayers can respond to all dimensions of the Four E's, thereby serving the members of the congregation in one of their most important places of need. Indeed, relevant sermon illustrations and meaningful prayer content can be gleaned from the ministry of presence and listening. Moreover, other parts of Sunday liturgy can incorporate awareness of and support for faith-and-work issues, including commissioning services for businesspeople, music selection, and lay participation in worship.

Clergy who wish to equip their people to integrate faith and work will also need to develop a *ministry of teaching* that includes all dimensions of the Four E's. A ministry of teaching for integrating faith and work can take place in many forms, including adult education, small groups, special seminars, and retreats. It can also take many formats, including lectures, case study analyses, reading books, and sharing real workplace situations and dilemmas. Even traditional Bible studies can be reframed to reach the world of commerce and business. Toward that end, I propose that clergy learn a hermeneutic of the marketplace. This will ensure that the parables and biblical narratives gain a fresh sense of relevance and applicability to modern business situations. This ministry of teaching can be on specific workplace topics (e.g., affirmative action policies, responsible investment portfolios, money and profits, minimum wage, executive compensation, offshore manufacturing, marketing, competition, and downsizing) and on theological doctrines and teachings on topics relevant to the workplace (e.g., creation, humanity, calling, ethics, justice, and prayer). Experience suggests that clergy should jointly coordinate and teach such sessions in partnership with a lay businessperson. This will ensure a relevant selection of topics and issues drawn from all Four E's, as well as validating, equipping, and encouraging those called to the business world.

Clergy who wish to equip their people to integrate faith and work will also need to develop a *ministry of spiritual integration* that ensures that laity are trained to utilize personal prayer and devotional study in their daily lives. Just as prayer and devotion form a central part of the Sunday liturgy to prepare adherents of a particular faith to worship and celebrate God, so too can personal prayer and scriptural study prepare people in the workplace to engage in and respond to issues such as the Four E's. This ministry of spiritual integration asserts that developing spiritual disciplines, such as prayer and the devotional study of Scripture, can be a source of great succor and wisdom for ethical guidance and personal comfort in the business world. As we have seen in this volume, there is a growing body of study materials and devotional literature aimed at Christians in the marketplace. Indeed, if churches looked into their own liturgical history and theology, they would find rich resources to help a ministry of spiritual integration, ranging from Brother Lawrence in the 1600s to the Daily Offices (daily prayers) from the 1979 Book of Common Prayer in the Episcopal Church USA.

Additionally, clergy who wish to equip their people to integrate faith and work will need to find or develop a *ministry of gatherings* of businesspeople to help address the Four E's. Such gatherings provide forums for businesspeople to share, reflect, pray, witness, challenge, and encourage one another in the common desire to be faithful and effective in their work. The now nearly ubiquitous nature of the FAW movement may mean that a local church need not necessarily start its own organization but simply participate in an existing group. However, based on its size and demographic profile, a church may choose to develop an in-house FAW group. As with other parts of this proposed ministry of integration, clergy wishing to launch an FAW program should do it in partnership with a core group of lay leaders, as my research has found that lay-led and lay-founded groups are generally more effective at understanding and meeting workplace integration needs.

The participants and leaders in the FAW movement itself are not beyond critique. Despite the many benefits of faith at work described in this volume, there are also limitations and dangers if the movement develops in isolation, without engaging the structure of church and the ideas of the academy. For instance, some conservative Christian FAW groups are suspicious of intellectualism and secular insights, fearing that these may undermine confessional beliefs, thereby missing out on many opportunities for learning and growth. And some secular spirituality groups are surprised to learn that Christianity has a long tradition of spiritual and contemplative practices and that questions of integration, faith, and work are not new to the Christian tradition. Some FAW participants and groups view faith merely as a "feel good" bromide or to rationalize their marketplace actions, thus ignoring the ethical demands and challenges of authentic faith. However, the movement's decentralized and loosely networked nature impedes the ready receipt of such dialogue, proposals, or suggestions. For these reasons, the leaders of the movement should seek more intentionally to draw on the theological resources of the academy and the infrastructure of the church. This could take the form of personal exchanges, conferences, support for theological research into marketplace issues, creation and distribution of FAW resources for congregations, and other shared projects with the church and the academy. Moreover, leaders in the movement should convene conferences and seminars for themselves to engage in mutual conversation, illumination, and growth. Through such gatherings, FAW leaders could broaden their understandings of the diversity of the FAW movement, particularly as manifested through the Four E's of ethics, evangelism, experience, and enrichment. Indeed, just as for individual participants, groups should be challenged to grow beyond their current Integration Box orientation. Through closer cooperation, possibilities might emerge for operational efficiencies, financial stability, shared content, additional distribution channels, and market expansion through new affiliations or confederations.

To date, the movement has largely been lay-driven and has operated under the radar screen of corporate policies and practices. But as more and more M.B.A. programs engage the question of spirituality in the workplace, as more management scholars study the impact of FAW, as more executives go public about the question of integrating faith and work, as companies are forced to accommodate the religious needs of new immigrants (particularly Islam and Eastern religions), and as the business press continues to provide visibility and legitimization of FAW, it is only a matter of time before human relations professionals and academicians adopt and adapt the movement as a formal part of corporate best practices.

Perhaps this is the logical unfolding of an inevitable historical pattern. The 1960s erupted with the Civil Rights movement, and soon leading companies sought to develop race-friendly or affirmative action policies to encourage integration and racial equality in the workforce. The 1970s gave birth to the modern feminist movement, which confronted corporations with women's rights to equal pay and equal opportunity to compete for jobs and positions historically thought suitable only for men. Enlightened companies, instead of fighting this, sought to develop gender-friendly policies to attract and retain women in all levels of the organization. The 1980s gave rise to many single-parent families, families where both parents worked outside the home, and blended families composed of remarried couples and children from different marriages living under one roof. Forward-thinking companies, instead of bemoaning the disruption to typical work patterns and norms, created a range of family-friendly policies, including flex-time, day care centers, and paternity leave. The 1990s, building on this pattern of social changes and revised corporate practices, presented business with questions of gender and sexual orientation and medical benefits for same-sex partners, convincing many companies to offer gay-friendly policies which sought at a minimum to eliminate discriminatory policies and at a maximum to validate or even promote gay lifestyles. Thus, we see a pattern where leading companies chose to embrace holistic policies and constructively engage the often personal and emotional topics of race, gender, extended family, and sexual orientation. So, looking back over the past four decades we now find that most companies who compete for top talent in the global marketplace have a mixture of race-friendly, female-friendly, family-friendly, and sexual-orientation-friendly policies. So what is next?

Faith at work appears to be one of the final taboos to be broken in the corporate world. Just as the industrial age and the development of specialization by Henry Ford broke apart social life and functions into separate compartments, the best business leaders and consultants of our time are seeking to reassemble the lives and job descriptions of employees to provide a more balanced and holistic work environment. It seems only logical that the next best-practice frontier for corporations is to develop faith-friendly policies to honor, respect, and dignify the spiritual dimension of employees' lives. Faith-friendly policies, if carefully designed and appropriately implemented, have the potential to be one of the more significant ethical and organizational changes to affect the business world. What is at stake is not just accommodating the requests for religion-based affinity groups, prayer or meditation rooms, flexible holidays for religious observances, expanded employee assistance programs, and workplace chaplaincy initiatives—valuable though these all may be. At stake is also preparing companies and their employees to understand different religious practices and orientations in our increasingly pluralistic American workforce and thereby to avoid situations of religious discrimination and harassment. Moreover, this question is only magnified when considered on a global basis, where each country's religious practices often have a deep impact on business ethics, human dealings, and social customs. Businesses that embrace the general concerns of the FAW movement, and develop faith-friendly policies and practices, are likely to be more effective and culturally comfortable whether doing business in Buffalo, Bonn, Beijing, Bahrain, or Bangalore. If companies embrace the concept of developing faith-friendly workplaces with the same vigor as they embraced other programs now seen as status quo or "best practice" in the marketplace, the Faith at Work movement will expand exponentially.

Looking Ahead: Open Questions and Areas for Further Research

This book, while perhaps providing a foundation for future research into the FAW movement, is hardly complete. Moreover, the dynamic nature of the movement means that new shapes, forms, and issues will emerge in response to the needs and changing circumstances it encounters. Even as this volume was going through its final editing, I had to add references to new technological changes (blogging and iPod downloads) now widely employed by those in the movement. These and other changes will raise new questions and considerations that will invite further theological, ethical, sociological, and ecclesiastical study and reflection.

With or without the evolution of the movement and the factors that drive it, further research into the Integration Box framework and the Four E's appears in order. The framework seems to offer great analytical potential, yet additional research is necessary to consider such questions as what modifications and refinements are necessary to ensure universal application of the framework; whether certain vectors or continuums can be measured within each quadrant to indicate the degree or intensity of orientation; whether there is a statistical pattern of how many people fall into each quadrant; what the variables are that determine one's quadrant (personality type, race, gender, geography, childhood church, current church, work context); whether measurable criteria can be developed for each quadrant that recognizes an ideal type and unacceptable deviations; and similarly, whether the earlier mentioned EI (everywhere integrator) type is a measurable overall ideal type toward which to strive.[11]

In addition, the academy should explore whether some forms of theological orientation (e.g., Protestant, Catholic, liberal, mainline, evangelical, Pentecostal, fundamentalist) predispose their adherents to a particular quadrant or quadrants, whether any are more effective at achieving integration,[12] and if so, why. Valuable research could also be conducted as to whether there is, as I have posited based on anecdotal evidence, a link between the steady gradual decline of the mainline denominations and the church's general lack of attention to, or involvement in FAW. In the formal discipline of theological ethics, creative parallels might be found between schools of ethics (e.g., deontology, teleology, and ethology) and certain ethical standards in the marketplace (e.g., business and regulatory laws, corporate objectives, and marketplace norms or standards of best practice). Finally, valuable insights might be gained from the extension of certain theological studies into other spheres of society, such as Reinhold Niebuhr's concept of Christian realism, to develop analogues such as "workplace realism" for Christians engaged in shaping and transforming the workplace.

Of particular value for further study would be to apply these same questions across cultural lines to other countries, including research into non-Christian cultures. My own preliminary research suggests that there is a global FAW movement taking root in other cultures and countries. If the American FAW movement is part of a larger global movement, this raises many questions, including whether they have the same organizing principle and, if so, whether others' quests for integration have the same manifestations as seen in the Four E's; whether the Integration Box framework applies; whether different cultural, economic, and political contexts influence formulations of the movement; whether each country's movement has its own culturally unique characteristics and variables; and if there are different phases or waves of development as we have seen in Europe and America. In a similar vein, scholars should study the cross-religious applications of these questions to explore the parallels and variances in the Jewish, Christian, Muslim, Hindu, and Buddhist traditions as regards the FAW movement. How will FAW activity in each of these faith traditions inform and be informed by interreligious and intercultural business encounters, political dialogue, and theological research?

Conclusion

The goals of this book have been to recognize the Faith at Work movement as a movement; to understand its roots and historical trajectory leading to its current form and substance; to offer a framework and language to analyze it, challenge it, and assist it to realize its significant social possibilities; and to raise questions for further research. This movement has the potential to influence and give new ethical shape to marketplace activity, business institutions, the church, and the academy. The potential ripple effect of positively affecting people in the workplace, the surrounding corporate context, the broader marketplace, and even society at large is staggering. Indeed, the Faith at Work groups and participants and their various modes of expression constitute a significant social movement worthy of continued scholarly analysis to advance knowledge, provide theological clarity and critique, and offer new models for integrating faith and work. And it appears that participants in the FAW movement, as this quote from the *Fortune* magazine cover story "God at Work" indicates, are eager and willing to seek help and find partners in their quest to integrate faith and work.

> Executives are in the vanguard of a diverse, mostly unorganized mass of believers—a counterculture bubbling up all over corporate America—who want to bridge the traditional divide between spirituality and work. Historically, such folk operated below the radar, on their own or in small workplace groups where they prayed or studied the Bible. But now they are getting organized and going public to agitate for change.[13]

Once religious leaders and theologians decide to engage the FAW movement—to get into the Integration Box, so to speak—great possibilities exist for the church writ large and the society it serves. The church and the theological academy have a choice: they can sit on the sidelines, ignore the movement, and let it pass them by, or they can learn from it, engage it, and help shape the theology and practice of faith at work. The church and the theological academy, too often seen as remote in responding to the issues of the day, have the chance here to participate in the FAW dialogue, help set the agenda, address the Four E's, and thereby influence societal structures by affecting and even transforming individual lives, corporations, and the broader marketplace. The church and the academy can offer theological resources and practical tools to equip those whose calling is to serve in and through the marketplace. For the church to do anything less is to abandon millions of Christians for five-sevenths of their week, and to abdicate responsibility for and influence over this important sphere of society. Indeed, active participation in the transformation of individual employees, their workplaces, and the overall marketplace may be one of the most powerful means to help feed the hungry, clothe the naked, and welcome the stranger.

NOTES

INTRODUCTION

1. See the bibliography for a sample listing of such articles.

2. Marc Gunther, "God and Business: The Surprising Quest for Spiritual Renewal in the American Workplace," *Fortune*, July 9, 2001, 58–80; Michelle Conlin, "Religion in the Workplace: The Growing Presence of Spirituality in Corporate America," *BusinessWeek*, November 1, 1999, 150; Laura L. Nash, "How the Church Has Failed Business," *Across the Board*, July–August 2001.

3. One of the few essays recognizing the movement's existence and history is found in Pete Hammond, R. Paul Stevens, and Todd Svanoe, *The Marketplace Annotated Bibliography: A Christian Guide to Books on Work, Business & Vocation* (Downers Grove, Ill.: InterVarsity, 2002). Pete Hammond, a lay author, has been active since 1979 with InterVarsity's Marketplace Ministry.

4. See Gilbert C. Meilaender, ed., *Working: Its Meaning and Its Limits* (Notre Dame, Ind.: University of Notre Dame Press, 2000); Kenan B. Osborne, *Ministry: Lay Ministry in the Roman Catholic Church: Its History and Theology* (New York: Paulist, 1993); David J. Bosch, *Transforming Mission: Paradigm Shifts in Theology of Mission* (Maryknoll, N.Y.: Orbis, 1991); Stephen Charles Neill and Hans-Ruedi Weber, eds., *The Layman in Christian History* (London: SCM, 1963); Karl Marx and Friedrich Engel, *Manifesto of the Communist Party* (originally published London, 1848; edited by David McClellan, Oxford and New York: Oxford University Press, 1992), and *Das Kapital: Kritik der politischen Oekonomie* (originally published Hamburg, 1867; translated by Ben Fowkes. *Capital: Vol. 1: A Critique of Politcal Economy*. London: Penguin Classics, 1990); Ernst Troeltsch, *Social Teachings of the Christian Churches* (originally published Tübingen, 1912; translated by Olive Wyon, Louisville, Ky.: Westminster/John Knox Press, 1992); and Max Weber, *The Protestant Ethic and the Spirit of Capitalism* (originally published Tübingen, 1905; translated by Talcott Parsons, Los Angeles, Calif.: Roxbury, 1996).

5. This is not to say that paid work is more or less important than unpaid or volunteer work (e.g., homemaker or hospital volunteer). Further, while outside the scope of this book, the evidence suggests that many of the issues driving the FAW

movement in the arena of for-profit companies are also applicable to those who work in the nonprofit sector and voluntary associations.

6. The pursuit of integration and a holistic life is generally recognized as a beneficial and valid aim. Indeed, even cursory research into the social sciences and other fields reveals findings confirming the benefits of integration to both the individual and society, including in the disciplines of psychology (e.g., Jung's theory of psychological development spoke of reintegrating ourselves into a balanced person, saying that those who fail to integrate may be psychologically unhealthy; see Nancy Di Tomasao, "Cognitive Styles—the Integrated Self and the Integrated Work Place," Rutgers University, http://newark.rutgers.edu/~ditomaso/ob3_4/sld001.htm); theology (e.g., doctrine of the Trinity); sociology (e.g., racial integration); medicine (e.g., holistic medicine); economics (see Hugh Kerr's "Holistic Economics" in *Theology Today*, April 1984); and technology (e.g., integrated software and hardware architecture).

CHAPTER 1

1. Scholars differ in what they call these spheres, how many there are, and what their relationship is to each other. For instance, Martin Luther calls them "offices" and "orders of creation"; Dietrich Bonhoeffer calls them "mandates"; Abraham Kuyper, Karl Barth, and Michael Walzer call them "spheres of life"; Ernst Troeltsch calls them "departments of society"; and Niklas Luhmann calls them "systems." Some scholars, such as Max Stackhouse, argue for several "clusters" of cultural expression, whereas Daniel Bell identifies just three "sectors" (the "techno-economic," polity, and culture).

2. See Max L. Stackhouse and Peter Paris, eds., *God and Globalization: Religion and the Powers of the Common Life* (Harrisburg, Pa.: Trinity Press International, 2000); and Max L. Stackhouse and Don S. Browning, eds., *God and Globalization: The Spirit and the Modern Authorities* (Harrisburg, Pa.: Trinity Press International, 2001).

3. Several criticisms have emerged from within the business and extended business communities, expressing concern over the growing power and influence of the commercial sector over other parts of society, including Michael L. Budde and Robert W. Brimlow, *Christianity Incorporated: How Big Business Is Buying the Church* (Grand Rapids, Mich.: Brazos, 2002); Business Roundtable, *A New Ethic of Responsibility* (Washington, D.C., 2002); George Soros, *Open Society: Reforming Global Capitalism* (New York: Public Affairs, 2000); David Korten, *When Corporations Rule the World* (San Francisco, Calif.: Kumarian/Berrett-Koehler, 1995); and Caux Roundtable, *Principles for Business* (St. Paul, Minn., 1994).

4. See William H. Swatos, "Protestant Ethic Thesis," in *Encyclopedia of Religion and Society* (William H. Swatos, ed.; Walnut Creek, Calif.: AltaMira Press, 1998); Gustaf Wingren, *Luther on Vocation* (Philadelphia: Muhlenberg, 1957); John Oliver Nelson, ed., *Work and Vocation: A Christian Discussion* (New York: Harper, 1954); W. R. Forrester, *Christian Vocation: Studies in Faith and Work* (London: Lutterworth, 1951); Karl Holl, *Gesammelte Aufsätze zur Kirchengeschichte*, vol. 3 (Tübingen: Mohr, 1921); and John Dillenberger, ed., *Martin Luther: Selections from His Writings* (Garden City, N.Y.: Doubleday, 1962).

5. See Douglas Ottati, "Kingdom of God," in *Encyclopedia of the Reformed Faith*, ed. Donald K. McKim (Louisville, Ky.: Westminster/John Knox, 1992); Jürgen Moltmann,

The Coming of God: Christian Eschatology (translated by Margaret Kohl; Minneapolis, Minn.: Fortress, 1996); and Walter Rauschenbusch, *A Theology for the Social Gospel* (New York: Macmillan, 1917), and *The Righteousness of the Kingdom* (Nashville, Tenn.: Abingdon, 1968).

6. See John Calvin, *Institutes of the Christian Religion* (Grand Rapids, Mich.: Baker Book House, 1987); Miroslav Volf, *Work in the Spirit* (New York: Oxford University Press, 1991); Wade H. Boggs, *All Ye Who Labor: A Christian Interpretation of Daily Work* (Richmond, Va.: John Knox, 1961); Alfred P. Klausler, *Christ and Your Job: A Study in Christian Vocation* (St. Louis, Mo.: Concordia, 1956); Gustaf Wingren, *Luther on Vocation* (Philadelphia: Muhlenberg, 1957); and Karl Holl, *Gesammelte Aufsätze zur Kirchengeschichte*, vol. 3 (Tübingen: Mohr, 1921).

7. See Reinhold Niebuhr, *The Nature and Destiny of Man* (1941; rpt., Louisville, Ky.: Westminster/John Knox, 1996), *Christian Realism and Political Problems* (New York: Scribner's, 1953), and *The Self and the Dramas of History* (New York: Scribner's, 1955).

8. H. Richard Niebuhr, *Christ and Culture* (New York: Harper and Row, 1951).

9. Laura L. Nash and Scotty McLennan, *Church on Sunday, Work on Monday: The Challenge of Fusing Christian Values with Business Life* (San Francisco, Calif.: Jossey-Bass, 2001), xxix.

10. Other twentieth-century movements, such as the Social Gospel movement, had a similar evolution in naming. It went by many different names during its life (e.g., applied Christianity, practical Christianity, Christian sociology) and only later, in the movement's more mature stage, did scholars settle on "the Social Gospel" as its generally accepted name. See Charles H. Lippy, "Social Christianity," in *Encyclopedia of the American Religious Experience* (New York: Scribner's, 1988); Robert T. Handy, ed., *The Social Gospel in America, 1870–1920* (New York: Oxford University Press, 1966); and Charles Howard Hopkins, *The Rise of the Social Gospel in American Protestantism, 1865–1915* (New Haven, Conn.: Yale University Press, 1940).

11. The selection of this descriptive term for the movement is not meant to cause confusion with or reference to the organization and journal *Faith at Work, Inc.* (referred to elsewhere in this study) or the book by David Johnson Rowe, *Faith at Work: A Celebration of All We Do* (Macon, Ga.: Smyth & Helwys, 1997).

12. Notably, an informal poll I conducted in June 2002 of some seventy leaders in the Faith at Work movement (members of the Coalition for Ministry in Daily Life) revealed that, by a three-to-one ratio, members preferred the term "faith at work" to "faith in the workplace" (another popular term) to describe the movement.

13. For example, some words, such as "piety" and "pious," have taken on pejorative meanings, while other words, such as "gay," have taken on completely new meanings.

14. Increasingly, New Age religions and the world's other religious or philosophical systems, such as Hinduism, Buddhism, and Confucianism, are also understood by these terms.

15. Don A. Saliers, "Spirituality," in *A New Handbook of Christian Theology*, ed. Donald W. Musser and Joseph L. Price (Nashville, Tenn.: Abingdon, 1992), 460–62.

16. Robert C. Fuller, *Spiritual but Not Religious: Understanding Unchurched America* (New York: Oxford University Press, 2001), 5.

17. Fuller, *Spiritual but Not Religious*.

18. Fuller, *Spiritual but Not Religious*; Robert Wuthnow, *After Heaven: Spirituality in America since the 1950s* (Berkeley: University of California Press, 1998).

19. Ian I. Mitroff and Elizabeth A. Denton, *A Spiritual Audit of Corporate America: A Hard Look at Spirituality, Religion, and Values in the Workplace* (San Francisco, Calif.: Jossey-Bass, 1999), xvi.

20. Mitroff and Denton, *Spiritual Audit of Corporate America*, 22–25.

21. Mitroff and Denton, *Spiritual Audit of Corporate America*, xv.

22. Nash and McLennan, *Church on Sunday*, xxix.

23. Nash and McLennan, *Church on Sunday*, xxix.

24. Nash and McLennan, *Church on Sunday*, xxix.

25. Nash and McLennan, *Church on Sunday*, xxix.

26. Nash and McLennan, *Church on Sunday*, xxix.

27. William Q. Judge, *The Leader's Shadow: Exploring and Developing Executive Character* (Thousand Oaks, Calif.: Sage, 1999).

28. Judge, *Leader's Shadow*, 82.

29. Nash and McLennan, *Church on Sunday*, 16.

30. John Dillenberger, "Faith," in *A New Handbook of Christian Theology*, ed. Donald W. Musser and Joseph L. Price (Nashville, Tenn.: Abingdon, 1992), 182–84; and Daniel L. Migliore, "Faith," in *Encyclopedia of the Reformed Faith*, ed. Donald K. McKim (Louisville, Ky.: Westminster/John Knox, 1992), 133–35.

31. While this inquiry presupposes a Western democratic political model and a capitalistic economic model, inasmuch as they are the concrete social reality and context of the movement, it is outside the scope of this study to engage in the debate as to the relative strengths and weaknesses of various political and economic organizational schemes for society.

32. Although FAW activity in the business world is the focus of this book, many of the issues driving the FAW movement can also be found in the nonprofit sector or in organizations that are not strictly associated with the profit motive (e.g., education, government, and charities).

33. Notably, due to changing family patterns and worker preference, many businesspeople today choose to work from home. This choice is facilitated by more flexible company policies and new technologies that enable remote connectivity to and communication with office colleagues, clients, and suppliers.

34. Keith Thomas, ed., *The Oxford Book of Work* (Oxford: Oxford University Press, 1999), xiii.

35. Thomas, *Oxford Book of Work*, xvi.

36. Consider, for instance, *Ethics* and *Politics* (Aristotle); *Rule for Monks* (Saint Benedict, c. 540); Thomas Aquinas, *Summa Theologiae* (ca. 1273; New York: Blackfriars and McGraw-Hill, 1964); *Wealth of Nations* (Adam Smith; London, 1776); *Democracy in America* (Alexis de Tocqueville; Paris, 1835); *The Principles of Political Economy* (John Stuart Mill; London, 1848); *Das Kapital* (Karl Marx; originally published Hamburg, 1867; translated by Ben Fowkes. *Capital: Vol. 1: A Critique of Politcal Economy*. London: Penguin Classics, 1990); *Rerum Novarum* (Pope Leo XIII; Vatican, 1891); *Up from Slavery* (Booker T. Washington; New York, 1901); Walter Rauschenbusch, *A Theology for the Social Gospel* (New York: Macmillan, 1917); *Civilization and Its Discontents* (Sigmund Freud; Vienna, 1930); Otto Piper, "The Meaning of Work," in *Theology Today* (1957); *The Affluent Society* (John Kenneth Galbraith; Boston: Houghton Mifflin, 1958); *Gaudium et Spes* (Second Vatican Council; Vatican, 1965); Studs Terkel, *Working* (New York: Pantheon, 1974); Robert N. Bellah, *Habits of the Heart: Individualism and Commitment in American Life* (Berkeley, Calif.: University of California

Press, 1985); *Laborem Exercens* and *Centesimus Annus* (Pope John Paul II; Vatican, 1981 and 1991); Miroslav Volf, *Work in the Spirit* (New York: Oxford University Press, 1991); and Gilbert Meilaender, *Working: Its Meaning and Its Limits* (Notre Dame, Ind.: University of Notre Dame Press, 2000).

37. See Max L. Stackhouse, Dennis P. McCann, and Shirley Roels, *On Moral Business* (Grand Rapids, Mich.: Eerdmans, 1995).

38. "Facing the Challenge of a New Age," in *A Testament of Hope: The Essential Writings and Speeches of Martin Luther King, Jr.* (New York: HarperCollins, 1986), 139.

39. It is outside the scope of this volume to develop a theology of work. However, renewed systematic attention to a theology of work could assist the Faith at Work movement in its self-understanding and ethical focus. Indeed, many of the historical definitions are limited and no longer sufficient for the modern globalized economy. Such an inquiry could be pursued through a number of paths or traditions, including, along the Catholic lines of Pope John Paul II's social teachings, the Reformed tradition of calling and work ethic, the Lutheran tradition of vocation and orders of creation, or in newer conceptions such as Moltmann's eschatological interpretation, Volfs pneumatological framework, or Stackhouse's framework that focuses on vocation and profession.

40. See Gustaf Wingren, *Luther on Vocation* (Philadelphia: Muhlenberg, 1957); Karl Holl, *Gesammelte Aufsätze zur Kirchengeschichte*, vol. 3 (Tübingen: Mohr, 1921); Martin Luther, *Treatise on Good Works* (1519), *Kirchenpostille* (1522), *Treatise on Secular Authority* (1523); John Calvin, *Institutes of the Christian Religion* (1536; Grand Rapids, Mich.: Baker Book House, 1987); Max Weber, *The Protestant Ethic and the Spirit of Capitalism* (first English edition: London, 1930; Los Angeles, Calif.: Roxbury, 1996); Michael Novak, *Business as a Calling* (New York: Free Press, 1996); Pope John Paul II, *Laborem Exercens* (Vatican, 1981), *Centesimus Annus* (Vatican, 1991); Miroslav Volf, *Work in the Spirit* (Oxford, 1991); and Stackhouse, McCann, and Roels, *On Moral Business* (Grand Rapids, Mich., 1995).

41. R. Paul Stevens, *The Other Six Days: Vocation, Work, and Ministry in Biblical Perspective* (Grand Rapids, Mich.: Eerdmans, 1999), 107. While an improvement, even this proves insufficient, as it omits work that is (or seems to be) without purpose, and risks confusion with the concept of "play."

42. Volf, *Work in the Spirit*, 7.

43. Volf, *Work in the Spirit*, 119.

44. Stackhouse, McCann, and Roels, *On Moral Business*; Max L. Stackhouse, "Jesus and Economics: A Century of Reflection," in *The Bible in American Law, Politics, and Political Rhetoric*, ed. James Turner Johnson (Philadelphia: Fortress, 1985), 107–51.

45. The movement under examination is akin to other historical social movements in that they also merited theological and ethical reflection (e.g., early American Puritanism, the Social Gospel, fundamentalism, black theology, liberation theology, and feminist theology).

46. For a view questioning the ability to define social movements, see A. Morris and C. Herring, "Theory and Research in Social Movements: A Critical Review," *Annual Review of Political Science* 2 (1987): 137–98. Much has changed since the Chicago School elevated social movement theory to an area of specialty within sociology in the 1920s. The basic definition of social movement has evolved since then, to include Smelser's "mobilization on the basis of a belief which redefines social action"; see Neil J. Smelser, *Theory of Collective Behavior* (New York: Free Press, 1962), 8; and

Turner and Killian's "a collectivity acting with some continuity to promote a change or resist a change in the society or group of which it is a part." See Ralph H. Turner and Lewis M. Killian, *Collective Behavior* (Englewood Cliffs, N.J.: Prentice-Hall, 1957), 308. Diani identifies four main trends within social movement theory since the 1960s, as represented by four perspectives: collective behavior (e.g., Turner and Killian); resource mobilization theory (e.g., Zald and McCarthy); the political process (e.g., Tilly); and the new social movements (e.g., Touraine and Melucci).

47. Mario Diani, "The Concept of Social Movement," *Sociological Review* 40, no. 1 (February 1992): 17.

48. Diani, "Concept of Social Movement," 1.

49. Diani, "Concept of Social Movement," 1.

50. Diani, "Concept of Social Movement," 7.

51. Luther P. Gerlach and Virginia H. Hine, *People, Power: Change Movements of Social Transformation* (Indianapolis, Ind.: Bobbs-Merrill, 1970); Donatella Della Porta and Mario Diani, *Social Movements: An Introduction* (Malden, Mass.: Blackwell, 1999).

52. The organizing principle appears to be a common quest to integrate faith claims and workplace demands, particularly when the two seem unrelated or in conflict. Or, more broadly put, the central organizing question is to ponder what it means to be a believer, and for the majority of this book, this means a Christian, and to be engaged in the marketplace.

53. Diani, "Concept of Social Movement," 11.

54. Della Porta and Diani, *Social Movements: An Introduction*, 20.

CHAPTER 2

1. I would like to acknowledge and thank George Bauer, Dick Broholm, Howard E. Butt, Jr., Buddy Childress, Bill Diehl, Pete Hammond, Buck Jacobs, Mike McLoughlin Paul Minus, Shirley Roels, Martin Rutte, and Sally Simmel for being conversation partners with me, and sharing their insights into this movement, which has been a big part of their own lives and work.

2. Gibbs and Diehl are leading lay figures who advanced the interest in and practice of lay ministry in wave two. Gibbs authored several books and articles, including (with Ralph T. Morton), *God's Frozen People: A Book for and about Christian Laymen* (Philadelphia: Westminster, 1965), (with Ralph T. Morton), *God's Lively People: Christians in Tomorrow's World* (London: Fontana/Collins, 1971), *Christians with Secular Power* (Philadelphia: Fortress, 1981), and "The Development of a Strong and Committed Laity" (paper presented at the First Vesper/Audenshaw Lecture on the Laity, New York, April 1982), and he was head of the London-based Audenshaw Foundation. Diehl wrote several books and essays, including *Christianity and Real Life* (Philadelphia: Fortress, 1976), *In Search of Faithfulness* (Philadelphia: Fortress, 1987), and *The Monday Connection: On Being an Authentic Christian in a Weekday World* (New York: HarperCollins, 1991), and in 1991 he was the founding president of the Coalition for Ministry in Daily Life.

3. Robert Wuthnow, *Poor Richard's Principle: Recovering the American Dream through the Moral Dimensions of Work, Business and Money* (Princeton, N.J.: Princeton University Press, 1996).

4. Wuthnow, *Poor Richard's Principle*, 300f.

5. This is not incompatible with Laura Nash's typology of evangelical business executives and their view of the relation between faith teachings and business pressures (*Believers in Business*) or H. R. Niebuhr's five-part typology of the approaches a Christian could take toward culture in *Christ and Culture* (New York: Harper and Row, 1951).

6. David J. Bosch, *Transforming Mission: Paradigm Shifts in Theology of Mission* (Maryknoll, N.Y.: Orbis, 1999).

7. The goal here is not to join the millennialist debate, but rather to employ the theological framework and its results in furtherance of this study.

8. Bosch, *Transforming Mission*, xv.

9. Bosch, *Transforming Mission*, xv.

10. Bosch's employment of Thomas Kuhn's paradigm theory helps to illuminate why in theology (as opposed to the natural sciences) multiple paradigms can be operative at the same time. This helps explain the dissension and rancor often seen among Christians who claim to share the same core beliefs.

11. One could say that today, many theologians are "amillennial," in that they are not driven by nor defined by millennial thought in their theological reflection or daily praxis. Yet millennialism offers a helpful framework to analyze and interpret the theological and ecclesiastical motivations operative in the early waves of the movement. Indeed, millennialist questions were part of theological discourse in that period, in a way that questions of transubstantiation versus consubstantiation were in an earlier period of the life of the church.

12. Bosch, *Transforming Mission*, 315f.

13. Bosch, *Transforming Mission*, 318.

14. Bosch, *Transforming Mission*, 319.

15. Bosch, *Transforming Mission*, 321.

16. Max L. Stackhouse, "Jesus and Economics: A Century of Reflection." In *The Bible in American Law, Politics, and Political Rhetoric*, ed. James Turner Johnson (Philadelphia: Fortress, 1985), 108.

17. This parallels the formation of the Protestant Evangelical Social Congress in Europe and the formation of the Brotherhood of the Kingdom among the early Social Gospelers, many of whom wrote favorable comments on Leo's encyclical.

18. Pius XI's encyclical *Quadragisimo Anno: After Forty Years* (1931), written in the post–World War I context during the Great Depression, no longer shares the optimism of Leo's *Rerum Novarum* and the era of liberal capitalism. Instead, akin to the Protestant Social Gospel movement, *Quadragisimo Anno* lays out a vision of a just Christian social order. For the first time, Catholic social teachings used the phrase "social justice." This teaching was an attempt to find a third way between the Left (socialism, communism) and the Right (fascism, injustices of capitalism).

19. Walter Rauschenbusch, *The Righteousness of the Kingdom*, ed. Max L. Stackhouse (Nashville, Tenn.: Abingdon, 1968).

20. Wuthnow, *Poor Richard's Principle*, 332.

21. Wuthnow, *Poor Richard's Principle*, 80.

22. A full exploration and analysis of the Social Gospel and its diverse forms of expression is beyond the scope of this book. The aim here is to recognize the Social Gospel as a significant stream of activity in wave one and that the heirs of the Social

Gospel tradition can be seen in later waves of the Faith at Work movement. See Charles Hopkins, *The Rise of the Social Gospel in American Protestantism, 1865–1915* (New Haven, Conn.: Yale University Press, 1940); Robert Handy, ed., *The Social Gospel in America, 1870–1920* (New York: Oxford University Press, 1966); Walter Rauschenbusch, *A Theology of the Social Gospel*, intro. Donald K. Shriver (Louisville, Ky.: Westminster John Knox, 1997); Max Stackhouse's introduction to Rauschenbusch's *The Righteousness of the Kingdom* (Nashville, Tenn.: Abingdon, 1968); and Stackhouse, "Jesus and Economics."

23. Charles H. Lippy, "Social Christianity," in *Encyclopedia of the American Religious Experience* (New York: Scribner's, 1988), 918.

24. Another way to describe the types of religious responses to social conditions is to use the categories of rescuer, radical, and reformer, drawing on Martin Marty, *Righteous Empire: The Protestant Experience in America* (New York: Dial, 1970).

25. Walter Rauschenbusch, *Christianizing the Social Order* (New York: Macmillan, 1912), 315.

26. Rauschenbusch, *Righteousness of the Kingdom*.

27. Walter Rauschenbusch, "Wanted: A New Kind of Layman," *Rochester* (N.Y.) *Democrat and Chronicle*, February 21, 1906.

28. While grating to the modern ear, I have not modified any of the gender language employed by figures during waves one and two, as it often accurately captures the sexist nature of the society it describes, although we might presume that the concepts apply to both men and women.

29. Rauschenbusch, "Wanted: A New Kind of Layman."

30. Rauschenbusch, "Wanted: A New Kind of Layman."

31. Howard Grimes, "The United States: 1800–1962," in *The Layman in Christian History*, ed. Stephen Neill and Hans-Ruedi Weber (London: SCM, 1963), 250.

32. Rauschenbusch, "Wanted: A New Kind of Layman."

33. Rauschenbusch, "Wanted: A New Kind of Layman."

34. Grimes, "The United States: 1800–1962," 250.

35. Lippy, "Social Christianity."

36. Janet F. Fishburn, "Social Gospel," in *Encyclopedia of the Reformed Faith*, ed. Donald K. McKim (Louisville, Ky.: Westminster/John Knox, 1992), 354–55; and Henry Farnham May, *Protestant Churches and Industrial America* (New York: Harper, 1949).

37. Stackhouse, "Jesus and Economics."

38. Consider, for instance, that in 1912 the recently formed Federal Council of Churches published "Social Creed of the Churches," which echoed both *Rerum Novarum* and Rauschenbusch. Moreover, Social Gospel teachings found later form in the Religion and Labor movement and in the rural ministries movement, the precursor bodies to the American Federation of Labor (AFL), and in aspects of the New Deal legislation.

39. Robert Wuthnow, *The Restructuring of American Religion: Society and Faith since WWII* (Princeton, N.J.: Princeton University Press, 1988), 100.

40. Grimes, "The United States: 1800–1962," 247.

41. The YMCA and YWCA, in some ways, straddle the Social Gospel and the special-purpose group streams, in that their original goals were to provide safe homes and Christian support for children and adults as they migrated to the cities in search of factory work in the mid-1880s.

42. Additional examples of other influential special-purpose groups include industrial chaplains and the men's brotherhood movement (i.e., the laymen's movement); see Charles Hopkins, *The Rise of the Social Gospel* (New Haven, Conn.: Yale University Press, 1940).

43. A full genealogical accounting of these groups is outside the current project. However, in many ways, these special-purpose groups are the forerunners of what became known as the ecumenical movement in wave two. The Student Volunteer movement (founded in the late 1880s) led to the founding of the World Student Christian Federation (Sweden, 1895), which had links to John R. Mott of the YMCA, which in turn contributed to the development of the First World Mission Conference (Edinburgh, 1910) and, after the interruption of World War I, to the First Life and Work World Conference (Stockholm, 1925), followed by the Faith and Order World Conference (Lausanne, 1927), which led to the formal founding of the Life and Work and Faith and Order groups (1932), and finally to the Second Life and Work World Conference (Oxford, 1937).

44. Quoted in Hans-Ruedi Weber, *A Laboratory for Ecumenical Life: The Story of Bossey, 1946–1996* (Geneva: WCC Publications, 1996), 17 (hereafter, *Story of Bossey*).

45. Weber, *Story of Bossey*, 17.

46. Karl A. Olsson, *The History of Faith at Work* (Falls Church, Va.: Faith at Work, 1997), 13.

47. Olsson, *History of Faith at Work*, 13.

48. This shift also attracted Brunner and sharpened the Barthian critique of Buchman. Further, it became focused on interpersonal dynamics, and Reinhold Niebuhr joined the attack.

49. Shoemaker's groups are today known as the Pittsburgh Experiment and Faith at Work, Inc. Buchman's groups are known today as *Initiatives of Change* (formerly Moral Re-Armament) and the Caux Roundtable.

50. *The Gideons International: About Us* (2001), available at http://www.gideons .org; accessed January 9, 2001.

51. *The Gideons International.*

52. *The Gideons International.*

53. *The Gideons International.*

54. *CBMC: Christian Business Men's Committee*, available at http://www.cbmc.com; accessed January 17, 2001.

55. *CBMC.*

56. *CBMC.*

57. In addition to these groups, there also existed lay-founded and lay-led businessmen's Bible study groups. While usually within the context of the church and oriented toward the interior life of the church, such groups were (and in some circles still are) popular among businessmen. Notable among such examples was a large Bible study group for businessmen that John D. Rockefeller led for many years at Riverside Church in New York City.

58. Charles M. Sheldon, *In His Steps: What Would Jesus Do?* (Westwood, N.J.: Revell, 1967).

59. Charles Howard Hopkins, *The Rise of the Social Gospel in American Protestantism, 1865–1915* (New Haven, Conn.: Yale University Press, 1940), 148.

60. This is perhaps due to the thesis of the book, which takes the scriptural account of Jesus' teachings largely in literal terms, which is theologically more

compatible with evangelicals than with mainstream Protestants in the contemporary times of wave three.

61. Laurie Beth Jones, *Jesus CEO: Using Ancient Wisdom for Visionary Leadership* (New York: Hyperion, 1995).

62. Bruce Barton, *The Man Nobody Knows* (Indianapolis, Ind.: Bobbs-Merrill, 1925), iv.

63. Barton, *Man Nobody Knows*, iv.

64. Bruce Barton, "The Man Nobody Knows," available at http://www.amazon.com/exec/obidos/tg/stores/detail/-/books/0965289419/reviews; accessed June 6, 2002.

65. Agnes Rush Burr, *Russell H. Conwell and His Work: One Man's Interpretation of Life* (Philadelphia: Winston, 1926), 165.

66. Burr, *Conwell and His Work*, 414.

67. Burr, *Conwell and His Work*, 415.

68. Elton Trueblood, *The Common Ventures of Life: Marriage, Birth, Work, and Death* (New York: Harper, 1949), 88.

69. Trueblood, *Common Ventures of Life*, 88.

70. Some of the most active wave three groups are city-based (see chapters 4–7).

CHAPTER 3

1. Francis O. Ayres, *The Ministry of the Laity* (Philadelphia: Westminster, 1962), 15.

2. William E. Diehl, *Christianity and Real Life* (Philadelphia: Fortress, 1976), viii.

3. Studs Terkel, *Working* (New York: Pantheon, 1974).

4. See William H. Whyte, *The Organization Man* (New York: Simon & Schuster, 1956); Charles H. Kepner and Benjamin B. Tregoe, *The Rational Manager* (New York: McGraw-Hill, 1965).

5. Harold Lindsell, ed., *The Church's Worldwide Mission: An Analysis of the Current State of Evangelical Missions, and a Strategy for Future Activity* (Waco: Word Books, 1966).

6. John R. W. Stott, *Christian Mission in the Modern World* (London: Falcon, 1975), 23.

7. Vinay Samuel and Chris Sugden, eds., *The Church in Response to Human Need* (London: Paternoster, 1986).

8. Hans-Ruedi Weber, *A Laboratory for Ecumenical Life: The Story of Bossey, 1946–1996* (Geneva: WCC Publications, 1996), 64.

9. Kenan B. Osborne, *Ministry: Lay Ministry in the Roman Catholic Church, Its History and Theology* (New York: Paulist, 1993).

10. Weber, *Story of Bossey*.

11. Weber, *Story of Bossey*, 17.

12. Hendrik Kraemer, *A Theology of the Laity* (Philadelphia: Westminster, 1958), 32.

13. Kraemer, *Theology of the Laity*, 33.

14. J. H. Oldham, *Work in Modern Society* (Published for the Study Dept., World Council of Churches, London: SCM Press, 1950).

15. Keith Clements, *Faith on the Frontier: A Life of J. H. Oldham* (Geneva: WCC Publications, 1999), 445.

16. Kraemer, *Theology of the Laity*, 33.

17. Kraemer, *Theology of the Laity*, 37.

18. Kraemer, *Theology of the Laity*, 37.

19. Kraemer, *Theology of the Laity*, 127.

20. Hans-Ruedi Weber, *Salty Christians* (New York: Seabury, 1963).

21. Hans-Ruedi Weber, "The Rediscovery of the Laity in the Ecumenical Movement," in *The Layman in Christian History*, ed. Stephen Neill and Hans-Ruedi Weber (London: SCM, 1963), 388f.

22. Weber, "Rediscovery of the Laity in the Ecumenical Movement," 389.

23. Weber, "Rediscovery of the Laity in the Ecumenical Movement," 390.

24. Miroslav Volf, *Work in the Spirit: Toward a Theology of Work* (New York: Oxford University Press, 1991).

25. Clements, *Faith on the Frontier*, 445.

26. Quoted in Weber, *Story of Bossey*, 27.

27. The absence of prominent females in the movement in waves one and two can probably be attributed to the traditional gender roles assigned to women in society. While women emerged as lay leaders in other early twentieth-century movements (e.g., missionary work, community chest programs, shelters, orphanages, temperance, and suffrage), the business community and professional workplace outside the home remained largely out of bounds for women. This makes de Diétrich's role all the more impressive.

28. Hans-Ruedi Weber, *The Courage to Live: A Biography of Suzanne de Diétrich* (Geneva: WCC Publications, 1995).

29. Weber, *Story of Bossey*, 51.

30. Weber, *Story of Bossey*, 51.

31. Weber, *Story of Bossey*, 56.

32. Weber, *Story of Bossey*, 78–79.

33. Weber, *Story of Bossey*, 41.

34. *Evanston Speaks: Reports from the Second Assembly of the World Council of Churches, August 15–31, 1954* (New York: World Council of Churches, 1955), 64–65.

35. Hendrik Kraemer, quoted in J. Geraint Morse, "Standing in the Mud" (Mark Gibbs, ed., London: Audenshaw Foundation, 1985), 1.

36. Kraemer, in Morse, "Standing in the Mud," 2.

37. Weber, *Story of Bossey*, 27.

38. Scholars in the United States, including Yale's John O. Nelson (*Work and Vocation: A Christian Discussion* [New York: Harper, 1954]) and Robert L. Calhoun, were writing in a similar vein and interested in emulating the European "academies" and "conference centres" (e.g., North American Lay Conference, Buffalo, 1952).

39. Elton Trueblood, *The Common Ventures of Life: Marriage, Birth, Work, and Death* (New York: Harper, 1949), 85.

40. Trueblood, *Common Ventures of Life*, 85.

41. Trueblood, *Common Ventures of Life*, 87.

42. Elton Trueblood, *Your Other Vocation* (New York: Harper, 1952).

43. Trueblood, *Your Other Vocation*.

44. Trueblood, *Your Other Vocation*, 58.

45. Trueblood, *Your Other Vocation*, 69.

46. William E. Diehl, letter to David W. Miller, July 14, 2001.

47. William E. Diehl, *The Monday Connection: On Being an Authentic Christian in a Weekday World* (New York: HarperCollins, 1991), 178.

48. Austin Flannery, ed., *Vatican Collection*, vol. 1, *Vatican Council II: The Conciliar and Post Conciliar Documents*, rev. ed. (Northport, N.Y.: Costello, 1992), 903f., 350f., 766f.

49. See Yves Congar's *Christians Active in the World* (New York: Herder and Herder, 1968) and *Lay People in the Church: A Study for a Theology of the Laity*, trans. Donald Attwater (Westminster, Md.: Neman Press, 1957).

50. See Lillemor Erlander, "Faith in the World of Work: On the Theology of Work as Lived by the French Worker-Priests and British Industrial Mission" (Ph.D. diss., Uppsala University, 1991); Stan Windass, *Chronicle of the Worker-Priests* (London: Merlin, 1966); John Rowe, *Priests and Workers: A Rejoinder* (London: Darton, Longman & Todd, 1965); David L. Edwards, ed., *Priests and Workers: An Anglo-French Discussion* (London: SCM, 1961); and Gregor Siefer, "Die Mission der Arbeiterpriester: Ereignisse und Konsequenzen" (Ph.D. diss., University of Essen, 1960).

51. Rodger Van Allen, "The Chicago Declaration and the Call to Holy Worldliness," in *Rising from History: U.S. Catholic Theology Looks to the Future*, ed. Robert J. Daly (Lanham, Md.: University Press of America, 1987), 157–70.

52. Ronald J. Sider, ed., *The Chicago Declaration* (Carol Stream, Ill.: Creation House, 1974).

53. Diehl, *Monday Connection*, 179.

54. Diehl, *Monday Connection*, 180.

55. Robert Wuthnow, *The Restructuring of American Religion: Society and Faith since WWII* (Princeton, N.J.: Princeton University Press, 1988), 107.

56. Wuthnow, *Restructuring of American Religion*, 107.

57. See chapters 6 and 7 for a more extensive description and analysis of wave three Faith at Work groups, many of which formed toward the end of wave two, and for evidence of the explosive growth of special-purpose FAW groups in wave three.

58. Abraham Vereide was a successful businessman whose life of ministry through his work was chronicled in Norman Grubb, *Modern Viking: The Story of Abraham Vereide, Pioneer in Christian Leadership* (Grand Rapids, Mich.: Zondervan, 1961).

59. Fred Remington, "The Pittsburgh Experiment," in *Faith at Work*, ed. Samuel M. Shoemaker (New York: Hawthorn, 1958), 302.

60. Remington, "The Pittsburgh Experiment," 302.

61. Samuel M. Shoemaker, *The Experiment of Faith* (Grand Rapids, Mich.: Zondervan, 1957), 56.

62. Helen Smith Shoemaker, *I Stand by the Door: The Life of Sam Shoemaker* (New York: Harper & Row, 1967), 194.

63. *Full Gospel Business Men's Fellowship International*; available at http://www.fgbmfi.org; accessed January 20, 2001.

64. Demos Shakarian, *The Happiest People on Earth* (Chappaqua, N.Y.: Steward, 1975).

65. *FCCI*; available at http://www.fcci.org; accessed June 18, 2006.

66. *FCCI*; available at http://www.fcci.org; accessed June 18, 2006.

67. Verna J. Dozier, *The Calling of the Laity: Verna Dozier's Anthology* (Washington, D.C.: Alban Institute, 1988), 1.

68. Mark Gibbs and Ralph Morton, *God's Frozen People: A Book for and about Christian Laymen* (Philadelphia: Westminster, 1965).

69. Mark Gibbs and Ralph Morton, *God's Lively People: Christians in Tomorrow's World* (London: Fontana/Collins, 1971).

70. Mark Gibbs, *Christians with Secular Power* (Philadelphia: Fortress, 1981).

71. The publication *Laity Exchange* frequently included writings from Catholic laypeople, such as Delores Leckey, the executive director of the U.S. Bishops' Committee on the Laity, representing the interfaith cooperation and spirit of the movement.

72. Wuthnow observes that reliance on a strong or charismatic leader is one of the characteristics of special-purpose groups. They rise up quickly and have remarkable focus on a given task, but can also fold up after the task is done or the founder ceases to be involved. This observation echoes the earlier findings of Ernst Troeltsch and his work on sects, and Weber and his work on charisma.

73. Richard J. Mouw, *Called to Holy Worldliness* (Philadelphia: Fortress, 1980).

74. William E. Diehl, telephone interview by David W. Miller, December 28, 2000.

75. This author has served on CMDL's board of directors and continues to be involved with its annual consultations.

76. Howard E. Butt, Jr., ed., *At the Edge of Hope: Christian Laity in Paradox* (New York: Seabury, 1978), 7.

77. Butt, *At the Edge of Hope*, 7.

78. Butt, *At the Edge of Hope*, 7–8.

79. The congress was conceived and underwritten by three related Butt family charities (the H. E. Butt Foundation, Christian Men, Inc., and the Laity Lodge Foundation).

80. Butt, *At the Edge of Hope*, 9.

81. Butt, *At the Edge of Hope*, 11.

82. See www.laitylodge.org.

83. See H. E. Butt's *The Velvet Covered Brick* (San Francisco, Calif.: HarperCollins, 1974), *At the Edge of Hope: Christian Laity in Paradox* (1978), *Renewing America's Soul* (New York: Continuum, 1996), and *Renewing the Spirit, Healing the Soul* (Dallas, Tex.: Laicom, 2000).

84. "The High Calling of Our Daily Work" is the name of a weekly radio spot produced and read by Butt, as well as the name of a Web site (www.TheHighCalling.org). The Web site and radio spots were launched in 2002. Note: this author sits on the advisory board of this Web site and has attended and spoken at several Laity Lodge and Leadership Forum events.

85. Quoted in Frederick K. Wentz, *Getting into the Act: Opening Up Lay Ministry in the Weekday World* (Nashville, Tenn.: Abingdon, 1978), 16.

86. Wentz, *Getting into the Act*.

87. For instance, see Bruce C. Birch and Larry L. Rasmussen, *The Predicament of the Prosperous* (Philadelphia: Westminster, 1978); Carnegie Samuel Calian, *The Gospel according to the Wall Street Journal* (Atlanta, Ga.: John Knox, 1975); John Daniel, *Labor, Industry, and the Church* (St. Louis, Mo.: Concordia, 1957); and Floyd Doud Shafer, *Liturgy: Worship and Work: A Study Book for United Presbyterian Church Officers* (Philadelphia: Board of Christian Education, 1966).

88. For instance, see James D. Anderson and Ezra Earl Jones, *Ministry of the Laity* (San Francisco, Calif.: Harper & Row, 1986); Francis Ayres, *The Ministry of the Laity: A Biblical Exposition* (Philadelphia: Westminster, 1962); Mouw, *Called to Holy Worldliness*; George Peck and John S. Hoffman, eds., *The Laity in Ministry: The Whole People of God for the Whole World* (Valley Forge, Pa.: Judson, 1984); Richard Taylor, *Christians in an Industrial Society* (London: SCM, 1961); Frederick K. Wentz, *The Layman's Role Today* (Garden City, N.Y.: Doubleday, 1963); and Wentz, *Getting into the Act*.

89. For instance, see W. Maxey Jarman, *A Businessman Looks at the Bible* (Westwood, Conn.: Revell, 1965); and Marion Wade, *The Lord Is My Counsel: A Businessman's Personal Experience with the Bible* (Englewood Cliffs, N.J.: Prentice-Hall, 1966). This substream of writing (i.e., lay-authored texts by commercially successful businesspeople) merits a deeper and more reflective analysis than can be offered here. Further research might suggest that this genre of writing had a lasting and large influence on the Faith at Work movement.

90. See R. G. LeTourneau, *Mover of Men and Mountains* (Englewood Cliffs, N.J.: Prentice-Hall, 1960); George Shinn, *Good Morning Lord!* (New York: Hawthorn, 1977); Stanley Tam, *God Owns My Business* (Waco, Tex.: Word, 1969); and Shakarian, *Happiest People on Earth*.

91. See William E. Diehl, *Christianity and Real Life* (Philadelphia: Fortress, 1976). In addition, former AT&T executive Robert Greenleaf spawned a new substream of the FAW movement (more prominent in wave three) that focuses on business ethics and management consulting, while also avoiding overt Christian language; see Robert K. Greenleaf, *Servant Leadership: A Journey into the Nature of Legitimate Power and Greatness* (Mahwah, N.J.: Paulist, 1977). In this regard, Greenleaf foreshadows wave three authors such as Stephen Covey.

92. Kraemer, *Theology of the Laity*, 115.

93. Kraemer, *Theology of the Laity*, 115.

94. Kraemer, *Theology of the Laity*, 83.

95. Mark Gibbs, "The Development of a Strong and Committed Laity," paper presented at the First Vesper/Audenshaw Lecture on the Laity, New York, April 1982.

96. Weber, *Story of Bossey*, 15.

97. Bosch argues that the early Reformers fell short of their goal and in many cases substituted new forms of clericalism for old (e.g., the accent on the pastor giving the authoritative Word replaced the Catholic accent on the priest's special powers to administer the sacraments).

98. Laity Exchange, *Newsletter*, Mark Gibbs, ed., (London: Audenshaw Foundation, 1985), 2.

99. Sally Simmel, telephone interview by David W. Miller, December 19, 2000.

100. Laity Exchange, *Newsletter*, 2 (Mark Gibbs, ed., London: Audenshaw Foundation, 1985).

101. Indeed, several key transitional lay figures helped to bridge waves two and three, including Howard E. Butt, Jr. (Laity Lodge), Buddy Childress (Needle's Eye Ministry), William Diehl (Coalition for Ministry in Daily Life), Pete Hammond (InterVarsity's Marketplace Ministry), Buck Jacobs (C12), Paul Minus (professor; CMDL) and Sally Simmel (ELCA Department of Ministry in Daily Life).

CHAPTER 4

1. Robert William Fogel, *The Fourth Great Awakening and the Future of Egalitarianism* (Chicago: University of Chicago Press, 2000).

2. Fogel, *Fourth Great Awakening*, 9.

3. Fogel asserts that the First Great Awakening of the 1730s laid the ideological foundation for the American Revolution and the democratic values on which this

country was founded. The Second Great Awakening of the early 1800s led to many social reforms and constitutional amendments, including the abolition of slavery. The Third Great Awakening of the Social Gospel from 1890 to 1930 emphasized social justice, leading to improved labor conditions and New Deal policies. Fogel argues that we are now in the Fourth Great Awakening, which was launched in the 1960s and which accents spiritual rather than material reforms. Spiritual assets and knowledge capital are now seen as more important than, and even prior to, access to material assets. He also argues that this Fourth Great Awakening reasserts egalitarianism as "equal opportunity for all" (as in the first two awakenings) and not "equal conditions for all" (as in the Third Great Awakening). Fogel sees the return to the principle of equality of opportunity as a healthy development. Fogel argues that these awakenings and changes are driven in large part by religious motivation and in particular by evangelical Protestant thinking. If he is correct, this is a major paradigm shift with significant corporate and public policy ramifications.

4. Fogel, *Fourth Great Awakening*, 1.

5. I find his theory would be enriched by a more concrete definition of "spiritual resources." Moreover, the avoidance of references to God, Holy Scriptures, prayer, and the relationships among self, God, and neighbor is problematic, particularly bearing in mind his linking of evangelical Christian theology to the awakenings. On the other hand, his more general definition of spirituality allows secular humanists and people of all religious traditions to find access points. Indeed, in an interview I conducted with him on February 8, 2002, he said that he did not use the words "religion" or "religious assets" because he rejects them, but simply because as a secular intellectual he does not think in those terms. However, he said, there is a strong correlation between spiritual assets and religious assets (e.g., religious virtues and teachings on character, ethics, honesty, integrity, meaning, purpose, vocation, and education).

6. This is consistent with Weber's and Troeltsch's findings of a century ago and with renewed scholarship that recognizes the role of culture and religion in shaping society, including work by economic historian David Landes, *The Wealth and Poverty of Nations: Why Some Nations Are So Rich and Some So Poor* (New York: Norton, 1999); public policy theorists Lawrence Harrison and Samuel Huntington, *Culture Matters: How Values Shape Human Progress* (New York: Basic, 2000); sociologist David Martin, *Tongues of Fire* (Cambridge: Blackwell, 1990); Rodney Stark, *The Victory of Reason: How Christianity Led to Freedom, Capitalism, and Western Success* (New York: Random House, 2005); and scholars of religion and business such as David Krueger, Dennis McCann, Shirley Roels, Max Stackhouse, and Oliver Williams.

7. Nash is familiar with the issues involved with the Faith and Work movement from her earlier study of evangelical business leaders; see Laura L. Nash, *Believers in Business* (Nashville, Tenn.: Thomas Nelson, 1994).

8. Nash and McLennan's work is helpful in describing the gap between clergy and businesspeople, the likely causes, and the danger of the church becoming self-marginalized as the secular spirituality resources become the new teacher and moral reference point for businesspeople in their work. They frame this research as a follow-up to Wuthnow's *God and Mammon in America* (New York: Macmillan, 1994), which foresaw the explosion in the 1990s of spirituality and work; see Nash and McLennan, *Church on Sunday*, xxxi.

9. Nash and McLennan, *Church on Sunday*, 10f.

10. See Stephen Carter, *A Culture of Disbelief: How American Law and Politics Trivialize Religious Devotion* (New York: Basic, 1993); David Tracy, *The Analogical Imagination: Christian Theology and Pluralism* (New York: Crossroad, 1981); and Max Stackhouse, *Public Theology and Political Economy* (Grand Rapids, Mich.: Eerdmans, 1987), and "Public Theology and Ethical Judgment," *Theology Today* 54, no. 2 (July 1997): 165–79. Nicholas Wolterstorff, "The Role of Religion in Discussion and Decision of Political Issues," in *Religion in the Public Square: The Place of Religious Convictions in Political Debate* (Lanham, Md.: Rowman and Littlefield, 1996): 67–120.

11. Bishop Tutu and other religious figures and groups were central in publicly placing moral pressure on the apartheid government in South Africa. Similarly, Pope John Paul II and other religious figures played central roles in bringing down the Berlin Wall and in the subsequent dismantling of the USSR.

12. Tanenbaum Center for Interreligious Understanding, *Religion in the Workplace Survey* (Alexandria, Va.: Society for Human Resource Management, 2001).

13. Carter, *Culture of Disbelief*.

14. Michael Wolf, Bruce Friedman, and Daniel Sutherland, *Religion in the Workplace: A Comprehensive Guide to Legal Rights and Responsibilities* (Chicago: American Bar Association Publishing, 1998).

15. The Free Exercise and Establishment clauses of the First Amendment pertain primarily to public-sector workplaces, not private-sector workplaces. Moreover, President Clinton's Religious Freedom Restoration Act (subsequently declared unconstitutional in 1997 by the Supreme Court) and the resulting Guidelines on Religious Exercise and Religious Expression in the Federal Workplace sought to clarify and guarantee certain rights of religious expression even in the public-sector workplace, while recognizing the limitations of the Establishment Clause.

16. Some of the federal and constitutional laws and regulations include Title VII of the Civil Rights Act of 1964 (as amended in 1972, and including the Equal Employment Opportunity Commission), Executive Order 11246, the National Labor Relations Act, federal personnel laws and regulations, the First Amendment to the U.S. Constitution, the Religious Freedom and Restoration Act, and the resultant White House Guidelines on Religious Exercise and Religious Expression in the Federal Workplace. See Wolf, Friedman, and Sutherland, *Religion in the Workplace*.

17. Wolf, Friedman, and Sutherland, *Religion in the Workplace*, 2.

18. Wolf, Friedman, and Sutherland, *Religion in the Workplace*, 2.

19. Tanenbaum Center, *Religion in the Workplace Survey*.

20. Joe Queenan, *Balsamic Dreams: A Short but Self-Important History of the Baby Boomer Generation* (New York: Holt, 2001).

21. David Brooks, *Bobos in Paradise: The New Upper Class and How They Got There* (New York: Simon & Schuster, 2000).

22. Floyd Norris, "With Bull Market under Siege, Some Worry about Its Legacy," *New York Times*, March 18, 2001, 1, 18.

23. Riva D. Atlas, "What's an Aging 'Barbarian' to Do?" *New York Times*, August 26, 2001, 1, 10.

24. Lincoln Caplan, *Skadden: Power, Money, and the Rise of a Legal Empire* (New York: Farrar Straus Giroux, 1993).

25. William Taylor, "Crime? Greed? Big Ideas? What Were the '80s About?" *Harvard Business Review* vol. 70(1) (January–February 1992): 7.

26. Taylor, "Crime? Greed?" 7.

27. Atlas, "Aging 'Barbarian'," 1.

28. Roy Serpa, "The Often Overlooked Ethical Aspect of Mergers," *Journal of Business Ethics* 7 (1988): 359–62.

29. Taylor, "Crime? Greed?"

30. These incriminating financial exploits led to bestselling nonfiction books such as James B. Stewart's *Den of Thieves* (New York: Simon & Schuster, 1991), chronicling the true crimes of white-collar financiers, such as Martin Siegel, Dennis Levine, Ivan Boesky, and Michael Milken, and *Barbarians at the Gate* (by Bryan Burrough and John Helyar; New York: Harper & Row, 1990), which chronicles KKR's hostile takeover fight for RJR Nabisco. Fictional accounts, such as Tom Wolfe's *Bonfire of the Vanities* (New York: Farrar Straus & Giroux, 1987), and films, including *Wall Street* (1989) and *Other People's Money* (1991), also chronicle the *Geist* of this era. The popular dismay over managerial and corporate behavior in this period refueled old suspicions (from the 1930s and the 1960s) and brought sharp critiques of corporate life. This phenomenon appears to be repeating itself, as scandals at major corporations (e.g., Adelphia, Enron, Tyco, and WorldCom) again raise sharp questions about structural questions and corporate governance within democratic capitalism.

31. Taylor, "Crime? Greed?" 5.

32. Taylor, "Crime? Greed?" 12.

33. Daniel H. Pink, "Free Agent Nation," *FastCompany*, January 1998, 131–47; Nina Munk, "The Price of Freedom," *New York Times Magazine*, March 5, 2000, 50–54.

34. David Leonhardt, "Joy for Second-String M.B.A.'s: Elites and Internet Change Face of Campus Recruiting," *New York Times*, February 23, 2000.

35. Robert J. Shiller, *Irrational Exuberance* (Princeton, N.J.: Princeton University Press, 2000).

36. Maggie Jackson, *What's Happening to Home? Balancing Work, Life, and Refuge in the Information Age* (Notre Dame, Ind.: Sorin, 2002); *Wirthlin Report* 11, no. 6 (July 2001).

37. Robert Wuthnow, *After Heaven: Spirituality in America since the 1950s* (Berkeley: University of California Press, 1998), 3.

38. Wuthnow, *After Heaven*, 3.

39. Wuthnow, *After Heaven*, 3–4.

40. Wuthnow, *After Heaven*, 4.

41. Wuthnow, *After Heaven*, 6.

42. George Gallup, Jr., and D. Michael Lindsay, *Surveying the Religious Landscape: Trends in U.S. Beliefs* (Harrisburg, Pa.: Morehouse, 1999), 8.

43. Marilyn Elias, "New Ways Likely to Replace That Old-Time Religion," *USA Today*, February 28, 2001.

44. Gallup and Lindsay, *Religious Landscape*, 2.

45. Gallup and Lindsay, *Religious Landscape*, 1.

46. Gallup and Lindsay, *Religious Landscape*, 2.

47. Gallup and Lindsay, *Religious Landscape*, 2.

48. Gallup and Lindsay, *Religious Landscape*, 1.

49. Gallup and Lindsay, *Religious Landscape*, 4.

50. Gallup and Lindsay, *Religious Landscape*, 1.

51. See William H. Whyte, Jr., *The Organization Man* (New York: Simon & Schuster, 1956); Shirley Roels, *Organization Man, Organization Woman: Calling, Leadership, and*

Culture (Nashville, Tenn.: Abingdon, 1997). In effect, these books chronicle the bifurcated lives that businesspeople felt they had to lead to be successful in business, with accents on blind loyalty, sacrifice to the company, meaningless work, and the suppression of personality or beliefs.

52. Theologically expressed, the doctrine of sin ensures that humans and institutions will always fall short of the glory of God. Yet the doctrines of creation, justification, and sanctification lead one to seek betterment, transformation, and integration of all spheres of life.

53. Studies beyond those already mentioned include John Green and Kevin E. Schmiesing, *The State of Economic Education in United States Seminaries* (Grand Rapids, Mich.: Acton Institute, 2001); Stephen Hart and David A. Krueger, "Faith and Work: Challenges for Congregations," *Christian Century* (July 15–22, 1992): 683–86; William Q. Judge, *The Leader's Shadow: Exploring and Developing Executive Character* (Thousand Oaks, Calif.: Sage, 1999); MMA Stewardship Solutions, *Where Faith and Wall Street Intersect* (Goshen, Ind.: MMA Stewardship Solutions, August 2001); David W. Miller, "Faith in the Workplace: Issues, Themes, and Responses" (Princeton University, May 1999, unpublished paper); Ian I. Mitroff and Elizabeth A. Denton, *A Spiritual Audit of Corporate America: A Hard Look at Spirituality, Religion, and Values in the Workplace* (San Francisco, Calif.: Jossey-Bass, 1999); and Presbyterian Church (USA), *Social Issues in Investing* (Louisville, Ky.: Presbyterian Church [USA], 1995).

54. R. Paul Stevens, "The Marketplace: Mission Field or Mission?" *CRUX* 37, no. 3 (September 2001): 7–16.

55. See chapter 1 and Diani's three-part test of a social movement (i.e., it is a loose network of relations among a plurality of actors; it has a collective identity; and it deals with conflictual issues).

56. Mario Diani, "The Concept of Social Movement," *Sociological Review* 40, no. 1 (February 1992): 11.

57. Diani, "Concept of Social Movement," 11.

CHAPTER 5

1. Lisa Miller, "Can You Go Back? Many Professionals Return to Church or Synagogue: Having It All Isn't Enough," *Wall Street Journal*, April 10, 1998, W1.

2. *National Council of Churches: NCC at a Glance*; available at http://www.ncccusa.org/about/about_ncc.htm; accessed February 12, 2003.

3. *Top 10 Religious Bodies with Most Churches in the U.S., 1990*; available at http://www.adherents.com/rel_USA.html; accessed February 13, 2003.

4. Examples of church-based FAW ministry programs include the Center for Faith in the WorkPlace at St. Mark's Episcopal Church, San Antonio, Texas; the Nehemiah Ministry at Christ Church of Oak Brook, Illinois; Faith @ Work at Fifth Avenue Presbyterian Church in New York City; Job Transitions at the Fourth Presbyterian Church in Chicago; Marketplace Ministry at Redeemer Presbyterian Church (PCA) in New York City; Marketplace Ministry at Park Street Church in Boston; Center for Spirituality and Ethics in the Workplace at St. Paul's Episcopal Cathedral in Buffalo, New York; and Workplace at Willow Creek Community Church in South Barrington,

Illinois. Examples of other churches with intentional workplace ministry programs include Menlo Park Presbyterian Church, Menlo ParkCalifornia; Park Street Church, Boston; St. Andrew's Lutheran Church, Mahtomedi, Minnesota; St. Timothy's Episcopal Church, Mountain View, California; and Trinity Church Wall Street, New York City.

5. Stephen Hart and David A. Krueger, "Faith and Work: Challenges for Congregations," *Christian Century* (July 15–22, 1992): 683–86.

6. Hart and Krueger, "Faith and Work," 684.

7. Peter J. Paris, *The Social Teaching of the Black Churches* (Philadelphia: Fortress, 1985); C. Eric Lincoln and Lawrence H. Mamiya, eds., *The Black Church in the African American Experience* (Durham, N.C.: Duke University Press, 1990).

8. See David W. Miller, "King and the Economy: Getting Down to the Business of Business" (unpublished paper, Princeton Theological Seminary, 1998).

9. Consider, for example, the ministries of Jesse Jackson, T. J. Jakes, Kirbyjon Caldwell, and Buster Soaries. In contrast, some black clergy (like their white counterparts) accent the extremes of accepting poverty as divine will, or expecting the divine promise of wealth and material blessing (i.e., the so-called prosperity gospel).

10. Laura L. Nash and Scotty McLennan, *Church on Sunday, Work on Monday: The Challenge of Fusing Christian Values with Business Life* (San Francisco, Calif.: Jossey-Bass, 2001), 166.

11. See above and chapter 6.

12. Laura L. Nash, "How the Church Has Failed Business," *Across the Board*, July–August 2001.

13. See John Green and Kevin E. Schmiesing, *The State of Economic Education in United States Seminaries* (Grand Rapids, Mich.: Acton Institute, 2001); Robert William Fogel, *The Fourth Great Awakening* (Chicago: University of Chicago Press, 2000); George Gallup, Jr., and D. Michael Lindsay, *Surveying the Religious Landscape: Trends in U.S. Beliefs* (Harrisburg, Pa.: Morehouse, 1999); Hart and Krueger, "Faith and Work"; William Q. Judge, *The Leader's Shadow: Exploring and Developing Executive Character* (Thousand Oaks, Calif.: Sage, 1999); David W. Miller, "Faith in the Workplace: Issues, Themes, and Responses" (unpublished paper, Princeton University, 1999); Ian I. Mitroff and Elizabeth A. Denton, *A Spiritual Audit of Corporate America: A Hard Look at Spirituality, Religion, and Values in the Workplace* (San Francisco, Calif.: Jossey-Bass, 1999); Nash and McLennan, *Church on Sunday*; Presbyterian Church (USA), Congregational Ministries Division, *Social Issues in Investing* (Louisville, Ky.: Presbyterian Church [USA], 1995); Tanenbaum Center for Interreligious Understanding, *Religion in the Workplace Survey* (Alexandria, Va.: Society for Human Resource Management, 2001); and Wuthnow, *God and Mammon in America* (New York: Macmillan, 1994), and *The Crisis in the Church* (New York: Oxford University Press, 1997).

14. William E. Diehl, *Christianity and Real Life* (Philadelphia: Fortress, 1976), v–vi.

15. Perhaps this is one of the overlooked but root causes of the well-documented declining membership in the mainline church today. Pursuit of this question, however, is outside the scope of this volume.

16. The survey was of members of Chicago area churches and synagogues.

17. Hart and Krueger, "Faith and Work."

18. Hart and Krueger, "Faith and Work," 683.

19. Hart and Krueger, "Faith and Work," 683.

20. Hart and Krueger, "Faith and Work," 685.

21. Nash and McLennan, *Church on Sunday*, xix.

22. Hart and Krueger, "Faith and Work," 685.

23. Hart and Krueger, "Faith and Work," 684.

24. Hart and Krueger, "Faith and Work," 684.

25. Gallup and Lindsay, *Religious Landscape*, 4.

26. Gallup and Lindsay, *Religious Landscape*, 4.

27. Hart and Krueger, "Faith and Work," 684.

28. Hart and Krueger, "Faith and Work," 684.

29. Hart and Krueger, "Faith and Work," 684.

30. Wuthnow, *God and Mammon in America*, 56.

31. Nash and McLennan, *Church on Sunday*, xiii.

32. Presbyterian Church (USA), Office of the General Assembly, Advisory Committee on Social Witness, *God's Work in Our Hands: Employment, Community, and Vocation*, ed. Irvin S. Moxley (Louisville, Ky.: Presbyterian Church [USA], 1995), 14.

33. Presbyterian Church (USA), *God's Work in Our Hands*, 14.

34. While one of the best extant studies, their methodology and findings are not beyond critique. They acknowledge that their condemnatory assessment of the church is based on research that does not include sufficient survey samples of evangelical or black churches. In addition, they do not sufficiently distinguish among the conservative Right, the mainstream, and the liberal Left. Moreover, in rightly arguing that the church has chosen to self-marginalize from the business world and to abdicate pastoral responses to secular spirituality resources, they do not sufficiently acknowledge the significance of the Christian response in the form of the lay-founded and lay-led Faith at Work movement. In addition, the book does not offer a theological grounding or ecclesiastical rationale for why the church should minister to the business community. Finally, despite the generally strong analysis, the book does not offer the church new models of ministering to the business community. Essentially, the authors offer two solutions: issuing a call for a new "evolutionist language" and for integration based on new "mental maps" (Nash and McLennan, *Church on Sunday*, 2001, 184f., 213f.). The former fails to capture the imagination and utilize the church's existing vocabulary, and the latter lacks cohesion. A sound theoretical framework or a concrete model of what the church ought to do is lacking. In short, Nash and McLennan offer an excellent sociological description and diagnosis of the problem, but fail to develop a systematic theological, ethical, or ecclesiastical prescription.

35. Nash and McLennan, *Church on Sunday*, 260.

36. Nash and McLennan, *Church on Sunday*, 130f.

37. Presbyterian Church (USA), *God's Work in Our Hands*, 13.

38. While a complete cross-denominational evaluation is beyond the scope of this study, a brief review of PCUSA policy statements, if taken as indicative of most major denominations, is instructive.

39. Many of the staff members responsible for lay ministry or ministry in daily life became members of the Coalition for Ministry in Daily Life (CMDL). The CMDL was founded in 1991 by layperson William Diehl; it was designed as a networking and meeting place for early wave three collaborators, including individual lay members and lay groups from the FAW movement (see chapters 6 and 7).

40. Presbyterian Church (USA), Advisory Committee on Social Witness Policy, *Presbyterian Social Witness Policy Compilation*, ed. Peter A. Sulyok (Louisville, Ky.: Presbyterian Church [USA], 2000), 255–94.

41. After offering a theological rationale for social action, the compilation is organized around eleven areas, of which "economic issues" is one. The section on economic issues contains statements on such topics as poverty in the United States, the church as an agent in the economy, responsible corporate behavior, a just economic order, federal economic priorities, housing and urban renewal, work as vocation, industrial labor relations, and migratory and farm labor.

42. Presbyterian Church (USA), *Social Witness Policy Compilation*, 270.

43. Presbyterian Church (USA), *Social Witness Policy Compilation*, 269.

44. Presbyterian Church (USA), *Social Witness Policy Compilation*, 285–91.

45. Presbyterian Church (USA), *God's Work in Our Hands*, 273.

46. Robert Wuthnow, *Christianity in the 21st Century: Reflections on the Challenges Ahead* (New York: Oxford University Press, 1993), 200.

47. Wuthnow, *Christianity in the 21st Century*, 200.

48. World Council of Churches, *A Letter from Christ to the World: An Exploration of the Role of the Laity in the Church Today*, ed. Nicholas Apostola (Geneva: WCC Publications, 1998).

49. World Council of Churches, *Letter from Christ to the World*, ix.

50. World Council of Churches, *Letter from Christ to the World*, 12.

51. World Council of Churches, *Letter from Christ to the World*, 2.

52. World Council of Churches, *Letter from Christ to the World*, 12f.

53. World Council of Churches, *Letter from Christ to the World*, 17.

54. World Council of Churches, *Letter from Christ to the World*, 18.

55. Nash and McLennan, *Church on Sunday*, 258.

56. Mark Ellingsen, *The Cutting Edge: How Churches Speak on Social Issues* (Geneva: WCC Publications, 1993), xvi.

57. It is important to note—indeed, it is a central assertion of this volume—that the problem lies not in the theology of Christianity. Rather it lies in the interpretation of Christian theology as manifested in ecclesiological experience and practice.

58. Miroslav Volf, *Work in the Spirit: Toward a Theology of Work* (New York: Oxford University Press, 1991), 69.

59. See Oliver F. Williams, *Business, Religion, and Spirituality: A New Synthesis* (Notre Dame, Ind.: University of Notre Dame Press, 2003); Max L. Stackhouse, Dennis P. McCann, and Shirley Roels, *On Moral Business* (Grand Rapids, Mich.: Eerdmans, 1995); Michael Novak, *Will It Liberate?* (New York: Paulist, 1986); Peter L. Berger, *The Capitalist Revolution: Fifty Propositions about Prosperity, Equality, & Liberty* (New York: Basic, 1986), and *Pyramids of Sacrifice: Political Ethics and Social Change* (New York: Basic, 1975); and Dennis McCann, *Christian Realism and Liberation Theology: Practical Theologies in Conflict* (Maryknoll, N.Y.: Orbis, 1981).

60. World Council of Churches, *Letter from Christ to the World*, 35.

61. World Council of Churches, *Letter from Christ to the World*, 35.

62. Wuthnow, *God and Mammon in America*, 39.

63. Robert Wuthnow, *The Crisis in the Church: Spiritual Malaise, Fiscal Woe* (New York: Oxford University Press, 1997).

64. Wuthnow, *God and Mammon in America*, 55.

65. Hart and Krueger, "Faith and Work," 684.

66. See Davida Foy Crabtree, *The Empowering Church: How One Congregation Supports Lay People's Ministries in the World* (Washington, D.C.: Alban Institute 1990).

67. Loren B. Mead, *The Once and Future Church: Reinventing the Congregation for a New Mission Frontier* (Washington, D.C.: Alban Institute, 1991), 33.

68. Loren B. Mead, *Five Challenges for the Once and Future Church* (Bethesda, Md.: Alban Institute, 1996), 1.

69. Mead, *Five Challenges*, 8.

70. Mead, *Five Challenges*, 8.

71. Nash and McLennan, *Church on Sunday*, 190.

72. Nash and McLennan, *Church on Sunday*, 190.

73. Robert C. Fuller, *Spiritual but Not Religious: Understanding Unchurched America* (New York: Oxford University Press, 2001), 9–10.

74. See Christian Schumacher, *God in Work* (Oxford: Lion, 1998); Alexander Hill, *Just Business: Christian Ethics for the Marketplace* (Downers Grove, Ill.: InterVarsity, 1997); Nash, *Believers in Business* (1994); and Jay A. Conger, *Spirit at Work: Discovering the Spirituality in Leadership* (San Francisco, Calif.: Jossey-Bass, 1994).

75. While the focus of my inquiry here is teaching on the FAW movement and issues, there are also related areas, including theological and pastoral reflections on economic structures, globalization, public policy, social ethics, the moral roots of the corporation, lay ministry, vocation, and the nature and purpose of work.

76. I rely here on two leading empirical surveys of seminary and divinity school curricula, regarding FAW and economic issues, conducted by John Green and Kevin E. Schmiesing for the Acton Institute, *The State of Economic Education* (2001); Nash and MacLennan, *Church on Sunday* (2001); and my own qualitative and quantitative review of seminary curricula.

77. Examples include Dallas Theological Seminary (Center for Christian Leadership and master of arts in corporate chaplaincy); Fuller Theological Seminary (De Pree Center for Leadership); Gordon-Conwell Theological Seminary (Mockler Center for Faith and Ethics in the Workplace); and Regent College. See also chapter 6.

78. Green and Schmiesing, *Economic Education*.

79. The Yale Center for Faith & Culture (www.yale.edu/faith) was founded in 2003 by Miroslav Volf, with the support of YDS dean Harold Attridge, the YDS Advisory Board, and several business leaders, who encouraged the center's early focus on FAW matters through the Ethics and Spirituality in the Workplace program area. Volf became the center's director, and I joined the center at its inception as the executive director, bringing the work of the Avodah Institute with me.

80. A notable exception to this tendency of seminaries to ignore or devalue the issues and concerns of those engaged in the marketplace comes from Catholic universities and business schools (e.g., Gonzaga, Loyola, Notre Dame, and Santa Clara). In addition, some Protestant Christian undergraduate schools, largely out of the evangelical tradition, including Calvin, Millsaps, John Brown, and Wheaton, treat FAW concerns in their business department curricula. See chapter 6.

81. Nash and McLennan, *Church on Sunday*, xxxi.

82. Nash and McLennan, *Church on Sunday*, 162.

83. Nash and McLennan, *Church on Sunday*, 161–62.

84. Nash and McLennan, *Church on Sunday*, 147.

85. Nash and McLennan, *Church on Sunday*.

86. Nash and McLennan, *Church on Sunday*, 129–30.

87. Nash and McLennan, *Church on Sunday*, 129–30.

88. Green and Schmiesing, *Economic Education*.

89. Conducted by external researchers, the study was commissioned by the Acton Institute. Approximately 250 seminaries and theological institutions were surveyed with 129 responding.

90. Green and Schmiesing, *Economic Education*, 2.

91. Green and Schmiesing, *Economic Education*, 29.

92. Green and Schmiesing, *Economic Education*, 5.

93. Green and Schmiesing, *Economic Education*, 29.

94. Green and Schmiesing, *Economic Education*, 29.

95. Green and Schmiesing, *Economic Education*, 1.

96. Green and Schmiesing, *Economic Education*, 1.

97. Supplemental to the survey instrument, the researchers

> examined the course catalogs for approximately 175 seminaries and graduate schools of theology. Forty-five showed courses in which the word economic or economics were mentioned in the course description. Of these, most dealt with economic justice; only nine appeared to contain any explicit treatment of economics as a distinct discipline. (Green and Schmiesing, *Economic Education*, 130)

98. Green and Schmiesing, *Economic Education*, 15.

99. Green and Schmiesing, *Economic Education*, 19.

100. Green and Schmiesing, *Economic Education*, 26.

101. Green and Schmiesing, *Economic Education*, 30.

102. Acton Institute; available at http://www.acton.org/press/2001jul/templeton .html; accessed August 24, 2001.

103. A notable exception was the 2002 AAR annual meeting in which the Religion and the Social Sciences Section and the Christian spirituality group held sessions called "Religion in the Workplace" and "Spirituality in the Workplace," respectively. While in general this is a positive development, the overall quality and content of the six papers were disappointing, from the perspective of this study of the FAW movement qua movement. With the exception of two papers, the focus was generally not on the FAW movement, the factors and issues driving the movement, or the ensuing problems and potentialities. Notably, the papers that came closest to addressing issues in the movement were given by business scholars, not theologians. Two of the papers focused on traditional labor rights and worker exploitation questions.

104. For example, during the four decades of wave two, *Theology Today* only had two issues that included articles on the role of business and religion ("Symposium: Business and Religion," April 1984; and an article by Catholic theologian Oliver F. Williams, "Christian Formation for Corporate Life," October 1979). Notably, *Theology Today* produced a special issue on "Business and Theology" (October 2003). It was conceived and edited by Ellen Charry, who has been attentive to FAW concerns; I served as special advisor to help shape and design the issue.

105. Barbara Brown Taylor, *The Preaching Life* (Boston: Cowley, 1993), 26.

106. The theological entry points for seminaries to address these questions traditionally fall under the doctrines of the church, creation, humanity, work, stewardship, sanctification, and the kingdom of God. From a curriculum perspective, the

headings under which these questions fall vary, including social ethics, personal ethics, leadership, pastoral care, lay ministry, and continuing education.

107. *De Pree Leadership Center*, "De Pree Leadership Center: History and Vision"; available at http://www.depree.org/aboutdplc.html; accessed May 6, 2002.

108. Robert Banks and Kimberly Powell, eds., *Faith in Leadership: How Leaders Live Out Their Faith in Their Work and Why It Matters* (San Francisco, Calif.: Jossey-Bass, 2000); Robert Banks, "The Protestant Work Ethic," *Faith in Business Quarterly* 2, no. 2 (1998): 5–7; Robert Banks and R. Paul Stevens, eds., *The Complete Book of Everyday Christianity: An Every Day Guide to Following Christ in Every Aspect of Life* (Downers Grove, Ill.: InterVarsity, 1997); Robert Banks, *God the Worker: Journeys into the Heart, Mind, and Imagination of God* (Valley Forge, Pa.: Judson, 1994); Robert J. Banks, *Faith Goes to Work: Reflections from the Marketplace* (Washington, D.C.: Alban Institute, 1993).

109. *Mockler Center for Faith and Ethics in the Workplace*; available at http://www.gcts.edu/ockenga/mockler/index.html; accessed May 6, 2002.

110. *Mockler Center*.

111. *Mockler Center*.

112. *Mockler Center*.

113. *Regent College*; available at http://www.gospelcom.net/regent/regentnew/index.html; accessed May 6, 2002.

114. Other theological schools that have developed a center or curricular focus on the question of faith and work include Dallas Theological Seminary (through the Center for Christian Leadership and its lay ministry curriculum); Pittsburgh Theological Seminary (through the Center for Business, Religion, and Public Life); Columbia Theological Seminary (through the Lay Institute of Faith and Life and its affiliation with the independent nonprofit the Southern Institute for Business and Professional Ethics); and Luther Seminary (through Jack Fortin's directorship of the Center for Lifelong Learning in collaboration with Seeing Things Whole, one of the well-established nonprofit FAW groups). Yale Divinity School has developed a Center for Faith & Culture with an accent on ethics and spirituality in the workplace.

115. Hart and Krueger, "Faith and Work," 684.

116. The genre of self-help books that are imbued with vague forms of spirituality has become so popular that it has merited a lampoon of the genre itself; see Brother Ty, with Christopher Buckley and John Tierney, *God Is My Broker: A Monk-Tycoon Reveals the 7½ Laws of Spiritual and Financial Success* (New York: HarperPerennial, 1998).

CHAPTER 6

1. Delbecq in Marc Gunther, "God and Business: The Surprising Quest for Spiritual Renewal in the American Workplace," *Fortune*, July 9, 2001, 61.

2. Partially helpful but not definitive projects include Pete Hammond, "Some Wonderful North American 'Stirrings'" (Madison, Wisc.: InterVarsity Marketplace Ministry, Spring 2001, photocopied); Michael L. Budde and Robert W. Brimlow, *Christianity Incorporated: How Big Business Is Buying the Church* (Grand Rapids, Mich.: Brazos, 2002); Mike McLoughlin, *The Scruples Directory of Marketplace Ministry* (Kelowna, B.C., Canada: YWAM, 2002); Laura L. Nash and Scotty McLennan, *Church*

on Sunday, Work on Monday: The Challenge of Fusing Christian Values with Business Life (San Francisco, Calif.: Jossey-Bass, 2001); and Michael Skelley, "Work as Spiritual Practice: Spirituality in Organizational Life," paper presented at the American Academy of Religion Annual Meeting, Toronto, November 20, 2002.

3. Mike McLoughlin, with Neal Johnson, Os Hillman, and David W. Miller, eds., *2003 International Faith & Work Directory* (Cumming, Ga.: Aslan, 2003).

4. Discovery of and access to many of these sources are challenging for those both inside and outside the movement. Participants within the movement do not always have ready access to other sources of information, as member profile differences sometimes cause de facto limitations to intergroup awareness and dialogue. Outsiders to the movement are often unaware of the range of participant types and accents. In this regard, my role as a participant in the movement as the president and cofounder of the Avodah Institute, gave me unusual access to the full typological range of participants in the movement, and helped provide useful internal perspectives and access to a variety of FAW networks, including many that prefer to operate confidentially and outside the public spotlight.

5. Scruples is part of Youth with a Mission (YWAM), a Canadian-based mission-oriented para-church organization.

6. McLoughlin et al., eds., *Faith & Work Directory*.

7. This was was an online directory that was compiled by Mike McLoughlin and presented on his web site www.scruples.org

8. Mike McLoughlin, ed., *The Scruples Directory of Marketplace Ministry: Millennium 2000 Edition* (Kelowna, B.C., Canada: YWAM, 2000).

9. McLoughlin et al., eds. *Faith & Work Directory*.

10. Larger FAW organizations include the FCCI, FGBMFI, and CBMC with staff and members around the globe.

11. Examples include the C12 Group, Eads Management Development Associates, and the Ethical Leadership Group.

12. Examples include the C12 and the Christian Entrepreneurs Organization.

13. Examples include the CBMC, the Christian Entrepreneurs Organization, and the Forge.

14. Special TV segments include "Spirituality in the Workplace" (October 15, 2001) and "Searching for the Soul in Business" (September 23, 1993), both on "The McCuiston Program"; "Nightly Business Report with Paul Kangas" (August 6, 2001); and "NJ Network News" (April 9, 1998). Special radio segments include the three-part series "Faith and Fortune" (December 17–19, 2001) on Public Radio International; and "Overcoming the Sunday-Monday Gap" (September 18, 2001) on the Moody Broadcasting Network.

15. Gunther, "God and Business."

16. Richard McGill Murphy, "Jesus at Work," *FSB: Fortune Small Business*, February 2006.

17. Michelle Conlin, "Religion in the Workplace: The Growing Presence of Spirituality in Corporate America." *BusinessWeek*, October 25, 1999.

18. Susanne Alexander, "Spirituality," *Newsweek Japan*, September 9, 2001.

19. Sheila Sobell, "Soul Providers," *American Way*, November 15, 2001.

20. See Amy Lindgren, "Reasons Multiply for Keeping Religion Out of the Workplace," *Lancaster New Era*, December 17, 2001; and Amy Joyce, "Keep Personal Causes Far from Office," *Miami Herald*, August 19, 2002.

21. Daniel Akst, "When Business Gets Religion," *New York Times*, October 4, 1998; John Balzar, "Exploring Spiritual Approach to Business-World Challenges," *Los Angeles Times*, December 17, 1996; Cindy Bellinger, "New Spirit in the Workplace," *Crosswinds Weekly*, March 15–22, 2001; D. Briggs, "Serving the Ultimate Boss," *Plain Dealer*, December 25, 2000; Stephen Overell, "Souls Restored in the Workplace: Spirituality in Business," *Financial Times* (London), September 21, 2001; Jeffery Seglin, "Regulating Religious Life in the Office," *New York Times*, May 16, 1999; Gail Vaz-Oxglade, "Instilling Spiritual Values in the Workplace," *Investment Executive*, May 1998; Burton L. Visotzky, "Bible in the Boardroom?" *Inc. Magazine*, July 1998, 29–32.

22. Robert Wuthnow, *The Restructuring of American Religion: Society and Faith since WWII* (Princeton, N.J.: Princeton University Press, 1988).

23. A handful of ordained clergypersons have become involved in the FAW movement on a full-time basis, leading groups and no longer pastoring a church (e.g. David "Mac" McQuiston of the CEO Forum and David Williamson of Laity Lodge).

24. Some clergy are exceptions to this pattern, including Davida Foy Crabtree, *The Empowering Church: How One Congregation Supports Lay People's Ministries in the World* (Washington, D.C.: Alban Institute, 1990); Bill Hybels, *Christians in the Marketplace: Making Your Faith Work in the Secular World* (London: Hodder & Stoughton, 1993); Earl Palmer, *A Faith That Works* (Ventura, Calif.: Regal, 1985); Rich Marshall, *God @ Work: Discovering the Anointing for Business* (Shippensburg, Pa.: Destiny Image, 2000); Mark Slomka, *BizBreak: Weekly Reminders for the Workplace* (Camp Hill, Pa.: Horizon, 2000); and Jan Wood, *Christians at Work* (Scottsdale, Ariz.: Herald, 1999).

25. There is not yet an authoritative bibliography for this genre. It would be difficult to compile, as many books are from small private publishers and have minimal circulation and a short lifespan. Nevertheless, two helpful bibliographic resources that focus on spirituality and work (as opposed to religion and work) are J. Christina Smith, "Spirituality and Work: An Annotated Bibliography" (Boston: Boston University, 1998, photocopied); and Judi Neal, "Spirit at Work Bibliography"; available at http://www.spiritatwork.com/knowledgecenter; accessed January 18, 2001. Each contains hundreds of books yet each is incomplete and already dated.

26. Pete Hammond, R. Paul Stevens, and Todd Svanoe, *The Marketplace Annotated Bibliography: A Christian Guide to Books on Work, Business & Vocation* (Downers Grove, Ill.: InterVarsity, 2002).

27. *The Marketplace Annotated Bibliography* contains a theme index using the categories of case studies, congregational studies, especially for pastors, leisure studies, multiethnic and international, profiles, autobiographies and biographies, books with several profiles, and industry-specific (arts, business, calling, career and unemployment, church, communication, education, family, finance and economics, government, health, law, and technology).

28. For instance, Laurie Beth Jones, *Jesus, Inc.: The Visionary Path: An Entrepreneur's Guide to True Success* (New York: Crown Business, 2001); Larry Julian, *God Is My CEO: Following God's Principles in a Bottom-Line World* (Holbrook, Mass.: Adams Media, 2001); Gregory F. Pierce, *Spirituality @ Work: 10 Ways to Balance Your Life On-the-Job* (Chicago: Loyola Press, 2001); Stephen Graves and Thomas Addington, *The Fourth Frontier: Exploring the New World of Work* (Nashville, Tenn.: Word, 2000); Christian Schumacher, *God in Work* (Oxford: Lion, 1998); C. William Pollard, *The Soul of the Firm* (New York: HarperBusiness; Grand Rapids, Mich.: Zondervan, 1996);

Thomas Smith, *God on the Job: Finding God Who Waits at Work* (New York: Paulist, 1995); Laurie Beth Jones, *Jesus CEO: Using Ancient Wisdom for Visionary Leadership* (New York: Hyperion, 1995); Bob Buford, *Halftime: Changing Your Game Plan from Success to Significance* (Grand Rapids, Mich.: Zondervan, 1994); Bob Briner, *Roaring Lambs: A Gentle Plan to Radically Change Our World* (Grand Rapids, Mich.: Zondervan, 1993); Mark Greene, *Thank God It's Monday: Ministry in the Workplace* (London: Scripture Union, 1994); Tom Chappell, *The Soul of a Business: Managing for Profit and the Common Good* (New York: Bantam, 1994); William Diehl, *The Monday Connection* (New York: HarperCollins, 1991); and John D. Beckett, *Loving Monday: Succeeding in Business without Selling Your Soul* (Downers Grove, Ill.: InterVarsity, 1998).

29. Judi Neal, "Spirituality in the Workplace in Higher Education: A Global Phenomenon," paper presented at the Spirit in Business, Inc., Conference, April 21–23, 2002, New York.

30. Christine Leigh-Taylor, "Business Leadership as a Spiritual Discipline," *The Physician Executive*, March–April 2001.

31. "UMass to Host National Conference June 4–6 on Spirituality in the Workplace and Higher Education"; available at http://www.umass.edu/newsoffice/archive/2000/042400spirituality.html; accessed April 24, 2000.

32. "UMass to Host National Conference."

33. Marci McDonald, "Shush: The Guy in the Cubicle Is Meditating: Spirituality Is the Latest Corporate Buzzword," *U.S. News & World Report*, May 3, 1999, 46.

34. Marguerite Rigoglioso, "Spirit at Work: The Search for Deeper Meaning in the Workplace," *Harvard Business School Bulletin*, April 1999, 31–35.

35. Oliver F. Williams, *Business, Religion, and Spirituality: A New Synthesis* (Notre Dame, Ind.: University of Notre Dame Press, 2003).

36. Neal, "Spirituality in the Workplace."

37. Examples of universities that have offered courses or programs on FAW through the business curriculum include Babson College, Baylor University, Boston College, California Polytechnic University, Calvin College, Chapman University, Cranfield School of Management, DePaul University, Florida International University, George Washington University, Golden Gate University, Gonzaga University, Harvard Business School, John Brown University, Loyola, Miami University in Ohio, Notre Dame University, Ohio State University, Presidio College, Regent University, Santa Clara University, St. Edwards University, St. Mary's University (Canada), St. Thomas University, Seton Hall University, Tuck School of Business at Dartmouth, University of Alabama, University of Chicago Graduate School of Business, University of Massachusetts at Amherst, University of New Haven, University of the Redlands, University of Scranton, University of Southern California, Wake Forest, Wheaton College, and Yale University. See also the Spirit at Work Web site (www.spiritatwork.org).

38. Special issues of peer-reviewed journals include *American Behavioral Scientist*, "The Development of New Paradigm Values, Thinkers, and Business," May 2000; *Chinmaya Management Review*, "Spirituality at Work," June 1999; *Journal of Organization and Change Management*, "Spirituality in Organizations, Part I and Part II," 1999; *Journal of Management Education*, "Spirituality and Management Education," 2000; *Journal of Management Psychology*, "Spirituality and Management," 1994; *Management Education and Development*, "Working with Spirituality in Organizations," 1991. In

addition, a new, dedicated, international, blind-refereed journal, the *Journal of Management, Spirituality and Religion*, launched in 2003 to positive critical review. Finally, see the bibliography for a sample of articles in academic journals on FAW.

39. Many of the more secular centers in the spirituality and business movement intentionally avoid explicit reference to religion. For example, the Robert K. Greenleaf Center for Servant-Leadership (founded by the former AT&T executive) transposes distinctly Christian concepts like Christ as servant into secular analogues for business. Further, other teachers coming more out of Eastern religious traditions or modern repackagings, such as Deepak Chopra, *The Seven Spiritual Laws of Success: A Practical Guide to the Fulfillment of Your Dreams* (San Rafael, Calif.: Amber-Allen, 1994), reject religion's accent on truth claims and special revelation in favor of personal experience and determination. Examples of spiritual but not religious centers include the Center for Meaning and Work; the Forge Institute; the High Tor Alliance; the Chinmaya Institute of Higher Learning; and the Center for Spirit at Work.

40. See the Academy of Management's Management, Spirituality, and Religion (MSR) special-interest group; the International Academy of Business Disciplines' spirituality and organizations track; the Organizational Behavior and Teaching Conference's spirituality stream; and the American Society for Public Administration's initiatives on service, which include spirituality.

41. See the Spirit at Work Web site for sample academic and New Age conferences (www.spiritatwork.org). In addition, numerous local, regional, and national FAW conferences with a more specific Christian orientation are hosted annually by various FAW groups, including the Avodah Institute, CBMC, FGBMFI, CEO Forum, Inter-Varsity's Marketplace Ministry, Laity Lodge Leadership Forum, Navigator's Business & Professional Ministry, Pinnacle Forum, Priority Associates, Seeing Things Whole, the Southern Institute for Business and Professional Ethics, and the Yale Center for Faith & Culture's Ethics and Spirituality in the Workplace program.

42. Mario Diani, "The Concept of Social Movement," *Sociological Review* 40, no. 1 (February 1992): 9.

43. Pete Hammond, one of the long-standing lay leaders in the FAW movement, founded and leads InterVarsity's Marketplace Ministry initiative, aimed at M.B.A. students and businesspeople. Hammond is a frequent speaker and writer on FAW issues. In his unpublished essay, "Some Wonderful North American Stirrings," Hammond proposes organizing FAW activity into six categories: (1) products (books, videos, curricula, periodicals); (2) new ministries (guilds, regional and national ministry organizations, city-specific programs, and issues-driven groups); (3) special events (conferences and seminars); (4) congregational and denominational seminars, peer gatherings, the education industry (networks of Christians in higher education, professional schools, seminars); (5) changing structures (within and across denominations); and (6) new leaders (business authors, clergy, politicians, missionaries, and scholarly leaders). While helpful in its recognition of the variety of forms, it is ultimately insufficient as a means to analyze the substance, content, and theological accents of the movement. Further, it does not address the context and broader felt needs driving the movement. Moreover, Hammond's analysis focuses mostly on evangelical participants and issues, thereby missing mainstream, liberal, and New Age participants.

44. Other possible organizing schemes exist, such as Skelley's three types of spirituality ("Work as Spiritual Practice" 2002), Neal's four gateways (*The Four*

Gateways to the Enlightened Organization, 1999); Wuthnow's three orientations (*Poor Richard's Principle*, 1996); Nash's threefold typology (*Believers in Business*, 1994); Bosch's millennialist framework (*Transforming Mission*, 1990); and H. R. Niebuhr's fivefold typology in *Christ and Culture* (New York: Harper and Row, 1951). While helpful in other contexts, these organizing schemes also prove insufficient to provide insights into the underlying theological and business accents, content, motivators, and social ethics ramifications of the FAW movement. Nor do these models allow for the complex motion within the movement among the various modes of expression and manifestations. Thus, a framework is needed that acknowledges the organizing principle of integrating faith and work, diversity within certain boundaries, and allows for a perichoresis, or movement, between types. I propose such a framework, called the Integration Box, in chapter 7.

45. Examples include the CEO Institute in Dallas; City in Focus in Toronto; Marketplace Network, Inc., in Boston; Needle's Eye Ministry in Richmond, Virginia; and Spirituality at Work in Silicon Valley, California.

46. Examples include Christians in Commerce based in Falls Church, Virginia; Priority Associates based in Orlando, Florida; Spirit at Work based in New Haven, Connecticut; and Woodstock Business Conference based in Washington, D.C.

47. Examples include the FCCI and FGBMFI, which have broad global reaches; and the Trinity Forum, which have expanded into Europe.

48. Examples of FAW groups in professions or industry sectors include Affiliation of Christian Engineers (ACE); Christian Legal Society (CLS); Christian Medical and Dental Association (a society claiming membership of almost 11,000 physicians and dentists); Christian Management Association for leaders of Christian organizations; Fellowship of Christian Peace Officers; Fellowship of Christian Athletes for both amateurs and professionals; Genesis Arts for artists and entertainers; InterMission for actors and entertainers; the Master's Table for the furniture industry; and Nurses' Christian Ministry. See Mike McLoughlin et al., *International Faith & Work Directory* (Cumming, Ga.: Aslan, 2003), for the most complete listing. For another listing of Christian guilds, particularly academic guilds, see InterVarsity Ministry in Daily Life (www.ivmdl.org/dir.academic.cfm).

49. For instance, within the Academy of Management, there is an informal and unofficial group of Christian business professors who meet, discuss topical issues, and seek to influence the direction of their profession. Another example of an informal group within an industry is that organized by Anthony DiMaio, who has facilitated the NYSE (New York Stock Exchange) Bible Study for the several years. More recently, DiMaio launched a new outreach vehicle called IPO—Initial Public Offering: Market Outreach—aimed at seekers and new believers in the financial marketplace.

50. Examples include Christians in Commerce; the International Christian Chamber of Commerce (ICCC; founded by Gunnar Olson, a Swedish industrialist, in 1985); and *The Shepherd's Guide* (a "yellow pages" directory of Christian businesses customized for regional markets, now in more than 125 markets).

51. Examples include Opportunity International and MEDA (two leading Christian micro-lending organizations).

52. I coined the term *faith-friendly* as part of a similarly named CEO event hosted by the Avodah Institute ("Making Your Company Faith-Friendly: A Consultation for Leaders" in April 2002). Many executives see this as analogous to and a logical extension of other corporate policies on being race-friendly, female-friendly, family-

friendly, and gender-orientation friendly. Examples of privately held companies, many of whose founders or owners are Christians, and who strive to foster a faith-friendly atmosphere include Auntie Anne's, Barnhart Crane and Rigging, Beckett Manufacturing, Blistex, Cardone Industries, Chick-fil-A, Container Store, Covenant Transport, CR Trading Post, Flow Automotive, Herr Foods, Interstate Batteries, Reell Precision Manufacturing, Tires Plus, and Tom's of Maine.

53. Examples of publicly traded companies that have informal FAW groups include American Airlines, American Express, Boeing, Coca-Cola, Deloitte, Ford Motor Company, Hewlett Packard, HomeBanc Mortgage Corporation, King Pharmaceuticals, Intel, Microsoft, Texas Instruments, Tyco Electronics, ServiceMaster, Sunovas Bank, 3M, and Tyson Foods, Inc. I worked with Tyson Foods, Inc., to help its leadership design and create a new set of core values, which includes language about striving to be "faith-friendly" and to "honor God," and with Deloitte to help them consider the business value of being faith-friendly.

54. Examples include several of the companies in note 53, as well as Ameritech, Deloitte, Domino's Pizza, Entegris, FedEx, Ford Motor Company, MAC Tools, Motorola, Nortel Networks, Oracle, Southwest Airlines, Timberland, Toro Company, Tyco Electronics, Tyson Foods, Wal-Mart, and Xerox. Even some government agencies are active in the movement. For instance, the Centers for Disease Control (CDC) has an authorized Christian workplace group.

55. Consider what one of the founders of the Christian affinity group at American Express, related in a private e-mail to me on July 2, 2001:

> When we first started our efforts in 1995, the corporate environment here was very dark and not acceptable of Christianity in the workplace. We came up against enormous opposition and persecution, but God was victorious. Most of our criticism came from both the Gay and Lesbian employee community and (what was surprising to us) the Christian employee community. The Gay and Lesbian employees felt we were forming a network to attack their life style and maintain their stereotype of Christians as Bible bashers. The Christian employee community was cynical, because we weren't forming to stand up against the Gay and Lesbian community. In addition, senior management was very concerned over supporting a religious type network, since most of the advice and direction they were given was to avoid these types of networks like the plague. Over the last six years, we have more than silenced our critics. In fact, some of our greatest adversaries have become our strongest supporters. We have close partnerships with all of the other networks here and have made significant strides in senior management's view of the value of faith as an essential part of an employee's work ethics.

56. Steve Hyland, "The Coca-Cola Company Christian Fellowship," paper presented at the International Coalition of Marketplace Ministries, Atlanta, Ga., May 9, 2002.

57. The Coca-Cola statement reads:

> 1) We use the Holy Bible, which is the foundation of this fellowship to teach integrity, accountability, building relationships, respect and diversity, which are all essential to the company's long term success. . . . 2) We

are committed to living, working and supporting these values. We do this by embracing the "Heart and Soul" of our enterprise—Our People. We envision a community where morality is bred, integrity is lived, and diversity is deliberate. 3) We further endeavor to foster a sense of belonging such that each associate feels personally accountable for the consistent quality of every service and product that the Company produces. We believe this will be obtained and maintained through our sincere commitment to serve our customers, associates and above all—our Savior, JESUS CHRIST. (Hyland, "The Coca-Cola Company Christian Fellowship")

58. Hyland, "The Coca-Cola Company Christian Fellowship."

59. With the return of interest in workplace chaplaincy, a professional guild, the National Institute of Business and Industrial Chaplains (NIBIC), has emerged to stress uniform standards, certification, and codes of conduct. Yet even NIBIC is not generally accepted by all workplace chaplains as a fully representative professional association. Indeed, there is no uniform standard or accrediting organization to approve and certify corporate chaplains. Typically, but not necessarily, these chaplains are ordained by denominational bodies. Some work full time as corporate chaplains, but it appears that most do corporate chaplaincy on a part-time basis, while also serving a church.

60. See the Corporate Chaplains of America Web site, www.imchap.org.

61. The main themes emerging from the conference that deserve further research and study include legal considerations, multiculturalism and interfaith considerations, internally versus externally sourced chaplains, relationship to local churches and other religious communities, whether and how to measure the performance and value of a chaplaincy program, and whether and what accreditation standards should be imposed.

62. See www.workandsoul.com.

63. Examples include Tom Cooper's City in Focus ministry in Vancouver, which works full time with a group of business leaders; Joyce Avedisian and David Prescott in Princeton, New Jersey, who keep their corporate position but in their free time conduct research, write, and lead seminars on FAW; and Chip Weiant in Ohio, a former CBMC staffperson, who now is a character and ethics consultant to government, academic, and business officials, using that as a mechanism to infuse Christian principles into leadership positions. I also undertake some advisory work with and provide informal pastoral guidance to several CEOs and senior executives.

64. Examples of such groups include the Avodah Institute, the C12 Group, the Christian Entrepreneurs Organization, Christian Executive Leadership Forum (hosted by BGEA), the CEO Forum, the CEO Institute, Executive Ministries, GLF (Greenwich Leadership Forum), GOLF (Greater Orlando Leadership Foundation), Laity Lodge's Leadership Forum, Pinnacle Forum, Time Out, and aspects of the Yale Center for Faith & Culture's Ethics and Spirituality program.

65. Examples of historically men-only groups include the Christian Business Men's Committee (CBMC) and the Full Gospel Business Men's Fellowship International (FGBMFI). Others, while not explicit, appear to have a de facto orientation toward men. Some, such as CEO Forum, began with male membership but are changing. In many cases, the male leadership orientation is grounded in the parts of the Bible that teach "male headship," patriarchy, and traditional gender roles.

66. Indeed, several founders and FAW group leaders are women. Examples include Julie Cowie (Congruency), Dorie Griggs (Centre for Faith and Journalism), Andria Hall (SpeakEasy M.E.D.I.A., Inc.), Laurie Beth Jones (Jesus CEO Foundation), Judi Neal (Spirit at Work), Whitney Roberson (Spirituality at Work), and Sally Simmel (ELCA).

67. Examples include the Christian Working Woman organization in Wheaton, Illinois, which produces a Web site (www.christianworkingwoman.org), newsletter, conferences, and a radio show; Christian Women Today (a ministry of Campus Crusade for Christ, Canada; www.christianwomentoday.com), which has a special section on working women); and *Today's Christian Woman* magazine ("dedicated to Godly women! Each issue of *Today's Christian Woman* magazine is loaded with inspiring and uplifting stories that will bring you great encouragement").

68. Para-church ministry examples include InterVarsity (sponsors Marketplace Ministry, which serves as a resource to businesspeople of all levels; it also has a related group called InterVarsity MBA Ministry, which focuses on business majors and M.B.A. students, employing more than twenty-five representatives at some of the nation's best M.B.A. campuses, providing discipleship, support, and evangelism and teaching students that the Gospel is relevant to the business world); Campus Crusade for Christ (sponsors an evangelizing and fellowship ministry for young professionals called Priority Associates and an evangelizing ministry aimed at business leaders and influencers called Executive Ministries); Youth with a Mission (YWAM; which has a business and marketplace ministry through an organization called Scruples, founded and led by Mike McLoughlin in Canada); and Navigators (with roots tracing back to the 1930s, it now has a Business and Professional Ministries Division, which seeks to equip business leaders to integrate their faith and work).

69. For example, Fellowship of Companies for Christ International, Priority Associates, and Executive Ministries.

70. For example, Spirit at Work.

71. For example, FaithWorks, National Workrights Institute, and Worklife Institute.

72. For instance, Legatus (founded by Tom Monaghan, former owner of Domino's Pizza) aims at Catholic CEOs and senior executives. Legatus now has chapters in several states, each of which has an assigned priest. Another Catholic FAW group, Woodstock Business Conference, also founded and led by a layman, a former lawyer, has Jesuit roots and is based in Georgetown. Woodstock now has more than a dozen city-based chapters. Aimed at Catholics, usually at middle and upper management levels, Woodstock blends contemplation, Bible study, and ethical application in their meetings. Finally, the sometimes-controversial group Opus Dei may arguably be seen as part of the movement. Founded in 1928, it is a personal prelature of the Catholic church. Opus Dei's Web site states the mission of "finding God in Work and Daily Life." I choose not to treat it here in further detail, as its accent on secrecy stands outside the movement's general characteristics of openness and accessibility by and to all.

73. Examples include the National Center for the Laity in Chicago and Gregory Pierce's Faith and Work in Cyberspace, which focuses on conversations related to spiritual practices in the workplace.

74. Examples include Wally Kroeker, *God's Week Has 7 Days: Monday Musings for Marketplace Christians* (Waterloo, Ontario: Herald, 1998); Ben Sprunger, Carol J. Suter, and Wally Kroeker, *Faith Dilemmas for Marketplace Christians: A Resource for*

Small Groups (Scottdale, Penn.: Herald, 1997); and the long-standing bimonthly Mennonite magazine *Marketplace*.

75. In California, Menlo Park Presbyterian Church hired former senior business executive Katherine Leary in 2001 as director of Marketplace Ministries. There she sought to explore the ministry of spirituality and work and to develop programs that address the issues that face both Christians and non-Christians at work. Redeemer Presbyterian Church in New York City recently hired her away to build and lead a similar program, Center for Faith & Work. In San Antonio Texas, St. Mark's Episcopal Church, under the leadership of John Lewis, lawyer turned theologian and priest, has founded the Center for Faith in the Workplace with a vision for "every work environment to become a place of spiritual life, where people discover meaning in the fruitfulness of their work and find wholeness in their work relationships" (see the center's promotional brochure). Another example is Workplace Ministries, directed by lay leader Sherri Adams at Christ Church of Oak Brook in Illinois. Adams's ministry has a three-pronged approach that includes an employment assistance program, a Faith@Work program accenting integration and practical issues, and Nehemiah Ministry, which is an intensive year-long study program to equip Christian men and women to be servant-leaders for Christ in the workplace. See chapter 5 for examples of other churches experimenting with lay-led FAW ministry programs. One of the prototypes of these wave three church-based, lay-led FAW groups was Bill Diehl's church group, the Monday Connection. Since 1985, members of his church have been meeting over breakfast once a month to listen to one person present a "case study" of a real business dilemma. As a community, the group discusses the problem, drawing on biblical teachings, reason, prayer, and business experience to help the person resolve the problem (Diehl, *The Monday Connection*).

76. Examples include the Reverend John Mason's Wall Street Ministry at Redeemer Presbyterian Church (PCA) in New York City; the Reverend Mark D. Hostetter at First Presbyterian Church (PCUSA) in New York City, who is the associate pastor for stewardship and mission to the corporate world; and the Reverend Whitney Roberson in the Episcopal Diocese of California, who is director of Spirituality at Work in San Francisco.

77. Examples that fall into this type include groups such as Spirit in Business Inc., the Association for Spirit at Work, and the International Conference on Business and Consciousness.

78. As noted earlier, one of AAR's few engagements with the FAW movement occurred at the 2002 annual meeting. Notably, several of the presenters were members of AOM's Management, Spirituality, and Religion special interest group, including business scholar André Delbecq, who gave one of the primary papers.

79. Typically, these scholars are in Christian colleges and universities, such as Baylor University, John Brown University, Calvin College, Dordt College, Eastern College, Loyola, Notre Dame, Santa Clara University, and Wheaton College. See also Alan Wolfe, "The Opening of the Evangelical Mind," *Atlantic Monthly*, October 2000.

80. Francis P. McHugh, *Keyguide to Information Sources in Business Ethics* (London: Mansell Nichols, 1988).

81. Peter Drucker, "Ethical Chic," *Public Interest*, no. 16 (Spring 1981): 18–36.

82. Bruce Rosenstein, "Scandals Nothing New to Business Guru: A Conversation with Peter Drucker," *USA Today*, July 5, 2002, 8B.

83. Milton Friedman, "The Social Responsibility of Business Is to Increase Its Profits," *New York Times Magazine*, September 13, 1970, 32–33.

84. Patrick E. Murphy, *Eighty Exemplary Ethics Statements* (Notre Dame, Ind.: University of Notre Dame Press, 1998).

85. Judi Neal and Joel Bennett, "Examining Multi-Level or Holistic Spiritual Phenomena in the Workplace," *Academy of Management: Management, Spirituality and Religion Newsletter* (Briarcliff Manor, N.Y.: MSR SIG, Winter 2000): 1.

86. Neal and Bennett, "Holistic Spiritual Phenomena in the Workplace," 1.

87. Neal, "Spirituality in the Workplace."

88. Laura L. Nash and Scotty McLennan, *Church on Sunday, Work on Monday: The Challenge of Fusing Christian Values with Business Life* (San Francisco, Calif.: Jossey-Bass, 2001), xxiv.

89. For example, Ken Blanchard, Jim Collins, Jay Conger, Stephen Covey, Peter Drucker, Elizabeth Denton, Charles Handy, Willis Harman, John Maxwell, Peter Vaill, and Margaret Wheatley.

90. Examples of hardcopy FAW newsletters include *Ethix*, aimed at business, technology, and ethics; *Woodstock Business Conference Report: Affirming the Relevance of Religious Faith to Business Practice*; *Connexion*, published by the Forum for Faith in the Workplace in Columbus; *Vocatio*, published by Regent College in Vancouver; and *LayNet*, published by the Coalition for Ministry in Daily Life. *LayNet* was one of the first newsletters of wave three, emerging in 1991, following the Catholic-based *Initiatives: In Support of the Christian in the World*, a long-standing newsletter produced by the National Center for the Laity. Another newsletter is *Ministry of Money*, published by an FAW group of the same name that focuses on growth in financial discipleship, compassion for the poor, and global stewardship.

91. For instance, Os Hillman of Marketplace Leaders in Atlanta has one of the largest daily e-mail newsletters, "TGIF: Today God Is First," which claims a membership list of 60,000. Hillman, a businessman, has written extensively on FAW matters (including *Today, God Is First* [Shippensburg, Pa.: Destiny Image, 2000] and *The 9 to 5 Window* [Ventura, Calif.: Regal, 2005]). Other FAW groups that publish electronic newsletters include the Avodah Institute (www.AvodahInstitute.com) with more than two thousand subscribers in 2003, and Marketplace Network in Boston (www.marketplace-network.org), which has more than six hundred members. Other large and well-read electronic newsletters include the *Scruples* newsletter (www.scruples.org), founded by Mike McLoughlin in Canada; *His Church at Work* (www.workplaceministry.org), developed by Doug Spada, and one produced by Laurie Beth Jones (www.lauriebethjones.com), bestselling author of popular books on Jesus as a management role model (*Jesus CEO* [New York: Hyperion, 1995], *The Path* [New York: Hyperion, 1996], and *Jesus, Inc.* [New York: Crown Business, 2001]). Older FAW organizations like CBMC (www.cbmc.com) and FGBMFI (www.fgbmfi.org) also have newsletters with large readerships, spanning many countries. FAW newsletters are not limited to Christian groups alone. For instance, Judi Neal's *Spirit at Work* newsletter, based in New Haven, has a large readership, particularly in the academic community and those interested in non-Christian conceptions of spirituality at work. A final example is the e-newsletter published by the Yale Center for Faith & Culture, that has over 8,000 subscribers who are a mixture of marketplace practitioners, clergy, and academics.

92. For example, TheHighCalling sends daily devotional messages from Eugene Peterson (*Praying with the Early Christians: A Year of Daily Prayers and Reflections on the Words of the Early Christians* [San Francisco: HarperCollins, 1994]). Another example is Os Hillman's daily e-mail message taken from his book, Hillman, *TGIF: Today God Is First* (2000).

93. For instance, Scruples has chat-room discussion topics of faith at work, spirituality in the workplace, table talk for marketplace Christians, prayer for people at work in the marketplace, small business forum, business and mission, ethics in business, enterprise and community development, ministry in the marketplace, and equipping events. The Web site www.theHighCalling.com has thematic chat rooms and threaded discussions designed to encourage conversation, support, and encouragement. Topics include career moves, downsizing, responsibility, family, prayer for people at work, business ethics, biblical business principles, business and mission, community development, faith at work, and spirituality in the workplace.

94. Gregory F. Pierce is a lay Catholic leader, head of a publishing business, and author of *Spirituality @ Work: 10 Ways to Balance Your Life On-the-Job* (Chicago: Loyola Press, 2001).

95. Examples include *Business Reform: Real Business Questions, Real Biblical Answers*; *The Cambridge Papers: Towards a Biblical Mind*; *Christian Business Men*; *Faith in Business Quarterly*; *Life @ Work Journal: Blending Biblical Wisdom with Business Excellence*; *The Marketplace: MEDA's Magazine for Christians in Business*; *Prism*; *Radix*; *Vocatio*; *Women at Work*; and *The Works: Your Source for Being Fully Alive*.

96. Note: *Faith at Work* magazine, published by Faith at Work in Virginia, is perhaps the oldest extant FAW magazine, tracing its roots to waves one and two with Samuel Shoemaker. Whereas *Marketplace* focuses on practical applications of Christian life in business, *Faith at Work*, under its recent leadership, has focused on contemplative practices and inner reflection on holistic living, in light of one's work, family, and faith.

97. The *Life @ Work Journal* designed each issue around a particular theme, including topics such as ethics, vocation, success, failure, rest, money, ambition, and relationships. Though no longer published, it helped to demonstrate a market for quality production and writing for Christians in the FAW movement. It failed not due to lack of demand or paid subscribers but due to its business model that precluded advertising revenue. Other FAW magazines that have come and gone include *Christian Businessman*; *Faith Works*; *Sunday/Monday Woman*; *Women at Work*; and *Vocatio*.

98. Notably, the theologically more conservative *Christianity Today* occasionally has written about some of the demand-side issues in the FAW movement, but it has not recognized the FAW movement qua movement. The closest connection occurred as part of a cover story called "The Higher Self Gets Down to Business" (February 2003), an inquiry into "New Age spirituality in business," including articles on "The Profit of God: Finding the Christian Path in Business"; "Utopia or Kingdom Come"; "Prosperity Conscious"; and "Bad Company Corrupts." The theologically more liberal *Christian Century* had its own recent cover story entitled "The Market: What Does God Have to Do with It?" (*Christian Century*, March 27–April 3, 2002). In contrast to the *Christianity Today* feature, the two articles in the *Christian Century* issue made no mention of the FAW movement qua movement, nor of the demand-side factors

fueling the movement. Rather, the two articles were favorable reviews of two new books that were critical of democratic capitalism. The closest *Christian Century* has come to recognizing the FAW movement was in "High-Tech Quest: Finding God in Silicon Valley" (August 1–8, 2001).

99. Diani, "Concept of Social Movement," 8.

100. Diani, "Concept of Social Movement," 12.

101. Diani, "Concept of Social Movement," 8.

102. Diani, "Concept of Social Movement," 9.

CHAPTER 7

1. I have presented the Integration Box framework and language to several individual businesspeople, corporate conferences, and administered a program based on it to two large, publicly traded corporations to test the validity of the theory and the practicality of the concept among businesspeople. The visualization of the theory via a diagram proved helpful. Without exception, people respond very positively to the language and framework, feeling it accurately captures the phenomenon as well as providing neutral language to discuss it.

2. While beyond the scope of the current volume, a question meriting further research is whether a correlation exists between Jungian-based personality types and Integration Box types and other variables that influence one's predisposition to a certain quadrant. The corollary question would also merit further study: does one's Myers-Briggs evaluation serve as a reliable predictor of which Integration Box quadrant a person is likely to be in?

3. As part of my field testing with two corporations to validate the Integration Box framework and language, I developed and administered instruments for people to self-assess their dominant quadrant or manifestation of integrating faith and work. The instrument also revealed their secondary style, and whether they stayed mostly in their primary quadrant or whether they moved between quadrants, based on circumstances and context. The experiments strongly validated the theory and praxis of the framework and language, allowing people to develop greater self-awareness and affirmation, freedom to consider other manifestations of integrating faith and work, and new respect for other types of integration that were alien to them.

4. This is similar to personality testing and typologies, where people are deemed to have a primary and a secondary type.

5. In one corporate setting where I tested the Integration Box concept, about 60 percent of the participants identified themselves as being in the ET quadrant as their dominant type. It remains unclear if this is representative of a national profile, or if other factors biased the outcome (e.g., Were there flaws in the test instrument? Is the language of "ethics" still more accessible to laypeople than other quadrant labels? Did the current climate of corporate governance scandals affect the focus? Was the culture of this company different than others?). These and other questions merit further research.

6. Max L. Stackhouse, Dennis P. McCann, and Shirley Roels, *On Moral Business* (Grand Rapids, Mich.: Eerdmans, 1995).

7. H. Richard Niebuhr, *The Responsible Self: An Essay in Christian Moral Philosophy* (San Francisco, Calif.: Harper & Row, 1963).

8. Examples include refusing to pay an import bribe in a foreign country, which may result in the loss of jobs in one's domestic plant; refusing to pay protection money for your plant and equipment, which may result in sabotage and costly damage; closing a plant in a one-factory town, which may devastate that community while providing fresh life for another community receiving the plant; and testing new pharmaceutical drugs on humans, which risks endangering lives in the short term while potentially saving lives in the long term.

9. Dietrich Bonhoeffer, *Ethics* (New York: Macmillan, 1986), 249.

10. For instance, the group Workplace Spirituality (www.workplacespirituality .com) addresses how spirituality affects business ethics and decision making. Business Executives for Economic Justice (BEEJ) is an organization

> founded by Catholic business people committed to integrating Christian values in their business practice. Members of BEEJ believe the Christian Tradition, particularly Catholic social teaching, contributes in significant ways to our evaluation, judgment and action in the marketplace. (www.crossroads-center.org)

Other examples include IBTE (Institute for Business, Technology & Ethics), whose mission is to transform business by advancing technology and ethical values (www.ethix.org); ESA (Evangelicals for Social Action), which seeks to "challenge and equip the church to be agents of God's redemption and transformation in the world" (www.esa-online.org); the Council for Ethics in Economics, which has a secular orientation but in which many Christian business leaders are active (www .businessethics.org); and the Woodstock Business Conference, a Catholic-based group that has formed nineteen city-based chapters as part of its "international program that brings business leaders together in monthly meetings to integrate faith, family, and business life, and to bring Judeo-Christian values to the marketplace" (www.georgetown.edu/centers/woodstock/wbc.htm).

11. Examples of ET groups with this accent include many company affinity groups and larger intercompany organizations, such as Connecting Business Men to Christ, CEO Forum, Christians in Commerce, and the Woodstock Business Conference.

12. Examples of ET groups with this accent include many company affinity groups, such as SALT, the Christian Employee Network group at American Express, the 3M Christian employee group, and FIN (Ford Interfaith Network), as well as noncompany groups, such as Legatus, the C12 Group, Christian Entrepreneur Organization, Spirituality at Work, and the Institute for Servant Leadership.

13. Examples of ET groups with this accent include the Southern Institute for Business and Professional Ethics and the Caux Roundtable.

14. See Ethical Leadership Group (www.ethicalleadershipgroup.com), a for-profit organization grounded in Christian principles but providing secular consulting for organizations interested in strengthening ethical leadership; Ethicom (www.ethi.com), a secular consulting business that draws explicitly on Christian principles; and Di Frances & Associates (www.difrances.com), providing Christian-based consulting to secular corporations and leaders.

15. Servant leadership is a popular and effective concept taught by many Christian FAW groups and secular groups with Christian foundations, including Servant-Leader Associates (www.servant-leaderassociates.com); the Greenleaf Center for Servant-Leadership (www.greenleaf.org), which approaches principles and practices of servant leadership from a secular perspective that is spirituality infused; and the Institute for Servant Leadership (www.servleader.org), an Episcopalian-based organization that "provide[s] opportunities for the spiritual formation and leadership development of people who are called to be servant leaders." Former academic turned consultant Ken Blanchard writes popular management books that fit in this ET type: Ken Blanchard and Phil Hodges, *Servant Leader* (Nashville: J. Countryman, 2003); and Ken Blanchard and Phil Hodges, *Lead Like Jesus: Lessons from the Greatest Leadership Role Model of All Time* (Nashville: W Publishing Group, 2006).

16. See the Southern Institute Web site (www.southerninstitute.org).

17. Examples include corporate governance after Enron; leading with values; the problem of privacy: how technology is raising new ethical issues for business, consumers, and employers; strategic morality and corporate reputation; and building a great place to work.

18. For instance, the EV quadrant contains groups such as FGBMFI (Full Gospel Business Men's Fellowship International) and FCCI (Fellowship of Companies for Christ International). In addition, many newer groups were founded during wave three, such as Priority Associates (www.iPriority.com), a division of Campus Crusade for Christ, which targets young professionals. Another EV group, albeit aimed more at senior executives, is the Center for FaithWalk Leadership (www.faithwalkleadership .com), founded by popular management consultant and author Ken Blanchard. While both Priority Associates and FaithWalk address issues found in the other types, their primary focus is often evangelizing and witnessing to Christ in the marketplace.

19. For example, CBMC (Connecting Business Men to Christ), formerly known as the Christian Business Men's Committee (see chapter 3). CBMC has retained its historic focus on evangelization, as shown by the mission statement: "to present Jesus Christ as Lord and Savior to business and professional men, and to develop men to carry out the Great Commission" (www.cbmc.com). While CBMC provides a range of resources that touch on other aspects of the Four E's, its primary focus is to use the business world as a venue to evangelize. CBMC provides resources and tools for seekers and new Christians, such as study texts (e.g., *Operation Timothy*), videotapes (e.g., *Evangelism as a Lifestyle* and *Discipleship as a Lifestyle*), and conferences.

20. This analysis was offered by an American executive, originally affiliated with Campus Crusade for Christ, who has lived in and been doing business in China for fifteen years.

21. Executive Ministries brochure.

22. Executive Ministries brochure.

23. Robin Stauffer Skur, "Look Who's Coming to Dinner," *Worldwide Challenge* (Orlando, Fla.), May–June 1996, 37.

24. Executive Ministries brochure.

25. Executive Ministries brochure.

26. Michael Wolf, Bruce Friedman, and Daniel Sutherland, *Religion in the Workplace: A Comprehensive Guide to Legal Rights and Responsibilities* (Chicago: American Bar Association Publishing, 1998).

27. Some recent writings have sought to redress this perception, including Michael Novak, *Business as a Calling* (New York: Free Press, 1996); Stackhouse, McCann, and Roels, *On Moral Business*; Gordon R. Preece, "Business as a Calling and Profession," in *Christianity and Entrepreneurship*, by Gordon R. Preece and Samuel J. Gregg (Grand Rapids Mich.: The Acton Institute, 1999); and Lake Lambert, "Called to Business: Corporate Management as a Profession of Faith" (Ph.D. diss., Princeton Theological Seminary, 1997).

28. Daniel J. Levinson, *The Seasons of a Man's Life* (New York: Ballantine, 1978).

29. Groups such as Navigators' Business & Professional Ministry host retreats and offer workshops designed to help people, particularly those in the business community, consider the nature and form of their calling. Forum for Faith in the Workplace is a Christian association whose mission is "to enrich the lives of individuals and institutions by helping people everywhere discover the presence and will of God in their places of work." FaithWorks, founded in 1998 by Bob Buford, successful businessman and author of *Halftime* (Grand Rapids, Mich.: Zondervan, 1994), is a Christ-centered program that helps committed Christian business leaders move "from success to significance." Through a structured method of biblical reflection and inquiry, FaithWorks helps business leaders to discover their gifts and passions, often linking them with social entrepreneurs to partner on good works and "bear much fruit for the Kingdom" (www.faithworks.net).

30. See www.listeninghearts.ang-md.org.

31. Suzanne G. Farnham, ed., *Listening Hearts: Discerning Call in Community* (Harrisburg, Pa.: Morehouse, 1991).

32. See www.listeninghearts.ang-md.org.

33. One such group, the Forge Institute, is a professional association of "transtraditional teachers and leaders" whose mission is to foster a "renaissance of spiritual wisdom in our pluralistic world" (www.theforge.org). In defining *spiritual wisdom*, the group notes that "there are many valid paths and no one of them, even our own, is the only true way" (www.theforge.org), thereby stating a truth claim while appearing to reject the claims of others who assert their own truth claims (e.g., there is only one true way to know God).

34. For example, Legatus is a Catholic FAW group for business executives with chapters in more than fifteen cities. Each chapter meeting opens with a prayer, a reading of Scripture, and a five-minute period of silent reflection prior to discussion. A group with Episcopal roots, the Shalem Institute for Spiritual Transformation (www .shalem.org), sponsors a program called the "Soul of the Executive," which focuses on personal renewal, contemplative spiritual traditions, and the fellowship of other executives. The word *shalem*, related to *shalom*, speaks of wholeness, and the institute seeks to help business leaders find wholeness in all aspects of their lives. In addition, the aforementioned Listening Hearts Ministry, while focusing on calling and vocation, uses contemplation and silence as key parts of the discernment process.

35. One example of this manifestation is CEO (Christ's Exceeding Opportunities) Ministries, which is unabashed prosperity gospel, full of promises of anointing and financial blessing (www.ceoministries.org). The founder, Ann Bandini, authored the book *Prayer Strategy: God's Provocative Plan for Wealth* (Irvine, Calif.: CEO/Christ's Exceeding Opportunities, 2000). Other FAW groups may be subtler, but the hint of financial reward can often be found. For instance, the work of Os Hillman may well be located here, with its linkage of faith and wealth, as well as the popularized

"Jesus-as-CEO" model (e.g., Jones, *Jesus CEO* [New York: Hyperion, 1995]) that accents the practical nature of Jesus' leadership style as a model for modern business success.

36. Deepak Chopra is one example of a New Age and secular spiritual leader, whose bestselling *The Seven Spiritual Laws of Success: A Practical Guide to the Fulfillment of Your Dreams* (San Rafael, Calif.: Amber-Allen, 1994) strongly suggests that obeying spiritual laws leads to material success. He runs conferences, retreats, and consulting services promising and promoting inner peace and financial reward.

37. Andrew Ferguson, "Founding Documents" (unpublished paper, April 2, 2001, photocopied).

38. Another example of this type, having an even stronger New Age orientation, is the International Conference on Business and Consciousness (www.bizspirit.com). This was one of the first gatherings, and remains one of the premier events, for the New Age and generic spirituality branch of the FAW movement. Attendees pay conference fees of more than $1,000 for the three-day event. From eighty-four attendees at the inaugural conference in 1995 in Mexico, the annual conference is now hosted in Santa Fe, New Mexico, and regularly attracts more than five hundred people. Speakers and participants are largely from the consciousness and human potential movement who are seeking personal transformation and success in their work. Many business consultants and spiritual advisors attend. Notably, a review of the past eight annual Business and Consciousness conferences reveals a distinct absence of speakers, writers, or theologians coming from Christianity or other orthodox monotheistic religions. Indeed, despite claims of openness to spirit and the virtues of tolerance, there is an ironic implied disapproval of and prejudice against religionists as being close-minded and rigid.

39. Examples of groups moving between and among more than one type include the Acton Institute (ET and EX); Center for FaithWalk Leadership (EV, ET, and EX); Coalition for Ministry in Daily Life (ET and EX); Forum for Faith in the Workplace (ET, EX, and EN); Jesus CEO Foundation (ET, EN, and EX); Legatus (ET and EN); Southern Institute for Business and Professional Ethics (ET and EN); TGIF: Today God Is First (EV, EX, and EN); Woodstock Business Conference (ET, EX, and EN); and Trinity Forum (EN and EX).

40. Examples of groups and organizations moving among all four types include the Avodah Institute; BLSN (Business Leadership and Spirituality Network); the *Business Reform* journal; the C12 Group; the CEO Forum; Laity Lodge; *Life @ Work Journal*; Marketplace Network; MEDA (Mennonite Economic Development Associates); and the Yale Center for Faith & Culture's Ethics and Spirituality in the Workplace program.

41. Originally know as the Layman's Institute in the 1950s, this group sponsored layman's crusades in conjunction with Billy Graham. The direction shifted from evangelism to helping people to understand lay ministry in daily life and hosting events called the Layman's Leadership Institute. Laity Lodge was founded in 1961. Keith Miller, Bill Mead, and Fred Smith assisted Howard E. Butt, Jr., in the early days of this lay ministry, which for Southern Baptist culture was in many ways very bold and ahead of its times. This commitment to lay ministry led to the North American Lay Congress in 1978 and many other FAW events and programs. See Butt, *At the Edge of Hope: Christian Laity in Paradox* (New York: Seabury, 1978); and Bruce McIver, *Riding the Wind of God: A Personal History of the Youth Revival Movement* (Macon, Ga.: Smyth & Helwys, 2002).

42. H. E. Butt, from the 1999 Leadership Forum invitation letter.

43. David McQuiston, "CEO Forum Activities" (unpublished paper, October 2002).

44. McQuiston, "CEO Forum Activities."

45. For instance, at one corporate testing of the Integration Box framework, a woman said:

> I am clearly an EN type. I find my day is not right if I have not started off with my private devotional time of prayer and Bible study. However, it is precisely that private time that enables me to have public strength and courage to take strong ethical stands on difficult issues. Were it not for my inner EN orientation, I could not do the outer ET things that people see.

Similarly, an EV person noted that having a personal relationship with God was prior to and necessary for finding meaning and purpose (EX) in what otherwise might seem like an empty job.

CHAPTER 8

1. For example, I teach a new course at Yale Divinity School designed for future clergy who do not have a marketplace background. The course is entitled, "A Theology and Praxis of Ministering to the Workplace: Overcoming the Sunday-Monday Gap."

2. For example, work as vocation, business as a calling, meaningful work in postmodernism's crisis of meaninglessness, workplace as community, social justice in global companies, entrepreneurialism as creative act, theologically informed business ethics, marketplace as ministry, economics as stewardship, technology as an iron cage and a liberating force, materiality versus materialism, business as mission field, pastoral nurture of businesspeople, integrity in unethical contexts, and the gathered church in support of the scattered church.

3. For example, the Acton Institute and the Trinity Forum have developed extensive curricula and course content, and they and groups like the Avodah Institute (now subsumed into the Yale Center for Faith & Culture's Ethics and Spirituality in the Workplace program; it continues as part of my work as the center's executive director) and the CEO Forum have extensive networks of business leaders.

4. Stephen Hart and David A. Krueger, "Faith and Work: Challenges for Congregations," *Christian Century* (July 15–22, 1992): 685.

5. Many of these ideas, while implemented at the local church, may be transferable to FAW-related initiatives of denominational bodies.

6. Hart and Krueger have suggested four things that "congregations could do to strengthen the interactions between faith and work." They recommend: (1) work issues and concerns should be addressed more frequently and deeply within the life of the congregations, (2) clergy must work harder to be perceived as resources for members struggling to relate faith and work, (3) awareness of the distinctive theological and ethical resources of one's faith tradition be developed, and (4) discipleship and accountability of members be supported and stressed ("Faith and Work").

7. This can easily be accomplished by visits to their office for lunch or coffee, requests for a tour of their facility, and general inquiries about the nature of the goods or services generated by the organization.

8. Hart and Krueger, "Faith and Work," 684.

9. Hart and Krueger, "Faith and Work," 685.

10. Sermons given by the Reverend Dr. Tom Tewell, formerly senior pastor of Fifth Avenue Presbyterian Church in New York.

11. I see further criteria for evaluation and research that would draw on several factors, including the extent to which the group or mode of expression is (a) oriented outwardly to the life of the church scattered (as opposed to an inward orientation to the life of the church gathered), (b) effective in establishing and sustaining vibrant organizational and institutional structures, (c) attentive to inner personal issues of meaning, purpose, calling, salvation, and ethical behavior in work, (d) focused outwardly on broader structural and ethical issues of business institutions and the marketplace, and (e) providing an accent on personal and institutional transformation to approach and more closely resemble the kingdom of God on earth.

12. Hart and Krueger found, "The high level of integration among Evangelical Covenant members constitute[s] a challenge to mainline Protestants, Catholics and Jews: they show that a much higher level of integration is possible" ("Faith and Work," 684–685).

13. Marc Gunther, "God and Business: The Surprising Quest for Spiritual Renewal in the American Workplace." *Fortune*, July 9, 2001, 61.

SELECTED BIBLIOGRAPHY

Abu-Nasr, Donna. "Company Chaplains: New Trend in Workplace." *Associated Press*, February 3, 1997.

Ackers, Peter, and Diane Preston. "Born Again? The Ethics and Efficacy of the Conversion Experience in Contemporary Management Development." *Journal of Management Studies* 34, no. 5 (September 1997): 677–701.

Adams, Helen Colwell. "Ministry Bridges Gap between the Almighty, Quest for Almighty Dollar." *Lancaster* (Pa.) *Sunday News*, November 14, 1999.

Adams, Susan. "God Is His Business Planner." *Forbes*, July 27, 1998, 90–91.

———. "Renaissance Man." *Forbes*, December 27, 1999, 166–167.

Akst, Daniel. "When Business Gets Religion." *New York Times*, October 4, 1998.

Alderson, Jeremy. "A Matter of Faith." *Meetings & Conventions*, June 2001.

Alexander, Susanne. "Spirituality." *Newsweek Japan*, September 9, 2001.

Alford, Helen J., and Michael Naughton. *Managing as If Faith Mattered: Christian Social Principles in the Modern Organization*. Notre Dame, Ind.: University of Notre Dame Press, 2001.

Anderson, James D., and Ezra Earl Jones. *Ministry of the Laity*. San Francisco, Calif.: Harper & Row, 1986.

Antczak, Marianne. "Attending to the Grief Associated with Involuntary Job Loss." *Journal of Pastoral Care* 53, no. 4 (Winter 2000): 447–4460.

Armour, Stephanie. "Chaplains-for-Hire Provide Services in Workplaces." *USA Today*, November 14, 1997.

Atlas, Riva D. "What's An Aging 'Barbarian' to Do?" *New York Times*, August 26, 2001.

Ayres, Francis O. *The Ministry of the Laity: A Biblical Exposition*. Philadelphia: Westminster, 1962.

Bader, Scott. "Ethics More Important than Money." *Financial Times* (London), August 22, 2000.

Baker, Sandra. "Faith at Work." *Ft. Worth Star-Telegram*, September 7, 1998.

Balzar, John. "Exploring Spiritual Approach to Business-World Challenges." *Los Angeles Times*, December 17, 1996.

Bandini, Ann. *Prayer Strategy: God's Provocative Plan for Wealth.* Irvine, Calif.: Christ's Exceeding Opportunities, 2000.

Banks, Robert. *Faith Goes to Work: Reflections from the Marketplace.* Washington, D.C.: Alban Institute, 1993.

———. *God the Worker: Journeys into the Heart, Mind, and Imagination of God.* Valley Forge, Pa.: Judson, 1994.

———. "The Protestant Work Ethic." *Faith in Business Quarterly* 2, no. 2 (1998): 5–7.

Banks, Robert, and Kimberly Powell, eds. *Faith in Leadership: How Leaders Live Out Their Faith in Their Work and Why It Matters.* San Francisco, Calif.: Jossey-Bass, 2000.

Banks, Robert, and R. Paul Stevens, eds. *The Complete Book of Everyday Christianity: An Every Day Guide to Following Christ in Every Aspect of Life.* Downers Grove, Ill.: InterVarsity, 1997.

Barton, Bruce. *The Man Nobody Knows.* Indianapolis, Ind.: Bobbs-Merrill, 1924.

Beckett, John D. *Loving Monday: Succeeding in Business without Selling Your Soul.* Downers Grove, Ill.: InterVarsity, 1998.

Beideman, Don. "At This Company, Latest Perk Is an On-Site Ministry." *Philadelphia Inquirer,* February 20, 1997.

Bellinger, Cindy. "New Spirit in the Workplace." *Crosswinds Weekly,* March 15–22, 2001.

Belluck, Pam. "Drivers Find New Service at Truck Stops: Old-Time Religion." *New York Times,* February 1, 1998.

Belsie, Laurent. "Businesses That Build Foundations on Faith." *Christian Science Monitor,* January 24, 2000.

Bennett, Brad. "Free to Pray as the Spirit Moves Me." *Miami Herald,* November 11, 2001.

Berger, Peter L. *The Capitalist Revolution: Fifty Propositions about Prosperity, Equality, & Liberty.* New York: Basic, 1986.

———. *Pyramids of Sacrifice: Political Ethics and Social Change.* New York: Basic, 1975.

Biber, Rick. E-mail to David W. Miller, July 2, 2001.

Bird, Kay. "Bringing Spirituality into the Workplace." *Reporter* (Santa Fe, N.M.), December 1994.

Blanchard, Ken, and Bill Hybels. *Leadership by the Book.* New York: William Morrow and Company, 1999.

Blanchard, Ken, and Phil Hodges. *Lead Like Jesus: Lessons from the Greatest Leadership Role Model of All Time.* Nashville, Tenn.: W Publishing Group, 2006.

———. *Servant Leader.* Nashville, Tenn.: J. Countryman, 2003.

Blomberg, Craig L. *Heart, Soul, and Money: A Christian View of Possessions.* Joplin, Mo.: College Press Publishing, 2000.

———. *Neither Poverty nor Riches: A Biblical Theology of Material Possessions.* Grand Rapids, Mich.: Eerdmans, 1999.

Boggs, Wade H. *All Ye Who Labor: A Christian Interpretation of Daily Work.* Richmond, Va.: John Knox, 1961.

Bokhari, Farhan. "Put Your Faith in the Internet." *Financial Times* (London), August 30, 2000.

Bonhoeffer, Dietrich. *Ethics.* New York: Macmillan, 1986.

Bosch, David J. *Transforming Mission: Paradigm Shifts in Theology of Mission.* Maryknoll, N.Y.: Orbis, 1991.

Boyce, Joseph N. "Leaps of Faith: More People Join Clergy after First Pursuing a Career in Business." *Wall Street Journal,* August 9, 1995.

Brandt, Ellen. "Corporate Pioneers Explore Spirituality." *HR Magazine* 41, no. 4 (April 1996): 82–87.

Bratt, James D. "God & Mammon, Inc." Review of *The Fourth Great Awakening and the Future of Egalitarianism*, by Robert William Fogel. *Books & Culture* 7, no. 2 (March–April 2001): 6.

Breuer, Nancy L. "When Workers Seek Pastoral Advice—How Will You Answer Them?" *Workforce* 76, no. 4 (April 1997): 44–51.

Briggs, D. "Serving the Ultimate Boss." *Plain Dealer* (Cleveland, Ohio), December 25, 2000.

Briner, Bob. *Roaring Lambs: A Gentle Plan to Radically Change Our World*. Grand Rapids, Mich.: Zondervan, 1993.

Briskin, Alan, and Cheryl Peppers. "Soul and Work: Back to the Future." *Journal for Quality and Participation* 24, no. 1 (Spring 2001): 6–14.

Broadway, Bill. "Good for the Soul—and the Bottom Line." *The Washington Post* (Washington, D.C.), August 16, 2001.

———. "Putting Soul in the Workplace." *Washington Post*, September 7, 2001.

Brooks, David. *Bobos in Paradise: The New Upper Class and How They Got There*. New York: Simon & Schuster, 2000.

Browning, Don S. *Religious Ethics and Pastoral Care*. Philadelphia: Fortress, 1983.

Bruzzese, Anita. "Chaplain Adds Presence to Workplace." *Gannett*, July 24, 1997.

———. "Divine Intervention." *Human Resource Executive*, May 20, 1997.

Budde, Michael L., and Robert W. Brimlow. *Christianity Incorporated: How Big Business Is Buying the Church*. Grand Rapids, Mich.: Brazos, 2002.

Buford, Bob. *Half Time: Changing Your Game Plan from Success to Significance*. Grand Rapids, Mich.: Zondervan, 1994.

Burch, Audra D. S. "A Brush with God." *Miami Herald*, June 15, 2002.

———. "From Businessman to Missionary." *Miami Herald*, October 3, 1997.

Burr, Agnes Rush. *Russell H. Conwell and His Work: One Man's Interpretation of Life*. Philadelphia: Winston, 1926.

Butt, Howard E., Jr., ed. *At the Edge of Hope: Christian Laity in Paradox*. New York: Seabury, 1978.

———. *Renewing America's Soul: A Spiritual Psychology for Home, Work, and Nation*. New York: Continuum, 1996.

———. *Renewing the Spirit, Healing the Soul: A Christian Exposition for Twenty-First Century Living*. Dallas, Tex.: Laicom, 2000.

———. *The Velvet Covered Brick: Christian Leadership in an Age of Rebellion*. San Francisco, Calif.: HarperCollins, 1974.

Calandra, Bob. "From on High." *Human Resource Executive*, January 2001.

Calhoun, Robert L. *God and the Day's Work: Christian Vocation in a Unchristian World*. New York: Association Press, 1957.

Calvin, John. *Institutes of Christian Religion*. Grand Rapids, Mich.: Baker Book House, 1987.

Campbell, Dana Adkins. "Doing God's Business." *Southern Living*, August 2000.

Caplan, Lincoln. *Skadden: Power, Money, and the Rise of a Legal Empire*. New York: Farrar Straus Giroux, 1993.

Carlin, David R. "Awakening to What?" Review of *The Fourth Great Awakening and the Future of Egalitarianism*, by Robert William Fogel. *First Things* 107 (November 2000): 55–58.

Carmody, John. *Holistic Spirituality*. New York: Paulist, 1983.

Carter, Stephen L. *A Culture of Disbelief: How American Law and Politics Trivialize Religious Devotion*. New York: Basic, 1993.

Cash, Karen C., George R. Gray, and Sally A. Rood. "A Framework for Accommodating Religion and Spirituality in the Workplace/Executive Commentary." *Academy of Management Executive* 14, no. 3 (August 2000): 124–134.

Cassidy, Suzanne, and Mary Warner. "Religion Moves into Workplace." *Times* (Trenton, N.J.), December 28, 1997.

Catholic Church, National Conference of Catholic Bishops. *Economic Justice for All: A Catholic Framework for Economic Life*. Washington D.C.: U.S. Catholic Conference, 1996.

Center for Faith in the Workplace. *Bridging WorkPlace and WorshipPlace*. San Antonio, Tex., 2001.

Chappell, Tom. *The Soul of a Business: Managing for Profit and the Common Good*. New York: Bantam, 1994.

Chen, David W. "Fitting the Lord into Work Tight Schedules." *New York Times*, November 29, 1997.

Chewning, Richard C. *Biblical Principles and Business: The Foundations*. Colorado Springs, Colo.: NavPress, 1989.

———. *Biblical Principles and Business: The Practice*. Colorado Springs, Colo.: NavPress, 1990.

———. *Biblical Principles and Economics: The Foundations*. Colorado Springs, Colo.: NavPress, 1989.

———. *Biblical Principles and Public Policy: The Practice*. Colorado Springs, Colo.: NavPress, 1990.

Childs, James M., Jr. *Ethics in Business: Faith at Work*. Minneapolis: Fortress, 1995.

Chopra, Deepak. *The Seven Spiritual Laws of Success: A Practical Guide to the Fulfillment of Your Dreams*. San Rafael, Calif.: Amber-Allen, 1994.

Christiansen, Stig. "The Second Servant." *Christian Science Journal*, May 2001.

Claringbull, Denis. *Front Line Mission: Ministry in the Market Place*. Norwich: Canterbury, 1994.

Clements, Keith. *Faith on the Frontier: A Life of J. H. Oldham*. Geneva: WCC Publications, 1999.

Cohen, Andy. "The Guiding Light." *Sales & Marketing Management*, August 1997, 46–54.

Cohn, Gordon, and Hershey H. Friedman. "Improving Employer-Employee Relationships: A Biblical and Talmudic Perspective on Human Resource Management." *Management Decision: Focus on Management History* 40, no. 10 (2002): 955–961.

Cole, William Albert. "Prayer in the Workplace." *Christian Science Journal*, May 2001.

Colston, Hal. "The Good News Garage." *Faith at Work*, Winter 1999.

Congar, Yves. *Christians Active in the World*. New York: Herder and Herder, 1968.

———. *Lay People in the Church: A Study for a Theology of the Laity*, trans. Donald Attwater. Westminster, Md.: Newan Press, 1957.

Conlin, Michelle. "Religion in the Workplace: The Growing Presence of Spirituality in Corporate America." *BusinessWeek*, November 1, 1999.

Connor, James L., S.J., "A Moral Vision for Corporate America." *Liguorian* (Mo.) *Magazine*, September 1997, 28–35.

Coombs, Ann. *The Living Workplace: Soul, Spirit, and Success in the 21st Century.* Toronto: HarperBusiness, 2001.

"Corporate World Gets Religion, New Esprit de Corps." *Lancaster* (Pa.) *Era*, August 26, 2001.

Crabtree, Davida Foy. *The Empowering Church: How One Congregation Supports Lay People's Ministries in the World.* Washington, D.C.: Alban Institute, 1990.

Crowley, Elizabeth. "Houses of Worship: Evangelical by the Elevator." *Wall Street Journal*, July 5, 2002.

Csillag, Ron. "To All Staff: Let Us Now Pray." *National Post* (Canada), June 2, 1999.

Culver, Virginia. "Church Groups Carry Gospel to Wall St." *Denver Post*, January 6, 1996.

Dale, Eric Steven. *Bringing Heaven Down to Earth: A Practical Spirituality of Work.* New York: Lang, 1991.

Dalton, R., and M. Kuechler, eds. *Challenging the Political Order: New Social and Political Movements in Western Democracies.* Cambridge, Mass.: Polity, 1990.

Darling, Jeri, and Christopher Schaefer. "What Is 'Spirituality in the Workplace?'" High Tor Alliance: Resource for Organizational and Community Renewal, unpublished report, Spring Valley N.Y., October 1997.

De Pree Leadership Center. "De Pree Leadership Center: History and Vision." Available at http://www.depree.org/aboutdplc.html; accessed May 6, 2002.

Delbecq, André L. "Spirituality for Executive Leadership: Reporting on a Pilot Course for MBAs and CEOs." Santa Clara, Calif.: Santa Clara University, 1998.

Della Porta, Donatella, and Mario Diani. *Social Movements: An Introduction.* Malden, Mass.: Blackwell, 1999.

"The Development of New Paradigm Values, Thinkers, and Business." Special issue of *American Behavioral Scientist*, May 2000.

Diani, Mario. "The Concept of Social Movement." *Sociological Review* 40, no. 1 (February 1992): 1–25.

Diehl, William E. *Christianity and Real Life.* Philadelphia: Fortress, 1976.

———. *In Search of Faithfulness: Lessons from the Christian Community.* Philadelphia: Fortress, 1987.

———. Interview by David W. Miller, December 28, 2000.

———. Letter to David W. Miller, July 14, 2001.

———. *The Monday Connection: On Being an Authentic Christian in a Weekday World.* New York: HarperCollins, 1991.

Dillenberger, John. "Faith." In *A New Handbook of Christian Theology*, ed. Donald W. Musser and Joseph L. Price, 182–84. Nashville, Tenn.: Abingdon, 1992.

Dittes, James E. *Driven by Hope: Men and Meaning.* Louisville, Ky.: Westminster/John Knox, 1996.

———. *Men at Work: Life beyond the Office.* Louisville, Ky.: Westminster/John Knox, 1996.

———. *When Work Goes Sour.* Philadelphia: Westminster, 1987.

Dobrzyndki, Judith H. "Chicken Done to a Golden Rule: Fast-Food Chain Treats Its Employees as Family." *New York Times*, April 3, 1996.

Dozier, Verna J. *The Calling of the Laity: Verna Dozier's Anthology*. Washington, D.C.: Alban Institute, 1988.

Dozier, Verna J., and Celia Allison Hahn. *The Authority of the Laity*. Washington, D.C.: Alban Institute, 1984.

Droel, William L., and Gregory F. Pierce. *Confident & Competent: A Challenge for the Lay Church*. Notre Dame, Ind.: Ave Maria, 1987.

Drucker, Peter. "Ethical Chic." *Public Interest*, no. 16 (Spring 1981): 18–36.

Dubin, Murray. "Out of Academe." *Philadelphia Inquirer*, January 16, 1997.

Duchon, Dennis, and Donde P. Ashmos. "Spirituality at Work: A Conceptualization and Measure." *Journal of Management Inquiry* 9, no. 2 (June 2000): 134–145.

Duchrow, Ulrich. *Global Economy: A Confessional Issue for the Churches?* 1986. Translated by David Lewis. Reprint. Geneva: WCC Publications, 1987.

Edwards, David Lawrence, ed. *Priests and Workers: An Anglo-French Discussion*. London: SCM, 1961.

Elias, Marilyn. "New Ways Likely to Replace That Old-Time Religion." *USA Today*, February 28, 2001.

Ellin, Abby. "In the Name of Peace at the Office." *New York Times*, June 21, 2000.

Ellingsen, Mark. *The Cutting Edge: How Churches Speak on Social Issues*. Geneva: WCC Publications, 1993.

Erlander, Lillemor. "Faith in the World of Work: On the Theology of Work as Lived by the French Worker-Priests and British Industrial Mission." Ph.D. diss., Uppsala University, Stockholm, Sweden, 1991.

Evanston Speaks: Reports from the Second Assembly of the World Council of Churches. New York: World Council of Churches, 1955.

Eyck, Mary Ten. "When the Supplier Doesn't Supply." *Christian Science Journal*, May 2001, 11–12.

Fairholm, Gilbert W. *Capturing the Heart of Leadership: Spirituality and Community in the New American Workplace*. Westport, Conn.: Praeger, 1997.

———. *Perspectives on Leadership: From the Science of Management to Its Spiritual Heart*. Westport, Conn.: Quorum, 1998.

Farnham, Suzanne G., ed. *Listening Hearts: Discerning Call in Community*. Harrisburg, Pa.: Morehouse, 1991.

Feder, Barnaby J. "Many Companies Hire Chaplains as Counselors: Ministers Who Work among Their Flock." *New York Times*, October 3, 1996.

Ferguson, Andrew. "Founding Documents." Unpublished paper, New York, April 2, 2001. Photocopied.

Fishburn, Janet F. "Social Gospel." In *Encyclopedia of the Reformed Faith*, ed. Donald K. McKim, 354–355. Louisville, Ky.: Westminster/John Knox, 1992.

Flannery, Austin, ed. *Vatican Collection*, vol. 1, *Vatican Council II: The Conciliar and Post Conciliar Documents*, rev. ed. Northport, N.Y.: Costello, 1992.

Flowers, Lois. *Women, Faith, and Work: How Ten Successful Professionals Blend Belief and Business*. Nashville, Tenn.: Word, 2001.

Fogel, Robert William. *The Fourth Great Awakening and the Future of Egalitarianism*. Chicago: University of Chicago Press, 2000.

————. Interview by David W. Miller, February 8, 2002.

Forrester, William Roxburgh. *Christian Vocation: Studies in Faith and Work.* London: Lutterworth, 1951.

Fox, Laurie. "Gil Stricklin—His Marketplace Ministries Brings Spirituality into the Workplace." *Dallas Morning News*, January 23, 2000.

Friedman, Milton. "The Social Responsibility of Business Is to Increase Its Profits." *New York Times Magazine*, September 13, 1970.

Fuller, Robert C. *Spiritual but Not Religious: Understanding Unchurched America.* New York: Oxford University Press, 2001.

Full Gospel Business Men's Fellowship International. Available at http://www.fgbmfi .org; accessed January 20, 2001.

Gabbay, Alyssa. "Ministers, Rabbis Serve as Reference in Business Deals." *Sunday News* (Lancaster, Pa.), February 4, 1996.

Gallup, George, Jr., and D. Michael Lindsay. *Surveying the Religious Landscape: Trends in U.S. Beliefs.* Harrisburg, Pa.: Morehouse, 1999.

Gelsinger, Pat. *Balancing Your Faith, Family, and Work.* Colorado Springs, Colo.: Cook Communications Ministries/Life Journey, 2003.

Gerlach, Luther P., and Virginia H. Hine. *People, Power: Change Movements of Social Transformation.* Indianapolis, Ind.: Bobbs-Merrill, 1970.

Giacalone, Robert A., and Carole L. Jurkiewicz, eds. *Handbook of Workplace Spirituality and Organizational Performance.* Armonk, N.Y.: Sharpe, 2003.

Gibbons, Paul. "Spirituality at Work: A Pre-Theoretical Overview." Ph.D. diss., Birkbeck College, University of London, 2000.

Gibbs, Mark. *Christians with Secular Power.* Philadelphia: Fortress, 1981.

————. "The Development of a Strong and Committed Laity." Paper presented at the First Vesper/Audenshaw Lecture on the Laity. New York, April 1982.

Gibbs, Mark, and Ralph T. Morton. *God's Frozen People: A Book for and about Christian Laymen.* Philadelphia: Westminster, 1965.

————. *God's Lively People: Christians in Tomorrow's World.* London: Fontana/Collins, 1971.

The Gideons International: About Us. Available at http://www.gideons.org; accessed January 9, 2001.

Gillett, Richard W. *The Human Enterprise: A Christian Perspective on Work.* Kansas City, Kans.: Leaven, 1985.

"God Decentralized." *New York Times Magazine*, December 7, 1997.

Goforth, Candace. "Spirituality in the Workplace." *New Mexican* (Santa Fe), September 30, 2001.

Goldscheider, Eric. "Religion Journal: Seeking a Role for Religion on Campus." *New York Times*, February 2, 2002.

————. "Spiritual Rebirth: Chancellor Foresees Return of Religion." *Boston Sunday Globe*, October 3, 1999.

Goodwin, Jeff, and James M. Jasper. "Caught in a Winding, Snarling Vine: The Structural Bias of Political Process Theory." *Sociological Forum* 14, no. 1 (March 1999): 27–54.

Graves, Stephen, and Thomas Addington. *The Fourth Frontier: Exploring the New World of Work.* Nashville, Tenn.: Word, 2000.

Green, John, and Kevin E. Schmiesing. *The State of Economic Education in United States Seminaries*. Grand Rapids, Mich.: Acton Institute for the Study of Religion and Liberty, 2001.

Greene, Mark. *Thank God It's Monday: Ministry in the Workplace*. London: Scripture Union, 1994.

Greenleaf, Robert K., Anne T. Fraker, and Larry C. Spears. *Seeker and Servant: Reflections on Religious Leadership*. San Francisco, Calif.: Jossey-Bass, 1996.

Gregg, Samuel. *Economic Thinking for the Theologically Minded*. Lanham, Md.: Acton Institute/University Press of America, 2001.

Grenz, Linda L., and J. Fletcher Lowe, Jr., eds. *Ministry in Daily Life: A Guide to Living the Baptismal Covenant*. New York: Episcopal Church Center, 1996.

Grimes, Howard. "The United States: 1800–1962." In *The Layman in Christian History*, ed. Stephen Neill and Hans-Ruedi Weber. London: SCM, 1963.

Grubb, Norman. *Modern Viking: The Story of Abraham Vereide*. Grand Rapids, Mich.: Zondervan, 1961.

Gunther, Marc. "God and Business: The Surprising Quest for Spiritual Renewal in the American Workplace." *Fortune*, July 9, 2001, 58–80.

Guptara, Prabhu. "Spirituality at Work: A Comparative Perspective," *Faith in Business Quarterly*, December 2001.

Hammel, Laury. "A Place for God?" *Christian Science Journal*, May 2001, 5.

Hammond, Pete. "Some Wonderful North American 'Stirrings'." Madison, Wis.: InterVarsity Marketplace Ministry, Spring 2001. Photocopied.

Hammond, Pete, R. Paul Stevens, and Todd Svanoe. *The Marketplace Annotated Bibliography: A Christian Guide to Books on Work, Business & Vocation*. Downers Grove, Ill.: InterVarsity, 2002.

Handy, Robert T., ed. *The Social Gospel in America, 1870–1920*. New York: Oxford University Press, 1966.

Hardy, Lee. *The Fabric of this World: Inquiries into Calling, Career, Choice, and the Design of Human Work*. Grand Rapids, Mich.: Eerdmans, 1990.

Harney, Alexandra. "Zen and the Art of Making Profits." *Financial Times* (London), August 29, 2000.

Harrison, Lawrence E., and Samuel P. Huntington. *Culture Matters: How Values Shape Human Progress*. New York: Basic, 2000.

Hart, Stephen, and David A. Krueger. "Faith and Work: Challenges for Congregations." *Christian Century*, July 15–22, 1992, 683–686.

Hauerwas, Stanley. *Character and the Christian Life: A Study in Theological Ethics*. Notre Dame, Ind.: University of Notre Dame Press, 1985.

Hauerwas, Stanley, and William H. Willimon. *Resident Aliens: Life in the Christian Colony*. Nashville, Tenn.: Abingdon, 1989.

Haughey, John C. *Converting Nine to Five: A Spirituality of Daily Work*. New York: Crossroad, 1989.

Hawn, Carleen. "A Second Parting of the Red Sea." *Forbes*, March 9, 1998, 138–146.

Henneberger, Melinda. "Putting a Christian Stamp on Congress." *New York Times*, November 6, 1997.

Herman, Stewart W., and Arthur Gross Schaefer, eds. *Spiritual Goods: Faith Traditions and the Practice of Business*. Charlottesville, Va.: Philosophy Documentation Center, 2001.

Hicks, Douglas A. *Religion and the Workplace: Pluralism, Spirituality, and Leadership*. Cambridge, U.K., and New York: Cambridge University Press, 2003.

Hillman, Os. *Today, God is First*. Shippensburg, Pa.: Destiny Image/Treasure House, 2002.

———. *The 9 to 5 Window*. Ventura, Calif.: Regal, 2005.

Hiltner, Seward. "Needed: A New Theology of Work." *Theology Today* 31 (October 1974): 243–247.

Himmelberg, Michele. "The Purpose of Work? To Serve One's Spirituality." *Orange County* (Calif.) *Register: At Work Extra*, August 1998.

———. "Workers Are Making a Soul Shift in Search of Satisfaction." *Orange County* (Calif.) *Register: At Work Extra*, August 1998.

"History—Not Bunk, but an Asset." *Marketplace* (Lancaster, Pa.), February 2000.

Holl, Karl. *Gesammelte Aufsätze zur Kirchengeschichte*. Tübingen: Mohr, 1921.

Holland, Joe. *Creative Communion: Toward a Spirituality of Work*. New York: Paulist, 1989.

Hollandsworth, Skip. "Religion in the News: 'My Faith Makes Me a Better Reporter.'" *Columbus* (Ohio) *Dispatch*, December 4–6, 1998, *USA Weekend*.

Hopkins, Charles Howard. *The Rise of the Social Gospel in American Protestantism, 1865–1915*. New Haven, Conn.: Yale University Press, 1940.

Hybels, Bill. *Christians in the Marketplace: Making Your Faith Work in the Secular World*. London: Hodder & Stoughton, 1993.

Hyland, Steve. "The Coca-Cola Company Christian Fellowship." Paper presented at the International Coalition of Marketplace Ministries, Atlanta, Ga., May 9, 2002.

Hymowitz, Carol. "Midlife Career Swaps: An Investment Banker Switches to Preaching." *Wall Street Journal*, June 12, 2000.

Iannone, A. Pablo, ed. *Contemporary Moral Controversies in Business*. Oxford: Oxford University Press, 1989.

Jackson, Maggie. *What's Happening to Home? Balancing Work, Life, and Refuge in the Information Age*. Notre Dame, Ind.: Sorin, 2002.

Jarman, W. Maxey. *A Businessman Looks at the Bible*. Westwood, N.J.: Revell, 1965.

Jones, Laurie Beth. *Jesus CEO: Using Ancient Wisdom for Visionary Leadership*. New York: Hyperion, 1995.

———. *Jesus, Inc.: The Visionary Path: An Entrepreneur's Guide to True Success*. New York: Crown Business, 2001.

———. *The Path: Creating Your Own Mission Statement for Work and Life*. New York: Hyperion, 1996.

Jordan, Pat. "In Deepak We Trust." *Sales & Marketing Management*, August 1997, 59–65.

Journal Staff Reporter. "Consultant Rejuvenates Spirituality in the Workplace." *Albuquerque* (N.M.) *Journal*, December 19, 1994.

Joyce, Amy. "Keep Personal Causes Far from Office." *Miami Herald*, August 19, 2002.

Judge, William Q. *The Leader's Shadow: Exploring and Developing Executive Character*. Thousand Oaks, Calif.: Sage, 1999.

Julian, Larry. *God Is My CEO: Following God's Principles in a Bottom-Line World.* Holbrook, Mass.: Adams Media, 2001.

Kepner, Charles H., and Benjamin B. Tregoe. *The Rational Manager.* New York: McGraw-Hill, 1965.

King, Martin Luther Jr.; James M. Washington, ed. *A Testament of Hope: The Essential Writings and Speeches of Martin Luther King Jr.* New York: HarperCollins, 1986.

Klandermans, B., H. Kriesi, and S. Tarrow. *From Structure to Action, Comparing Social Movements Research across Cultures.* Greenwich, Conn.: JAI, 1988.

Klausler, Alfred P. *Christ and Your Job: A Study in Christian Vocation.* St. Louis, Mo.: Concordia, 1956.

Klein, Eric, and John B. Izzo. *Awakening Corporate Soul: Four Paths to Unleash the Power of People at Work.* Toronto, Ont., Canada: FairWinds, 1999.

Korten, David C. *When Corporations Rule the World.* San Francisco, Calif.: Kumarian/ Berrett-Koehler, 1995.

Kowalczyk, Nick. "Religious Practices Establish Foothold at Certain Job Sites." *Cleveland Plain Dealer*, August 14, 2001.

Kraemer, Hendrik. *A Theology of the Laity.* Philadelphia: Westminster, 1958.

Kretchmar, Laurie. "Fortune People." *Fortune Magazine*, April 6, 1992.

Kroeker, Wally. *God's Week Has 7 Days: Monday Musings for Marketplace Christians.* Waterloo, Ontario: Herald, 1998.

Krueger, David A. *The Business Corporation and Productive Justice.* Edited by Max L. Stackhouse. Nashville, Tenn.: Abingdon, 1997.

Kuhn, James W., and Donald W. Shriver. *Beyond Success: Corporations and Their Critics in the 1990s.* New York: Oxford University Press, 1991.

Kunde, Diana. "Contract Chaplains." *Orange County* (Calif.) *Register*, February 10, 1996.

Küng, Hans. *A Global Ethic for Global Politics and Economics.* New York: Oxford University Press, 1998.

Laabs, Jennifer J. "Balancing Spirituality and Work." *Personnel Journal* (Boulder, Colo.), September 1995, 60–76.

La Ganga, Maria L. "Seeking Spirituality at Work." *Marin Independent Journal* (Novato, Calif.), June 7, 1998.

Lambert, Lake. "Called to Business: Corporate Management as a Profession of Faith." Ph.D. diss., Princeton Theological Seminary, 1997.

Lampman, Jane. "Competing Values: Faith-Based Groups Move to Help Professionals Close the Gap Between Personal Beliefs and Corporate Behavior." *Christian Science Monitor*, August 1, 2002.

Landes, David S. *The Wealth and Poverty of Nations: Why Some Nations Are So Rich and Some So Poor.* New York: Norton, 1999.

Larive, Armand. *After Sunday: A Theology of Work.* New York: Continuum, 2004.

Leckey, Dolores R. *Laity Stirring the Church: Prophetic Questions.* Philadelphia: Fortress, 1987.

———. *Practical Spirituality for Lay People.* Kansas City, Mo.: Sheed & Ward, 1987.

———. *Seven Essentials for the Spiritual Journey.* New York: Crossroad, 1999.

Lee, Susan. "Filling the God-Hole." *Forbes*, October 6, 1997, 148–149.

Leggat, Dick. "Principles & Interest." *Christian Businessman*, July–August 1998.

Leigh, Pamela. "The New Spirit at Work." *Training & Development* 51, no. 3 (March 1997): 26–33.

Leigh-Taylor, Christine, "Business Leadership as a Spiritual Discipline," *The Physician Executive*, March–April 2001.

Leland, John. "Searching for a Holy Spirit: Young People Are Openly Passionate about Religion—but They Insist on Defining It in Their Own Ways." *Newsweek*, May 8, 2000.

Leonhardt, David. "Joy for Second-String M.B.A.'s: Elites and Internet Change Face of Campus Recruiting." *New York Times*, February 23, 2000.

LeTourneau, R. G. *Mover of Men and Mountains*. Englewood Cliffs, N.J.: Prentice-Hall, 1960.

Levine, Joshua. "Let the Fruit Run Down Your Chin." *Forbes*, January 11, 1999, 270–271.

Levinson, Daniel J. *The Seasons of a Man's Life*. New York: Ballantine, 1978.

Lewis, Jeffrey S., and Gary D. Geroy. "Employee Spirituality in the Workplace: A Cross-Cultural View for the Management of Spiritual Employees." *Journal of Management Education* 24, no. 5 (October 2000): 682–694.

Light, David A. "Is Success a Sin? A Conversation with the Reverend Peter J. Gomes." *Harvard Business Review* 79 (September 2001): 63–66, 68–69.

Lightman, Alan. "In God's Place." *New York Times Magazine*, September 19, 1999.

Lincoln, C. Eric, and Lawrence H. Mamiya, eds. *The Black Church in the African American Experience*. Durham, N.C.: Duke University Press, 1990.

Lindgren, Amy. "Reasons Multiply for Keeping Religion Out of the Workplace." *Lancaster* (Pa.) *New Era*, December 17, 2001.

Lippy, Charles H. "Social Christianity." In *Encyclopedia of the American Religious Experience*, ed. Charles H. Lippy and Peter W. Williams, 917–931. New York: Scribner's, 1988.

Lofland, John, and James T. Richardson. "Religious Movement Organization: Elemental Forms and Dynamics." In *Research in Social Movements, Conflicts and Change*, ed. Lewis Kriesberg, vol. 7. Greenwich, Conn.: JAI, 1984.

Long, Edward LeRoy. *Conscience and Compromise: An Approach to Protestant Casuistry*. Philadelphia: Westminster, 1954.

Loy, David R. "The Religion of the Market." *Journal of the American Academy of Religion* 65, no. 2 (1997): 275–290.

Luther, Martin. *Martin Luther: Selections from His Writings*. Edited by John Dillenberger. Garden City, N.Y.: Doubleday, 1962.

Lynem, Julie. "Keeping the Faith . . . Er, Faiths: Companies Adjust to Growing Religious Diversity in the Workplace." *San Francisco Chronicle*, December 8, 2001.

Machalaba, Daniel. "More Employees Are Seeking Spiritual Fulfillment on the Job." *Wall Street Journal*, June 25, 2002. Available at http://online.wsj.com/article_email/0,SB102494861440781728o,oo.html.

Macy, Beth. " 'Spirituality' at Work: Author Motivates People to Be Their Best Selves on the Job." *Roanoke* (Va.) *Times*, September 12, 2001.

Marshall, Rich. *God @ Work: Discovering the Anointing for Business*. Shippensburg, Pa.: Destiny Image, 2000.

Martin, David. *Tongues of Fire: The Explosion of Protestantism in Latin America.* Cambridge: Blackwell, 1990.

Marx, Karl, translated by Ben Fowkes. *Capital: Vol. 1: A Critique of Politcal Economy.* London: Penguin Classics, 1990.

Marx, Karl and Frederick Engels. *Manifesto of the Communist Party,* ed. David McClellan. Oxford: Oxford University Press, 1992.

Mastony, Colleen. "Managing with God." *Forbes,* July 27, 1998, 20–22.

May, Henry Farnham. *Protestant Churches and Industrial America.* New York: Harper, 1949.

McCann, Dennis. *Christian Realism and Liberation Theology: Practical Theologies in Conflict.* Maryknoll, N.Y.: Orbis, 1981.

McCarthy, Michael. "An Ex-Divinity Student Works on Searching the Corporate Soul." *Wall Street Journal,* June 18, 1999.

McCormick, Brian. "Principles and Profit." *Crain's Chicago Business,* March 26, 2001.

McCormick, Donald W. "Spirituality and Management." Special issue of *Journal of Managerial Psychology: Spirituality and Management* 9, no. 6 (1994): 5–8.

McCoy, Bowen H. "Business, Faith, & Ethics: Making the Connection." *Real Estate Issues,* 2001, 54–57.

———. "Business, Religion, and Ethics: Inquiry and Encounter" [book review]. *Theology Today* 40 (July 1983): 226–229.

———. "CRE Perspective: Living beyond the Boundaries." *Real Estate Issues,* 2001, 47–50.

———. "The Parable of the Sadhu." *Harvard Business Review,* September–October 1983, 103–108.

———. "A Test-Case in Communication." *Theology Today* 41, no. 1 (1984): 42–46.

McDonald, Marci. "Shush: The Guy in the Cubicle Is Meditating: Spirituality Is the Latest Corporate Buzzword." *U.S. News & World Report,* May 3, 1999, 46.

McGraw, Dan. "The Christian Capitalists." *U.S. News & World Report,* March 13, 1995, 52–62.

McHugh, Francis P. *Keyguide to Information Sources in Business Ethics.* London: Mansell Nichols, 1988.

McIver, Bruce. *Riding the Wind of God: A Personal History of the Youth Revival Movement.* Macon, Ga.: Smyth & Helwys, 2002.

McLoughlin, Mike, ed. *The Scruples Directory of Marketplace Ministry.* Kelowna, B.C., Canada: YWAM, 2002.

———. *The Scruples Directory of Marketplace Ministry: Millennium 2000 Edition.* Kelowna, B.C., Canada: YWAM, 2000.

McLoughlin, Mike, Neal Johnson, Os Hillman, and David W. Miller, eds. *2003 International Faith & Work Directory.* Cumming, Ga.: Aslan, 2003.

McQuiston, David. "CEO Forum Activities." Unpublished paper, Colorado Springs, Colo., October 2002. Photocopied.

Mead, Loren B. *Five Challenges for the Once and Future Church.* Bethesda, Md.: Alban Institute, 1996.

———. *The Once and Future Church: Reinventing the Congregation for a New Mission Frontier.* Washington, D.C.: Alban Institute, 1991.

Medved, Michael. "The Left Prays, but the Right Pays." *Wall Street Journal,* August 11, 2000.

Meeks, M. Douglas. *God the Economist: The Doctrine of God and Political Economy*. Minneapolis, Minn.: Fortress, 1989.

Meilaender, Gilbert, ed. *Working: Its Meaning and Its Limits*. Notre Dame, Ind.: University of Notre Dame Press, 2000.

Midha, Harish. "Spirituality in the Workplace: The Sixth Discipline of a Learning Organization." Paper presented at the 18th Annual Conference of the Canadian Association for the Study of Adult Education. Sherbrooke, Quebec, Canada, June 10–11, 1999.

Migliore, Daniel L. "Faith." In *Encyclopedia of the Reformed Faith*, ed. Donald K. McKim, 133–35. Louisville, Ky.: Westminster/John Knox, 1992.

Miles, Madelon M. "The Workplace as Holy Ground." *Christian Science Journal*, May 2001, 7–10.

Miller, David W. "Faith in the Workplace: Issues, Themes, and Responses." Princeton University, May 1999, unpublished paper.

———. "King and the Economy: Getting Down to the Business of Business." Princeton Theological Seminary, December 1998, unpublished paper.

Miller, Keith. *The Taste of New Wine*. Waco, Tex.: Word, 1965.

Miller, Lisa. "Can You Go Back? Many Professionals Return to Church or Synagogue: Having It All Isn't Enough." *Wall Street Journal*, April 10, 1998.

———. "Pizza Magnate Mounts a Crusade to Restore Orthodox Catholicism." *Wall Street Journal*, June 21, 2000.

———. "Rebels with a Cause." *Wall Street Journal*, December 18, 1998.

Miller, Michael J., ed. *The Encyclicals of John Paul II*. Huntington, Ind.: Our Sunday Visitor, 1996.

Millman, Gregory J. "God on the Job: All in a Day's Work." *San Francisco Examiner*, September 5, 1999.

"Mini-Symposium: Social Movements." In *Sociological Forum*, ed. Richard H. Hall, vol. 14, no. 1. New York: Kluwer Academic/Plenum, March 1999.

Minus, Paul. *Taking Faith to Work*. St. Paul, Minn.: Centered Life, 2004.

———. *Walter Rauschenbush: American Reformer*. New York: Macmillan, 1988.

———. "Lay Movements." In *Encyclopedia of Christianity*. ed. Erwin Fahlbusch. Grand Rapids, Mich.: Eerdmans & Brill, 2003.

Mitroff, Ian I., and Elizabeth A. Denton. *A Spiritual Audit of Corporate America: A Hard Look at Spirituality, Religion, and Values in the Workplace*. San Francisco, Calif.: Jossey-Bass, 1999.

———. "A Study of Spirituality in the Workplace." *Sloan Management Review* 40 (Summer 1999).

Moch, Michael K., and James M. Bartunek. "Linking Business, Spirituality, and Religion," Manuscript submitted for publication, 2002. Material presented at the Annual Academy of Management meeting, Denver, Colo., August 2001.

Mockler Center for Faith and Ethics in the Workplace. Available at http://www.gcts.edu/ockenga/mockler/index.html; accessed May 6, 2002.

Moltmann, Jürgen. *The Coming of God: Christian Eschatology*, trans. Margaret Kohl. Minneapolis, Minn.: Fortress, 1996.

Monroe, Ann. "Investment Strategies: Keeping the Faith." *Bloomberg Wealth Manager*, December 2000–January 2001.

Morris, A., and C. Herring. "Theory and Research in Social Movements: A Critical Review." *Annual Review of Political Science* 2 (1987).

Morse, J. Geraint. "Standing in the Mud." In *Laity Exchange*, ed. Mark Gibbs. London: Audenshaw Foundation, 1985.

Mouw, Richard J. *Called to Holy Worldliness*. Philadelphia: Fortress, 1980.

———. *Consulting with the Faithful: What Christian Intellectuals Can Learn from Popular Religion*. Grand Rapids, Mich.: Eerdmans, 1994.

Munk, Nina. "The Price of Freedom." *New York Times Magazine*, March 5, 2000.

Murphy, Patrick E. *Eighty Exemplary Ethics Statements*. Notre Dame, Ind.: University of Notre Dame Press, 1998.

Murphy, Richard McGill. "Jesus at Work." *FSB: Fortune Small Business* 16, no. 1 (February 2006).

Murray, Matt. "A Faith of One's Own: Many People Are Finding Very Personal Ways to Express Spirituality." *Wall Street Journal*, January 1, 2000.

———."Tackling Workplace Problems with Prayer." *Wall Street Journal*, October 19, 1995.

Nash, Laura L. *Believers in Business*. Nashville, Tenn.: Thomas Nelson, 1994.

———. "How the Church Has Failed Business." *Across the Board*, July–August 2001.

Nash, Laura L., and Scotty McLennan. *Church on Sunday, Work on Monday: The Challenge of Fusing Christian Values with Business Life*. San Francisco, Calif.: Jossey-Bass, 2001.

National Council of Churches. Available at http://www.ncccusa.org/about/about_ncc.htm; accessed February 12, 2003.

Naylor, Thomas H., Rolf Österberg, and William H. Willimon. *The Search for Meaning in the Workplace*. Nashville, Tenn.: Abingdon, 1996.

Neal, Judi. http://www.fourgateways.com/uversity/Four_Gateways.htm. 1999.

———. "Letter from the Chair: Making a Difference." *Academy of Management, Management, Spirituality and Religion Newsletter*, Spring–Summer 2002, 1.

———. "Spirit at Work Bibliography." Available at http://www.spiritatwork.com/knowledgecenter; accessed January 18, 2001.

———. "Spirituality in the Workplace in Higher Education: A Global Phenomenon." Paper presented at the Spirit in Business, Inc., Conference. New York, April 21–23, 2002.

Neal, Judi, and Joel Bennett. "Examining Multi-Level or Holistic Spiritual Phenomena in the Workplace." *Academy of Management: Management, Spirituality and Religion Newsletter*, Winter 2000.

Neill, Stephen Charles and Hans-Ruedi Weber, eds. *The Layman in Christian History*. London: SCM, 1963.

Nelson, John Oliver Nelson, ed. *Work and Vocation: A Christian Discussion*. New York: Harper, 1954.

Nelson, Paul, and Sally Simmel, eds. *On Assignment from God: The Ministry of the Baptized*. Chicago: Evangelical Lutheran Church in America, 1991.

Nelson, Robert H. *Economics as Religion: From Samuelson to Chicago and Beyond*. University Park: Pennsylvania State University Press, 2001.

"New Program Designed for Working Folks." *New Mexican* (Santa Fe), March 31, 2001.

Newby, James R. *Eton Trueblood: Believer, Teacher and Friend*. San Francisco, Calif.: Harper & Row, 1990.

Niebuhr, Reinhold. *Christian Realism and Political Problems*. New York: Scribner's, 1953.

———. *The Nature and Destiny of Man: A Christian Interpretation*. 1941. Reprint. Louisville, Ky.: Westminster/John Knox, 1996.

———. *The Self and the Dramas of History*. New York: Scribner's, 1955.

Niebuhr, H. Richard. *Christ and Culture*. New York: Harper and Row, 1951.

———. *The Purpose of the Church and Its Ministry*. New York: Harper, 1956.

Norris, Floyd. "With Bull Market under Siege, Some Worry about Its Legacy." *New York Times*, March 18, 2001.

Novak, Michael. *Business as a Calling: Work and the Examined Life*. New York: Free Press, 1996.

———. "A Philosophy of Economics." Lecture at Baylor University, Waco, Tex., November 10, 2002.

———. *Will It Liberate? Questions about Liberation Theology*. New York: Paulist, 1986.

Nutter, James W. "Sacred or Secular No More." Available at www.palmertx.com/Sermons/Nutter/nutter02-03-02.htm; accessed February 3, 2002.

Oldham, J. H. *Work in Modern Society*. London: SCM Press, 1950.

Olney, Buster. "Baseball: Prayer Group Helps Some Yankees Bond." *New York Times*, August 23, 1998.

Olsson, Karl A. *The History of Faith at Work*. Falls Church, Va.: Faith at Work, 1997.

Osborne, Kenan B. *Ministry: Lay Ministry in the Roman Catholic Church, Its History and Theology*. New York: Paulist, 1993.

O'Steen, Robert. "Legatus Chapter Forming Locally." *Florida Catholic* (Miami), November 27, 1997.

Ottati, Douglas F. "Kingdom of God." In *Encyclopedia of the Reformed Faith*, ed. Donald K. McKim, 204–205. Louisville, Ky.: Westminster/John Knox, 1992.

———. *Reforming Protestantism: Christian Commitment in Today's World*. Philadelphia: Westminster/John Knox, 1995.

Overell, Stephen. "Plain Dealing Pays Dividends." *Financial Times* (London), August 22, 2000.

———. "Souls Restored in the Workplace: Spirituality in Business." *Financial Times* (London), September 21, 2001.

Palmer, Earl F. "Christians in Business." *Theology Today* 39 (1982): 199–200.

———. *A Faith That Works*. Ventura, Calif.: Regal, 1985.

Paris, Peter J. *The Social Teaching of the Black Churches*. Philadelphia: Fortress, 1985.

Peale, Norman Vincent. *The Power of Positive Thinking*. New York: Prentice-Hall, 1952.

Peck, George, and John S. Hoffman, eds. *The Laity in Ministry: The Whole People of God for the Whole World*. Valley Forge, Pa.: Judson, 1984.

Pedersen-Pietersen, Laura. "From Addict to Educator in Harlem." *New York Times*, May 16, 1999.

Peterson, Eugene H. *Praying with the Early Christians: A Year of Daily Prayers and Reflections on the Words of the Early Christians*. San Francisco: Harper Collins, 1994.

Pierce, Gregory F. *Spirituality @ Work: 10 Ways to Balance Your Life On-the-Job*. Chicago: Loyola Press, 2001.

Pierce, Gregory F., ed. *Of Human Hands: A Reader in the Spirituality of Work*. Minneapolis and Chicago: Augsburg ACTA, 1991.

Pink, Daniel H. "Free Agent Nation." *FastCompany*, January 1998, 131–147.

Piper, Otto A. "The Meaning of Work." *Theology Today* 14 (July 1957): 174–194.

Pollard, C. William. *The Soul of the Firm*. New York: HarperBusiness; Grand Rapids, Mich.: Zondervan, 1996.

Potter, Ralph B. *War and Moral Discourse*. Richmond, Va.: John Knox, 1969.

Potthoff, Harvey H., "The Christian at Work and Leisure in Today's World: Selected Readings." In *The Christian in Today's World*, ed. Harvey Potthoff, vol. 8. Nashville, Tenn.: Graded, 1969.

Powelson, John P. "Holistic Economics." *Theology Today* 41 (April 1984).

Preece, Gordon R., and Samuel J. Gregg. *Christianity and Entrepreneurship: Protestant and Catholic Thoughts*. Grand Rapids, Mich.: The Acton Insitute for the Study of Religion and Liberty, 1999.

Presbyterian Church (USA). *All the Livelong Day: Women and Work*. Louisville, Ky.: Office of the General Assembly, Presbyterian Church (USA), 1988.

Presbyterian Church (USA), Advisory Committee on Social Witness Policy. *Presbyterian Social Witness Policy Compilation*, ed. Peter A. Sulyok, 255–294. Louisville, Ky.: Presbyterian Church (USA), 2000.

Presbyterian Church (USA), Advisory Council on Church and Society. *Reformed Faith and Economics*, ed. Robert L. Stivers. New York: University Press of America, 1989.

Presbyterian Church (USA), Committee on Social Witness Policy. *Challenges in the Workplace: A Resource Paper Prepared by the Task Force on Issues of Vocation and Problems of Work in the United States*. Louisville, Ky.: Presbyterian Church (USA), 1990.

Presbyterian Church (USA), Congregational Ministries Division, Presbyterian Panel. *Social Issues in Investing*. Louisville, Ky.: Presbyterian Church (USA), 1995.

Presbyterian Church (USA), Office of the General Assembly, Advisory Committee on Social Witness. *God's Work in Our Hands: Employment, Community, and Vocation*, ed. Irvin S. Moxley. Louisville, Ky.: Presbyterian Church (USA), 1995.

Presbyterian Eco-Justice Task Force. *Keeping and Healing the Creation*. Louisville, Ky.: Committee on Social Witness Policy, Presbyterian Church (USA), 1989.

Prud'homme, Alex. "Taking the Gospel to the Rich. *New York Times*, February 2, 1999.

Putnam, Robert D. *Bowling Alone: The Collapse of American Community*. New York: Simon & Schuster, 2000.

Queenan, Joe. *Balsamic Dreams: A Short but Self-Important History of the Baby Boomer Generation*. New York: Holt, 2001.

Rauschenbusch, Walter. *Christianizing the Social Order*. New York: Macmillan, 1912.

———. *The Righteousness of the Kingdom*, ed. Max L. Stackhouse. Nashville, Tenn.: Abingdon, 1968.

———. *A Theology for the Social Gospel*. New York: Macmillan, 1917.

———. *A Theology of the Social Gospel*, intro. Donald K. Shriver. Louisville, Ky.: Westminster John Knox, 1997.

Regent College. http://www.gospelcom.net/regent/regentnew/index.html; accessed May 6, 2002.

"Religion Today", *New York Times*, January 20, 2000. http://www.nytimes.com/aponline/AP-Religion-Today.html.

Remington, Fred. "The Pittsburgh Experiment." In *Faith at Work*, ed. Samuel M. Shoemaker, 302–312. New York: Hawthorn, 1958.

Ribadeneira, Diego. "Bringing Your Faith to Work." *Boston Sunday Globe*, March 28, 1999.

———. "Religion Becomes an Oasis in Hectic Corporate World." *Boston Globe*, February 1998.

Rigoglioso, Marguerite. "Spirit at Work: The Search for Deeper Meaning in the Workplace." *Harvard Business School Bulletin*, April 1999, 31–35.

Rivera, Carrie T. "Religion in the Workplace." *Office Solutions*, February 2000.

Rodriguez, Orlando. "Miami Herald Religion Writer Brings Message of Faith to the Key." *Islander News* (Key Biscayne, Fla.), September 23, 1999.

Ronsner, Bob. "Is There Room for the Soul at Work?" *Workforce*, February 2001.

Roof, Wade Clark. *Spiritual Marketplace: Baby Boomers and the Remaking of American Religion*. Princeton, N.J.: Princeton University Press, 1999.

Rosenfeld, Jill. "If the Spirit Moves You." *Fast Company*, May 2001, 54–56.

Rosenstein, Bruce. "Scandals Nothing New to Business Guru: A Conversation with Peter Drucker." *USA Today*, July 5, 2002.

Rowe, David Johnson. *Faith at Work: A Celebration of All We Do*. Macon, Ga.: Smyth & Helwys, 1994.

Rowe, John. *Priests and Workers: A Rejoinder*. London: Darton, Longman & Todd, 1965.

Rowland, Mary. "Getting Professional Help." *Wealth Manager*, November–December 1999.

Rowthorn, Anne W. *The Liberation of the Laity*. Wilton, Conn.: Morehouse-Barlow, 1986.

Ruffle, Charlie. "The Experts: Faith and the Investment Process." *Plan Sponsor*, February 2001.

Ruth, Phil. "A Servant of God in a Business Suit." *Sharing*, Winter 1995, 3–6.

Rutte, Martin. "Spirituality in the Workplace." *Psychic Reader*, March 2001, 7.

Ryken, Leland. *Redeeming the Time: A Christian Approach to Work and Leisure*. Grand Rapids, Mich.: Baker, 1995.

———. *Work & Leisure in Christian Perspective*. Portland, Ore.: Multnomah, 1987.

Saliers, Don A. "Spirituality." In *A New Handbook of Christian Theology*, ed. Donald W. Musser and Joseph L. Price, 460–4462. Nashville, Tenn.: Abingdon, 1992.

Sampson, Ovetta. "More Than Just Hope and Prayer." *Gazette* (Colorado Springs, Colo.), May 1, 2000.

Samuel, Vinay, and Chris Sugden, eds. *The Church in Response to Human Need*. London: Paternoster, 1986.

Santora, Kathleen Curry. "Spirituality in the Workplace." *American Association for Higher Education Bulletin*, April 1999.

Schaefer, Christopher, and Jeri Darling. *Spirit Matters: Using Contemplative Disciplines in Work and Organizational Life*. High Tor Alliance for Organizational and Community Renewal, unpublished report, Spring Valley, N.Y., November 1996.

Schellhardt, Timothy. "Feeling Dispirited? Have Someone Read This Story to You." *Wall Street Journal*, February 10, 1997.

Schumacher, Christian. *God in Work*. Oxford: Lion, 1998.

———. *To Live & Work: A Theological Interpretation*. Bromley, Kent, England: MARC Europe, 1987.

Schweiker, William. *Power, Value, and Conviction: Theological Ethics in the Postmodern Age*. Cleveland, Ohio: Pilgrim, 1998.

Seglin, Jeffery. "Regulating Religious Life in the Office." *New York Times*, May 16, 1999.

Serpa, Roy. "The Often Overlooked Ethical Aspect of Mergers." *Journal of Business Ethics* 7 (1988): 359–362.

Shakarian, Demos. *The Happiest People on Earth*. Chappaqua, N.Y.: Steward, 1975.

Sheldon, Charles M. *In His Steps: What Would Jesus Do?* Westwood, N.J.: Revell, 1967.

Sheler, Jeffery L. "Is God Lost as Sales Rise?" *U.S. News & World Report*, March 13, 1995.

Sherrill, Martha. "The Buddha of Detroit." *New York Times Magazine*, November 26, 2000.

Sherwood, Melinda. "God's Bottom Line." *U.S. 1* (Princeton, N.J.), February 23, 2000.

Shiller, Robert J. *Irrational Exuberance*. Princeton, N.J.: Princeton University Press, 2000.

Shoemaker, Helen Smith. *I Stand by the Door: The Life of Sam Shoemaker*. New York: Harper & Row, 1967.

Shoemaker, Samuel M. *The Experiment of Faith*. Grand Rapids, Mich.: Zondervan, 1957.

Sider, Ronald J. *Just Generosity: A New Vision for Overcoming Poverty in America*. Grand Rapids, Mich.: Baker, 1999.

Sider, Ronald J., ed. *The Chicago Declaration*. Carol Stream, Ill.: Creation House, 1974.

———. *Rich Christians in an Age of Hunger*. Dallas, Tex.: Word, 1990.

Siegal, Nina. "New Yorkers Take Five from the Workday to Feed the Spirit." *New York Times* 1999.

Simmel, Sally. Interview by David W. Miller, December 19, 2000.

Skapinker, Michael. "Lessons in Avoiding Moral Bankruptcy." *Financial Times* (London), September 5, 2000.

Skelley, Michael. "Work as Spiritual Practice: Spirituality in Organizational Life." Paper presented at the American Academy of Religion Annual Meeting, Toronto, November 20, 2002.

Slade, Lorna. "Christians Ply Ethics at Work." *Intelligencer* (Doylestown, Pa.), January 30, 1996.

Slomka, Mark. *BizBreak: Weekly Reminders for the Workplace*. Camp Hill, Pa.: Horizon, 2000.

Smelser, Neil J. *Theory of Collective Behavior*. New York: Free Press, 1962.

Smith, J. Christina. "Spirituality and Work: An Annotated Bibliography." Unpublished paper, Boston University. September 1998. Photocopied.

Smith, Polly Weaver. "Living Stones: Bridging the Gap between Faith and Work." *Florida Catholic*, June 25, 1998.

Smith, Thomas. *God on the Job: Finding God Who Waits at Work*. New York: Paulist, 1995.

Sobell, Sheila. "Soul Providers." *American Way*, November 15, 2001.

"Some Corporate Execs Follow Spiritual Beliefs: Displays of Faith Can Be Beneficial to Companies, Advocates Say." *Dallas Morning News*, December 25, 2001.

Soros, George. *Open Society: Reforming Global Capitalism*. New York: Public Affairs, 2000.

Southwick, Ron. "More Ponder Road Not Taken, and Choose Seminary." *Trenton* (N.J.) *Times*, February 6, 2000.

"A Special Background Report on Trends in Industry and Finance." *Wall Street Journal*, August 13, 1998.

Spikereit, Fred, "Spirituality in the Workplace." *Business and Society Alliance*, no. 2 (May 1997): 2.

"Spiritual Directors Guide Catholic Hospitals." *Washington Times*, April 14, 1997.

"Spirituality and Management." Special issue of *Journal of Management Psychology* 9, no. 6 (1994).

"Spirituality and Management Education." Special issue of *Journal of Management Education*, October 2000.

"Spirituality in Organizations, Part I and Part II." Special issue of *Journal of Organization and Change Management* 12, nos. 3–4 (1999).

"Spirituality at Work." Special issue of *Chinmaya Management Review* (India), June 1999.

"Spirituality at Work Program Continues." *New Mexican* (Santa Fe), May 5, 2001.

Sprunger, Ben, Carol J. Suter, and Wally Kroeker. *Faith Dilemmas for Marketplace Christians*. Scottdale, Pa.: Herald, 1997.

Stackhouse, Max L. "Jesus and Economics: A Century of Reflection." In *The Bible in American Law, Politics, and Political Rhetoric*, ed. James Turner Johnson, 107–151. Philadelphia: Fortress, 1985.

———. "Public Theology and Ethical Judgment." *Theology Today* 54, no. 2 (July 1997): 165–179.

———. *Public Theology and Political Economy: Christian Stewardship in Modern Society*. Grand Rapids, Mich.: Eerdmans, 1987.

———. "Reforming Protestant Views." In *Christian Social Ethics in a Global Era*, ed. Max L. Stackhouse. Nashville, Tenn.: Abingdon, 1995.

Stackhouse, Max L., and Don S. Browning, eds. *God and Globalization: The Spirit and the Modern Authorities*. Harrisburg, Pa.: Trinity Press International, 2001.

Stackhouse, Max L., Dennis P. McCann, and Shirley Roels. *On Moral Business*. Grand Rapids, Mich.: Eerdmans, 1995.

Stackhouse, Max L., and Diane B. Obenchain, eds. *God and Globalization: Christ and the Dominions of Civilization*. Harrisburg, Pa.: Trinity Press International, 2002.

Stackhouse, Max L., and Peter J. Paris, eds. *God and Globalization: Religion and the Powers of the Common Life*. Harrisburg, Pa.: Trinity Press International, 2000.

Stark, Rodney. *The Victory of Reason: How Christianity Led to Freedom, Capitalism, and Western Success*. New York: Random House, 2005.

Steffens, Jeffrey A. "Prophets for Today." *Christian Science Journal*, May 2001, 25–26.

Stern, Gary M. "Soul at Work." *New Age Journal*, November–December 1996, 70ff.

Stevens, R. Paul. "The Marketplace: Mission Field or Mission?" *CRUX* 37, no. 3 (September 2001): 7–16.

———. *The Other Six Days: Vocation, Work, and Ministry in Biblical Perspective*. Grand Rapids, Mich.: Eerdmans, 1999.

Stewart, Christopher. "Soul Time." *Potentials Magazine*, September 2002, 92.

Stokes, Andrew. *Working with God: Faith and Life at Work*. New York: Mowbray, 1992.

Stott, John R. W. *Christian Mission in the Modern World*. London: Falcon, 1975.

Strasburg, Jenny. "Faith and the Workplace." *San Francisco Chronicle*, December 24, 2000.

Stringfellow, William. *An Ethic for Christians and Other Aliens in a Strange Land*. Waco, Tex.: Word, 1973.

Suarez, Ana Veciana. "Spirituality as Sound Management." *Miami Herald*, August 9, 1996.

Sullivan, Pat McHenry. "Gallup Survey Shows Growth in Spirituality." *San Francisco Examiner*, December 23, 1999.

Tanenbaum Center for Interreligious Understanding. *Religion in the Workplace Survey*. Alexandria, Va.: Society for Human Resource Management, 2001.

Tarrow, Sidney G. *Power in Movement Social Movements and Contentious Politics*, 2d ed. Cambridge: Cambridge University Press, 1998.

Taylor, Barbara Brown. *The Preaching Life*. Boston: Cowley, 1993.

Taylor, Richard. *Christians in an Industrial Society*. London: SCM, 1961.

Taylor, William. "Crime? Greed? Big Ideas? What Were the '80s About?" *Harvard Business Review*, Reprint No. 92110 (January–February 1992).

Terkel, Studs. *Working*. New York: Pantheon, 1974.

Terwilliger, Cate. "Faith at Work: Movement Seeks to Bridge Professional, Personal Beliefs." *Denver Post*, February 21, 2000.

Thomas Aquinas. *Summa Theologiae*. New York: Blackfriars and McGraw-Hill, 1964.

Thomas, Keith, ed. *Oxford Book of Work*. Oxford: Oxford University Press, 1999.

Thompson, William David. "Can Business Do Well by Doing Good?" *Performance Management Magazine* 14, no. 4 (1999).

———. "Can You Train People to Be Spiritual?" *Training and Development*, Alexandria Va., December 2000.

Timson, Judith. "Should Spirituality Be Reshaping the Workplace?" *Toronto Star*, June 25, 1998.

Todd, John Murray. *Work: Christian Thought and Practice: A Symposium*. London: Darton, Longman & Todd Helicon, 1960.

Toms, Michael, ed. *The Soul of Business*. Carlsbad, Calif.: Hay House, 1997.

Tracy, David. *The Analogical Imagination: Christian Theology and Pluralism*. New York: Crossroad, 1981.

Troeltsch, Ernst, translated by Olive Wyon. *Social Teaching of the Christian Churches*. Louisville, Ky.: Westminster/John Knox Press, 1992.

Trueblood, Elton. *The Common Ventures of Life: Marriage, Birth, Work, and Death*. New York: Harper, 1949.

———. *Your Other Vocation*. New York: Harper, 1952.

Tucker, Graham. *The Faith-Work Connection: A Practical Application of Christian Values in the Marketplace*. Toronto: Anglican Book Centre, 1987.

Turner, Ralph H., and Lewis M. Killian. *Collective Behavior*. Englewood Cliffs, N.J.: Prentice-Hall, 1957.

Ty, Brother, with Christopher Buckley and John Tierney. *God Is My Broker: A Monk-Tycoon Reveals the 7½ Laws of Spiritual and Financial Success*. New York: Harper-Perennial, 1998.

"UMass to Host National Conference June 4–6 on Spirituality in the Workplace and Higher Education." Available at http://www.umass.edu/newsoffice/archive/2000/042400spirituality.html; accessed April 24, 2000.

Vaill, Peter. "Introduction to Spirituality for Business Leadership." *Journal of Management Inquiry* 9, no. 2 (June 2000): 115–116.

Van Allen, Rodger. "The Chicago Declaration and the Call to Holy Worldliness." In *Rising from History: U.S. Catholic Theology Looks to the Future*, ed. Robert J. Daly, 157–170. Lanham, Md.: University Press of America, 1987.

Van Ness, Peter H. *Spirituality and the Secular Quest*. New York: Crossroad, 1996.

Van Niekerk, Anton A. "To Be a Christian and in Business." *Scriptura* 62, no. 3 (1997): 385–395.

Vaz-Oxglade, Gail. "Instilling Spiritual Values in the Workplace." *Investment Executive*, May 1998.

Vischer, Lukas, *Arbeit in der Krise: theologische Orientierungen*. Neukirchener: Neukirchen-Vluyn, 1966.

Visotzky, Burton L. "Bible in the Boardroom?" *Inc. Magazine*, July 1998, 29–32.

Volf, Miroslav. *Work in the Spirit: Toward a Theology of Work*. New York: Oxford University Press, 1991.

Von Bergen, Jane M. "Employees Pray for Guidance." *Philadelphia Inquirer*, March 25, 2002.

Wade, Marion E. *The Lord Is My Counsel: A Businessman's Personal Experience with the Bible*. Englewood Cliffs, N.J.: Prentice-Hall, 1966.

Warren, Rick. *The Purpose-Driven Life*. Grand Rapids, Mich.: Zondervan, 2002.

Wartzman, Rick. "Dual Ministry: A Houston Clergyman Pushes Civic Projects along with Prayers." *Wall Street Journal*, February 20, 1996.

Watanabe, Teresa. "The New Gospel of Academia." *Los Angeles Times*, October 18, 2000.

Weaver, Gary R., and Bradley R. Agle. "Religiosity and Ethical Behavior in Organizations: A Symbolic Interactionist Perspective." *Academy of Management Review* 27, no. 1 (January 2002): 77–97.

Weber, Hans-Ruedi. *The Courage to Live: A Biography of Suzanne de Diétrich*. Geneva: WCC Publications, 1995.

———. *A Laboratory for Ecumenical Life: The Story of Bossey, 1946–1996*. Geneva: WCC Publications, 1996.

———. *Salty Christians*. New York: Seabury, 1963.

Weber, Max. *The Protestant Ethic and the Spirit of Capitalism*, trans. Talcott Parsons. Los Angeles, Calif.: Roxbury, 1996.

———. *Economy and Society: An Outline of Interpretive Sociology*, ed. Guenther Roth and Claus Wittich, trans. Ephraim Fischoff et al. Berkeley: University of California Press, 1978.

Welles, Edward O. "Chaplain to the New Economy." *Inc. Magazine*, November 1997, 68–76.

Wellner, Alison. "Your Space Is the Place." *Inc. Magazine*, May 2001.

Wentz, Frederick K. *Getting into the Act: Opening Up Lay Ministry in the Weekday World*. Nashville, Tenn.: Abingdon, 1978.

———. *The Layman's Role Today*. Garden City, N.Y.: Doubleday, 1963.

Where Faith and Wall Street Intersect. Goshen, Ind.: MMA Stewardship Solutions, August 2001.

Whyte, Jr., William H. *The Organization Man*. New York: Simon & Schuster, 1956.

Williams, Oliver F. *Business, Religion, and Spirituality: A New Synthesis*. Notre Dame, Ind.: University of Notre Dame Press, 2003.

————. "Christian Formation for Corporate Life." *Theology Today* 36 (October 1979): 347–352.

Williams, Rhys H., and Timothy J. Kubal. "Movement Frames and the Cultural Environment." In *Research in Social Movements, Conflicts and Change*, ed. P. J. Coy, vol. 21. Stamford, Conn.: JAI, 1999.

Willmott, Hugh. "Strength Is Ignorance, Slavery Is Freedom: Managing Culture in Modern Organizations." *Journal of Management Studies* 30, no. 4 (July 1993): 515–552.

Windass, Stan. *Chronicle of the Worker-Priests*. London: Merlin, 1966.

Wingren, Gustaf. *Luther on Vocation*. Philadelphia: Muhlenberg, 1957.

Wirthlin Report 11, no. 6 (July 2001).

Wise, Mike. "Getting the Word Out." *New York Times*, May 1, 1999.

Wolf, Michael, Bruce Friedman, and Daniel Sutherland. *Religion in the Workplace: A Comprehensive Guide to Legal Rights and Responsibilities*. Chicago: American Bar Association Publishing, 1998.

Wolfe, Alan. "Faith and Diversity in American Religion." *Chronicle of Higher Education*, February 8, 2002.

————. "The Opening of the Evangelical Mind." *Atlantic Monthly*, October 2000.

Wolman, Richard. "Thinking with Your Soul: Spiritual Intelligence and Why It Matters." *Library Journal* 126, no. 2 (February 1, 2001): 102.

Wolterstorff, Nicholas, "The Role of Religion in Discussion and Decision of Political Issues" In *Religion in the Public Square: The Place of Religious Conviction in Political Debate*, ed. Robert Audi and Nicholas Wolterstorff. Lanham, Md.: Rowman and Littlefield, 1996.

Wood, Jan. *Christians at Work: Not Business as Usual*. Scottsdale, Ariz.: Herald, 1999.

"Working with Spirituality in Organizations." Special issue of *Management Education and Development*, August 1991.

World Council of Churches. *A Letter from Christ to the World: An Exploration of the Role of the Laity in the Church Today*, ed. Nicholas Apostola. Geneva: WCC Publications, 1998.

Wuthnow, Robert. *After Heaven: Spirituality in America since the 1950s*. Berkeley: University of California Press, 1998.

————. *Christianity in the 21st Century: Reflections on the Challenges Ahead*. New York: Oxford University Press, 1993.

————. *The Crisis in the Church: Spiritual Malaise, Fiscal Woe*. New York: Oxford University Press, 1997.

————. *God and Mammon in America*. New York: Macmillan, 1994.

————. *Poor Richard's Principle: Recovering the American Dream through the Moral Dimensions of Work, Business and Money*. Princeton, N.J.: Princeton University Press, 1996.

————. *The Restructuring of American Religion: Society and Faith since WWII*. Princeton, N.J.: Princeton University Press, 1988.

Wyszynski, Stefan. *All You Who Labor: Work and the Sanctification of Daily Life*. Manchester, N.H.: Sophia Institute Press, 1995.

"You Can Love Monday." Interview with John D. Beckett, *Real Issue*, September/October 1998, 8–10. Available: http://www.leaderu.com/menus/ri.html.

"You're on the Road." *Marketplace* (Lancaster, Pa.), January–February 2000, 2.

INDEX

Academy of Management (AOM) (*see also* Management, Spirituality, and Religion), 99–100, 110, 118–119, 144, 182, 183, 187
American Academy of Religion (AAR), 95, 99–100, 144, 177, 187
American Express, 113, 184
Anderson, James, 57
Attridge, Harold, 176
Audenshaw Foundation (*see also* Gibbs, Mark), 53–54, 160
Avodah Institute, vii, viii, 6, 19, 106, 176, 179, 182, 184, 185, 188, 194, 195
Ayres, Francis, 39, 167

Barth, Karl, 89–90, 156, 163
Barton, Bruce, 23, 35
Bifurcation, 6, 8, 71, 74, 78, 127, 172
Blanchard, Ken, 58, 119, 192
Bonhoeffer, Dietrich, 130, 156
Bosch, David, 24–25, 41–42, 60, 161, 168, 183
Bossey, Ecumenical Institute at, 32, 42–46, 145
Broholm, Dick, 54, 56
Buchman, Frank, 32, 50, 163
Buddhism, 4, 116, 128, 137–138, 152, 157
Butt, Howard E., Jr., vii, 55, 139, 160, 167, 168, 194

Campus Crusade for Christ, 116, 134, 186, 192
Capitalism, 5, 13, 26, 28, 65–66, 81, 90, 97, 144, 161, 171, 190

Carter, Stephen, 67, 169, 170
Catholic Church (*see* Roman Catholic Church, traditions of)
Catholic social teaching (*see* Roman Catholic Church, teachings of)
Chaplains, corporate (or workplace), 49–50, 113–115, 150, 162, 176, 185
Christian Business Men's Committee (CBMC) (*see also* Connecting Business Men to Christ), 31, 33–34, 179, 186, 192
Clericalism, 29, 45–47, 56, 59, 89, 92–94, 168
Coalition for Ministry in Daily Life (CMDL) (*see also* Diehl, William), 54, 174
Coca-Cola Inc., 113–114, 184, 185
Compartmentalization, 6, 24, 27–29, 41, 45, 60–61, 71, 74, 80, 89, 93–94, 127, 150
Connecting Business Men to Christ (CBMC) (*see also* Christian Business Men's Committee), 33, 192
Conwell, Russell, 35–36

de Diétrich, Suzanne, 43, 45–46
Delbecq, André, 105, 109–110, 187
De Pree Leadership Center, 102–103, 176
Diani, Mario, 20–21, 75, 77, 160, 172
Diehl, William (*see also* Coalition for Ministry in Daily Life), 23, 39, 48–49, 52–56, 81–82, 160, 174, 187

Discrimination, 7, 67–68, 118, 134, 141, 150, 175
Drucker, Peter, 55, 118

Ecumenism, 7, 13, 26, 31, 33, 36–37, 41–43, 45, 48, 50, 55, 81, 87–88, 90, 95, 99, 117, 132, 139, 163
eNewsletters (*see* Newsletters)
Enlightenment, 5, 17, 27
Enrichment (as quadrant of Integration Box, *q.v.*)
Episcopal Church (ECUSA), 47, 50, 84, 148, 172, 187, 192, 193, 196
Ethics
    business (or corporate), 32, 83, 96, 100, 102–103, 110, 112, 118, 121, 129, 130–131, 138, 150, 168, 181, 182, 189, 191, 195
    and FAW movement, 11–12, 173, 176, 178, 182, 185, 194, 195
    as quadrant of Integration Box, *q.v.*
    social, 11–12, 14, 56, 98, 101, 129, 176, 177, 183
Evangelical Lutheran Church of America (ELCA), 47, 84, 117, 172
Evangelism (as quadrant of Integration Box, *q.v.*)
Everywhere Integrator (*see* Integration Box)
Executive Ministries, 50, 134, 185, 186
Experience (as quadrant of Integration Box, *q.v.*)
Expression (in contrast to evangelism), 76, 128, 135

Faith, definitions of, 4, 5, 15, 17–18
"Faith-friendly," vii, 112, 150, 184
Farnham, Suzanne, 136
FAW affiliations
    Impact of gender, 116, 128, 186
    Impact of participants' management level, 115–116
    Impact of specific companies, 112–113
Fellowship of Companies for Christ International (FCCI), 51–52, 192
Fogel, Robert William, 64–66, 168, 169
Fortune (magazine), 3, 51, 107, 112, 114, 155, 178, 179, 196
Four E's (*see also* Integration Box), vii, 75, 77, 82, 84, 92, 96, 111, 117, 126–128, 136, 139–142

Fuller Seminary (*see* De Pree Leadership Center)
Fuller, Robert, 94
Full Gospel Business Men's Fellowship International (FGBMFI), 51–52, 186, 188, 192

Gallup, George, 72–73, 83
Gibbs, Mark, 23, 52–54, 58–59, 160
Gideons International, 31, 33–34, 36
Globalization, 7, 12, 99, 176
Gordon-Conwell Theological Seminary (*see* Mockler Center for Faith and Ethics)
Gospel, Social, 5, 7, 13, 23–37, 39, 43, 58, 60, 157, 159, 161, 162, 168

Hammond, Pete, 54, 109, 156, 160, 168, 178, 182, 183
Hart, Stephen, 80, 82–83, 91, 103, 147, 195, 196
Hillman, Os, 106, 188, 189, 194
Hinduism, 4, 116, 127, 138, 152, 157

Integration, 6, 8, 10, 12, 21, 42, 44, 60–61, 68, 74–75, 77, 80, 82, 94, 97, 110–111, 122, 126–128, 141, 143, 146–149, 151–152, 155, 168, 174, 187, 190, 196
Integration Box (*see also* Four E's), vii, 75, 111, 126–129, 134, 137, 139–142, 149, 151–153, 183, 190, 195
    Enrichment (as quadrant of Integration Box), 11, 75–76, 82, 84, 92–93, 96, 108, 111, 126, 127, 137–142, 145, 147, 149
    Ethics (as quadrant of Integration Box), 11, 75–76, 82, 84, 92–93, 96, 108, 111, 126, 127–132, 139–140, 141–142, 145, 147, 149
    Evangelism (as quadrant of Integration Box), 11, 75–76, 82, 84, 92–93, 96, 108, 111, 126–128, 132–134, 139–142, 145, 147, 149
    Everywhere integrator, 139, 151
    Experience (as quadrant of Integration Box), 11, 75–76, 82, 84, 92–93, 96, 108, 111, 126–127, 135–137, 139–142, 147, 148, 149

InterVarsity Christian Fellowship, 43, 116, 156, 168, 182, 183, 186
Islam, 4, 15, 127, 133, 137–138, 143, 149

Jones, Ezra, 57
Jones, Laurie Beth, 35, 109, 181, 186, 188, 194
Judaism, 4, 15, 127, 137, 138
Judge, William, 16

Kraemer, Hendrik, 43–48, 55, 57–58, 87
Krueger, David A., 80, 82–83, 91, 103, 147, 195, 196

Laity Lodge (*see also* Butt, Howard E., Jr.), 55, 139, 194
Lay ministry, 7, 13, 29, 39–61, 64, 81, 84, 87–88, 92, 95–97, 160, 174, 176, 177, 178, 194
Leo XIII, Pope (*see also* Roman Catholic Church, traditions of), 7, 26, 161
Life and Work Group, conferences, 31, 33, 43–44, 58, 163
Listening Hearts, 136, 193
Lutheran Church (*see* Evangelical Lutheran Church of America)

Magazines, 3, 50, 51, 81, 105, 107–108, 117, 120–121, 152, 179, 186, 187, 189
Management, Spirituality, and Religion (MSR) (*see also* Academy of Management), 99, 118–119, 182
Marketplace Ministries, 106, 113, 156, 168, 172, 178, 182, 185, 186, 187
Marxism, 5, 19, 27–28, 46, 48, 60, 66, 90
McLennan, Scott, 14, 16, 65–66, 82–84, 88, 93, 98, 100, 169, 174
McLoughlin, Mike, 105, 178, 179, 186, 188
Mead, Loren, 56, 92–93, 194
Mennonite Church, 117, 145, 187
Methodists (*see* United Methodist Church)
Ministry of laity (*see* Lay ministry)
Minus, Paul, 54, 96, 160
Mockler Center for Faith and Ethics, 102, 103, 176
Moody, D. L., 31, 179
Mouw, Richard, 53, 101–102

Movements, social
  Definitions of, 20–21
  Elements of: Conflict, political or cultural, 21, 77–78, 123, 172; Identity, collective 20, 111, 122–123, 172; Interactions, networks of informal, 20–21, 105, 122, 145, 172

Nash, Laura, 14, 16, 64–66, 82–84, 88, 93, 98, 100, 161, 169, 174, 183
Neal, Judi, 109–110, 183, 188
Niebuhr, H. Richard, 13–14, 58, 161, 183
Niebuhr, Reinhold, 13, 27, 30, 36, 48, 67, 90, 129, 152, 163
New Age, 15, 17–18, 103, 110, 115–117, 137–138, 157, 181, 182, 183, 189, 194
Newsletters, 3, 32, 50, 53, 74–75, 105, 111, 120–121, 133, 136, 146, 179, 186, 188, 189

Oldham, Joseph H., 31, 42–46
Oxford Group, 31–32

Peale, Norman Vincent, 57
Pentecostalism, 25, 51–52, 72, 80, 116, 151
Pettus, Robert, 114–115
Phillips, Tom, 103
Pollard, C. William, vii, 109, 181
Popularization of Jesus, 27, 34–37, 194
Postmillennialism, 24–26, 28, 31, 34, 41–42, 50, 52, 54, 60, 75–76, 90, 126, 140
Premillennialism, 24–25, 28, 30, 34, 41–43, 48, 50–54, 60, 76, 90, 126, 132, 140
Presbyterian Church (PCUSA), 30, 47, 83–87, 172, 187, 196
Prosperity gospel, 35, 52, 81, 90, 138, 173, 193

Raiser, Konrad (*see also* World Council of Churches), 88
Rauschenbusch, Walter, 23, 25–30, 48, 67, 90, 162
Reform tradition, 13, 25, 59, 86
Religion (*see also* Spirituality), 3–7, 11–12, 14–18, 34, 40–41, 50, 65, 67–68, 72–74, 83, 90–91, 94, 97–99, 107–110, 112, 117–119, 122, 125–126, 133, 137–138, 149, 157, 169, 177

Roman Catholic Church
  Social teachings of: *Rerum Novarum*, 7,
    26–27, 158, 161, 162; *Gaudium et Spes*,
    49, 158; *Laborem Exercens*, 159
  Traditions of 6–7, 13, 15, 26, 40–41, 43,
    48–50, 72, 80, 99, 106, 110, 116–117,
    159, 161, 166, 168, 176, 186, 188, 189,
    191, 193
Rutte, Martin, vii, 122, 160

Salvation, 13, 25, 28, 30, 34, 54–55, 60–61,
    90, 196
Scruples organization, 105–106, 178, 179,
    186, 188, 189
ServiceMaster Company, vii, 184
Shakarian, Demos, 51, 52
Sheldon, Charles, 34, 52
Shoemaker, Samuel, 32, 50–51, 59,
    163, 189
Simmel, Sally, 54, 117, 160, 168, 186
Southern Baptist Convention, 55, 84, 194
Special-purpose groups, 27, 30–34, 36–37,
    39, 42, 48–54, 108, 112, 119–120, 162,
    163, 166
Spirituality (*see also* Religion), 3, 4, 10,
    14–18, 65, 72–75, 96, 99, 102–103,
    105, 107–110, 115, 117–119, 122, 125,
    137–138, 148, 149, 153, 169, 174, 177,
    178, 180, 182, 183, 187, 189, 191,
    192, 194
Stackhouse, Max L., vii, 20, 96, 101–102,
    129, 156, 159
Stricklin, Gil, 113
Student Volunteer Movement (SVM), 31,
    43, 163
Sunday-Monday gap, 9–10, 14, 16, 53, 65,
    81, 84, 89, 91–94, 108, 123, 145–146

Theology
  Liberation, 13, 26, 56–57, 59, 89–90,
    95, 159

Of laity, 43–44, 48–49, 52
Of work, 12–13, 45, 89–90, 96–98,
    100–101, 103, 135, 157, 159
Theology Today, 156, 158, 170, 177
Transformation of society, 11, 20, 24, 28,
    30, 36, 42, 60–61, 77–78, 90, 146, 153,
    191, 196
Trueblood, Elton, 36–37, 48, 54
Tyson, John (*see* Tyson Foods)
Tyson Foods, vii, 114, 184

United Methodist Church, 47, 84

Vatican II Council, 41, 45, 48–49
Vocation, 5, 10, 12–13, 19, 36, 46–47, 76,
    79, 81, 85–87, 90, 97, 100–101, 103,
    108–109, 135–136, 145–147, 156, 157,
    159, 169, 174, 176, 189, 193, 195
Volf, Miroslav, vii, 20, 45, 89, 96,
    100–101, 159, 176

Warren, Rick, 34, 57
Weber, Hans-Ruedi, 43, 45–48, 54, 58–59,
    87, 90
Weber, Max, 5, 13, 65, 167, 169
Wolterstorff, Nicholas, 170
Work, definitions of, 5–6, 12–13, 18–20
World Council of Churches (WCC),
    26, 31, 40, 43–48, 54, 81, 84,
    87–90, 95
Wuthnow, Robert, vii, 24, 27, 29–30, 41,
    60, 72–73, 83, 87, 91–92, 100, 166,
    169, 183

Yale Center for Faith & Culture, vii, 96,
    102, 114, 176, 178, 182, 185, 189,
    194, 195
Yale Divinity School, vii, 96, 102, 114, 176,
    178, 195